W9-CQY-314

Discover how the ancient powers
of the universe can attract
more wealth and wellness!

Dr. Dhara Bhatt

1

This book is dedicated
to my
Dadaji
&
Naniba

I call my grandparents, Dadaji and Naniba,
with love and respect.

Your art of visualizing and designing is truly a wondrous gift any brother could give. You have always used your creativity in ways that enrich your life and those of people around you. You have given grace to the presentation of my little knowledge. Priyam, to me you are the greatest visual artist with such a yearning for creativity. Thank you "Buddy", without you my dream would never have come true so precisely and beautifully.

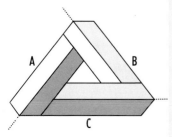

Published by:

Future Force Publication
336/43 GIDC Makarpura,
Baroda - 390 010, India

www.jitenpyramid.com
www.pyramidyantra.com

First edition: October 1997

Second edition: November 1997

Third edition: August 1998

Fourth edition: December 1999

Fifth edition: June 2000

Sixth edition: January 2001

Seventh edition: September 2001

Eighth edition: May 2003

Ninth edition: August 2003

All rights reserved.
No part of this book may be reproduced, stored in a retrieval system, or transmitted in any form or
by any means, electronic, electrostatic, magnetic tape, mechanical, photocopying, recording or
otherwise without prior permission in writing from the publishers.
Although every precaution has been taken in the preparation of this book, the publisher and
author assume no responsibility for errors or omissions.

This book is sold with the understanding that the author and the publisher are not engaged in
rendering legal, accounting, or other professional service. The author and publisher specifically
disclaim any liability, loss or risk, personal or otherwise, which is incurred as a consequence,
directly or indirectly, of the use and application of any of the contents of this book.

ISBN 81-88713-00-7

Foreword

Listening is learning. Most of the answers you are looking for are hidden within yourself. They may be anything from ideas, stories, images, movies, and experiences to composure and inner peace. But many of us are complete strangers to ourselves because we do not listen to ourselves. We have to re-learn from our existence. This book shows us how to create more wealth and wellness in our lives by applying our knowledge and capabilities in a slightly different perspective.

This book shares the experiences and knowledge Dhara and me have gained in all these years. I was amazed to see in this book the quotations from my lectures, which I delivered sometime, somewhere, here or abroad. Surprisingly some were from my lectures as far back as 15 years.

In all these years I have noticed Dhara's keen interest in learning more and more about this revolutionary technique and sharing it with others. Now with this book she gives some very fundamental and practical yet simple and easy-to-use steps to understand this technique. It has a very organized style of presentation with numerous illustrations. Here, I would like to recommend my special approach of reading this book, which I intuitively feel will help you optimize your personal knowledge.

Just relax more. Lose yourself in observing what is happening inside you. Life is closer to tune than to its notes, because notes are of mind, but life throbs in the tune of your heartbeats. So read not only the words as any message may be in form of written words, but also, its real meaning hides in what you understand of them. When reading, experience this melody of your heart and what your mind has to say about it.

One thing is definite Dhara has understood and presented the concept very well in this book. I have all the confidence that this book will become an 'eye-opener' to everyone who wishes to follow this path.

Prof. Dr. Jiten Bhatt

Prof. Dr. Jiten Bhatt

Founder of the PyraVastu, Pynergy
& Pyramid Yantra.
Ancient healing art consultant.
Health awareness promoter.
Bio-Energy scientist.

Also Friend, Philosopher and Guide
for thousands like me.

This book is based on knowledge
and experience I gained from my
dear father, Dr. Jiten Bhatt, by
being with him for almost all my
life till today. Also, I have learnt
from his way of life, his teachings,
workshops and researches.
Hereby, I reveal myself to you.

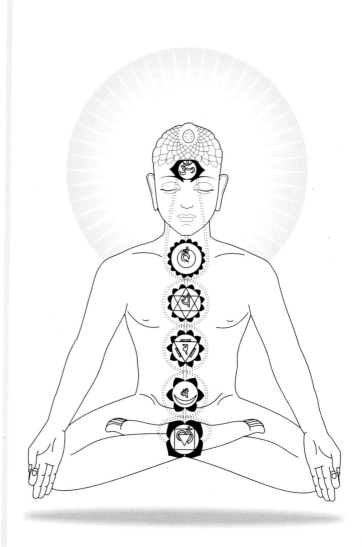

Our seven vital centers

Life is full of potential. Vital centers are our master keys to achieve our ultimate goal of bliss and self illumination.

1

"*Future doctors will depend less on medicine and more on energy. Focus of attention will be shifted from matter to the richness of mind.*
New dimension will be found out for the visible to experience the invisible."

Prof. Dr. Jiten Bhatt

New
Dimension

⋀ New Dimension

There was a rich gentleman, Ramchand, in Rampur, a small village. He was a reputed merchant of his village. He had worked hard all his life to earn wealth and fame. So now he decided to build a large villa. He put all his life's savings in the villa. The day came when his plans took shape as one of the most beautiful structures of his village. The merchant was very happy. One day a millionaire from town visited the village. The millionaire was amazed to see it. It was exactly the kind of villa he had been dreaming for years. So he made up his mind to purchase this instead of building one for himself. He offered a handsome price to Ramchand. As this was a very lucrative amount for a villager like Ramchand, he thought " Why not sell this villa for such a big amount? I can always build another more better than this for myself" He decided to sell this villa. Ramchand was in such happy state of mind that day.

Inspiration to Reality

The seed of all scientific inventions or outstanding work is creative perception. An innovative mind and deep desire in the heart leads towards success .

Ramchand's son went along with the millionaire to his town for fixing the deal of the villa. At midnight a villager came and told Ramchand that his villa was on flames, and that there was no chance of saving it. The merchant was aghast. He started crying and cursing his fortune. Just then a messenger came and told him that his son who was in the next town had fixed the deal of the villa at double the amount spent on villa. Hearing this the merchant considered himself to be the most fortunate man on earth, his happiness had no limits. The villa was still burning. But he was laughing and celebrating. Suddenly the phone rang. It was the merchant's son who said that the deal had been fixed but the payment was not yet done. The depressed merchant started crying and cursing again. But his son assured him that the person with whom the deal had been fixed was a thorough gentleman and once he had promised, he will accept the villa in any condition, whatsoever. The merchant became happy again and started rejoicing.

Now, consider this. The villa is still on fire. The situation has not changed. The only change is in perception. The merchant is unaware of the change but his condition is constantly changing. Similarly our body (our villa) is constantly on fire ever since we are born and its end is certain. All throughout the burning we are sometimes happy and at other times sad, sometimes healthy and at others ill. If only we change our perception we can be more contented in life. We cannot change others so why not change ourselves by merely changing our perception ?

⚠ The Inside Key

Let us fly together to re-discover ourselves in a fresh perspective. Let us try to understand the deeper meaning of life and explore a new dimension towards better health and happiness. Here starts our beautiful journey of realization of our environment through mind, body and emotion. The environment is not only made of things surrounding us but also includes us. The first and most powerful step is to refrom the inner,as the master-key is inside us. So we should go within ourselves to change our perception and in turn to make our world a better place to live in.

Here you will experience how we resonate with things around us and how inturn they affect us. There is a constant interaction between us and our environment. We face it every now and then, every moment. This interaction is so constant and subtle that we do not recognize it; that is to say, it is not very evident. It is like a sea where only high tides are noticed. Similarly, we also notice some distracting events occurring in our daily routine. But we do not realize the ocean of bliss and consciousness in and around us. We must now educate ourselves to experience this infinite contribution given by our surrounding.

It is impossible to exist solely without any support and co-operation of our surrounding environment. Our super consciousness is constantly busy in process of our evolution. It is we who have to change our attitude, actions and reactions towards our inner and outer momentum. You, me and all other living beings communicate with each other through a divine core link. To obtain optimum from our lives we must become aware and alert. We also must learn to reconnect with this divine tune and be in harmony with the core link.

Let us take a small step forward in understanding our core link system.

Our Spirit : A creative interpretation of prime force within.

Illumination to existence
What do you see? A candle or two faces?

Understanding the human matrix

We humans have an inborn reaction to any given situation-
1. Fight
2. Flight.
We utilize this under any condition of mental, physical or emotional stress. As this is a basic human response, we react very well to any problem having a 'bipolar' solution. Similar is the case for our problems related to health, happiness or prosperity. Let us understand this with the example of our health- when we are sick our prime goal is to achieve health as quickly as possible. There are a few of us who want health but in a simple yet safe and affordable yet healthy way.
There are two basic ways to achieve health-
1. Outer pole technique
2. Inner pole technique.
Both have their own advantages and limitations.

1. Outer Pole Technique- works from outside or physically, like allopathy. It starts to work from outside or on the body level and then goes inwards to bring about health.

2. Inner Pole Technique- works from inside like meditation, yoga naturopathy, Reiki or homoeopathy. They start to work from inside or at the vital force and then gradually on the physical level and brings about health.

Modern Science is developed on the Outer Pole Technique, depending more on the materialistic proofs and laboratory reports. The whole stress here is on sickness and disease. Whereas, on the other hand, New Age medicine gives importance to wellness and condition of the mind and spirit of the person who is sick. No doubt both methods are equally good and useful.

Inner Pole Technique is growing more popular today due to its positive approach towards achieving health. Similar is the case with happiness and prosperity; you achieve more when you start solving from within. All we need to do is to cross the threshold of being unable or unlucky and transform ourselves to new, positive, healthy, happy and prosperous human beings. We all are born with immense potential; all we need is to solve this matrix, which prevents us from opening the doors to the wide world of our capabilities. Come with me. Let us trace our path to personal growth with this fresh perception.

When we think of perception we instantly think of the ability to see something and understanding it. Sensing is the most important and constant function of our body. This sensing develops experience through which we interact with our surrounding environment. Without them we would be like any other non-living object, which is not moved by anything occurring in surrounding.

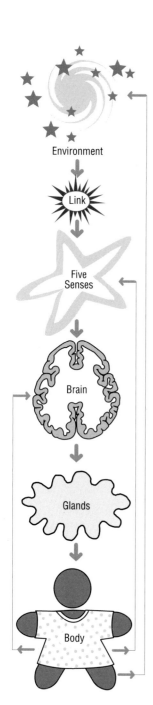

Environment

Link

Five Senses

Brain

Glands

Body

Our Universal Circuit
This critical Link is the only changeable variant between body & environment

Deeper Anatomy

Sensing can be understood in two ways-
1) Through gross/physical anatomy, and
2) Through subtle/unseen anatomy.

All of us know some basic physical anatomy. We have read it in our science books in school. Here let us make a simple effort to understand its deeper anatomy.

These five senses continuously interact with the outside environment as well as inner understanding. They act through body on command of the brain. These senses reach our brain via our body receptors. Our brain analyses them and sends information to their designated sites. These sites set up a program according to which there are chemical or electrical changes in the body. The chemical changes are the formation of hormones and their release while electrical changes initiate an impulse in a nerve. These changes ultimately monitor the functioning of the body. Here body and brain function rhythmically together .

To bring about harmony within us we must learn more about the finer ends of our existence. These finer ends or the senses are the bridge connecting our mind with matter. It is easier to manipulate at the finer ends than to achieve modifications at the gross ends. Out of the five powerful ends we possess, in this book we would understand only about one vital end, which is the eye.

Secret's of Jiten

Miracles are all over; one just needs a sensitive heart, a perceptive eye, and you will see matter and spirit dancing together everywhere.

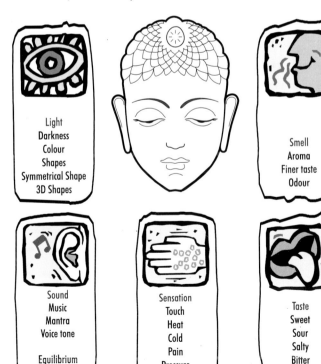

Light
Darkness
Colour
Shapes
Symmetrical Shape
3D Shapes

Smell
Aroma
Finer taste
Odour

Sound
Music
Mantra
Voice tone

Equilibrium
Atmospheric
pressure

Sensation
Touch
Heat
Cold
Pain
Pressure
Vibration

Taste
Sweet
Sour
Salty
Bitter
Metallic

Bridge connecting the mind with the matter

According to anatomy we have five senses. These five sense are - visual (light), auditory (sound), olfactory (smell), gustatory (taste) and tactile (touch). The five organs for these are -

- ◆ Visual : Eye
- ◆ Auditory : Ear
- ◆ Olfactory : Nose
- ◆ Gastatory : Tongue
- ◆ Tactile : Skin

Travel from Visible to Invisible

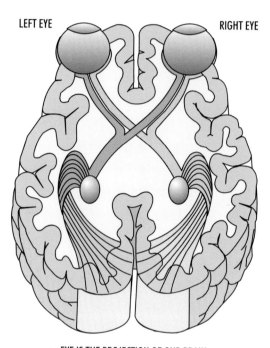

LEFT EYE   RIGHT EYE

EYE IS THE PROJECTION OF OUR BRAIN

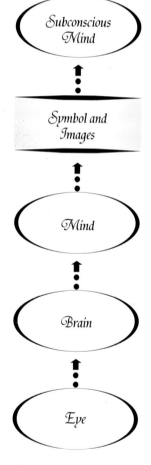

Subconscious
Mind

Symbol and
Images

Mind

Brain

Eye

The inner language

The subconscious mind only
understands the language of
symbols and images

Here we have taken up only the eye because 'sense' is a very vast topic, which we will discuss later. Eye is chosen because it is one of the most important input sources of our body. The eyes are responsible for 75 percent of all our perception. This shows how important eyes are to us and why is it that we believe in what we see. Sight is man's richest sense and vision begins with light on our first day in this world. Our eyes can sense about 10 million gradations of light and 7 million different shades of colours. Eye communicates with brain which in turn interacts with mind.

Our conscious mind can understand all the senses. Our subconscious mind controls the autonomous nervous system which in turn is responsible for functions like heartbeat and digestion. This subconscious mind only understands the language of symbols and images. Any other communication is foreign language for it. These symbols and images are sensed by our eyes. This shows how important the eye is in our inner dialogue with our subconscious mind and its memory. Also, the eye has maximum receptivity because it is the projection of our brain.

Let's learn more about this journey from the visible to the invisible action inside.

Eye : Map of the Mind, Body and Spirit

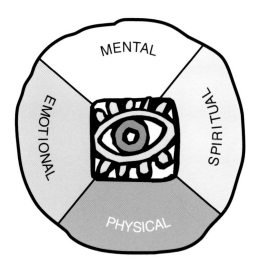

Our eye can sense three distinct things-
1) Light   2) Colour   3) Shape

All the three are very important. Out of these three many of us know much about the effect of light and colour on us. Very few people have ventured into knowing the effect of different shapes and forms on us. So today let's venture to that new dimension.

Our eye is not only a sharp receiver but also a very efficient transmitter. It transmits signals of all activity, whether on the physical, mental or emotional level. If you are physically exhausted, it takes no time for your eyes to reveal this. If you lie, you cannot face your opponent and look straight in his eyes. Your eyes reveal your mental condition. We somehow feel some clearly visible disturbance in the mentally challenged persons just by looking at their eyes. Eyes clearly reflect the inner feeling and emotion. Also, who can ever deny the role of eyes in love and benevolence?

Our eyes have a very vital role in our spiritual development. It has been nicely defined in all our ancient religious literatures. Also our eyes are important in : Sleep - movement of eyes during sleep are related to stages of Sleep, Hypnotism and Iridology.
Hypnotism - It is an important part of the modern psychiatry. It is considered to be one of the most powerful and practical tools for the journey from the eye to the deeper level of our subconscious mind. Psychiatrists tap this unlimited beneficial potential of the subconscious for therapeutic effect.
Iridology - It is the science of scanning a person by checking the iris. Thus, eye is the 'map' of our mind, body and spirit.

Eye is the mirror of our thoughts and feelings

The Egyptians believe in the lunar eye to be a symbol of divine protection.

In Hinduism, the third eye is the symbol of higher consciousness.

Buddhism believes eye to be the symbol of wisdom and omniscience.

Islam considers eye to be the spiritual gateway to the ultimate truth.

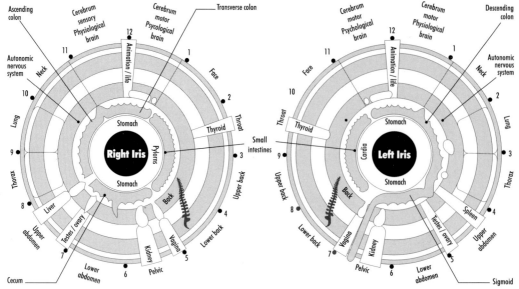

Iris Diagnostic chart

The Eye: Window of our Health

Visualizing the body in our eye is a comparatively new technique in alternative medicine, known as iridology. Our physical, mental and emotional health is clearly visible through this window of health. In this diagnostic method the color, condition, markings, patches or dots on the patient's iris are seen and with the help of that his health condition is assessed.

This is one technique where just by looking at the iris by a magnifying lens or with help of a magnified photograph of eye, mental or physical illness can be detected without any other examination.

Another benefit of this technique is that you can know the disorder quite before it manifests physically. Thus, it aids in impeding the ailment by giving us a chance for prophylactic treatment or changing our lifestyle. If the treatment or changes made were suitable it would be visible on the iris within a few days. This technique would equally benefit both doctors and healers. Hence, all this makes the eye a very intriguing yet a very vast subject.

To demonstrate how our brains construct what we perceive as reality, hold the illustration at eye level, close your left eye, and stare at the circle in the middle of the grid with your right eye. Slowly move the book back and forth along the line of your vision until the star vanishes (about 6 to 7 inches). The star disappears because it is falling on your blind spot. Now close your right eye and stare at the star. Move the book back and forth until the circle in the middle of the grid vanishes. When it does, notice that although the circle disappears, all the lines of the grid remain intact. This is because your brain is filling in what it thinks should be there.

A Creative Dip

Man carries the seed of misery or bliss, hell or heaven, within himself. Whatsoever happens to us, happens because of us.

This figure is not just any other figure even if you may see a skull and a bottle of alcohol. It is a reminder of changing our perception. You will encounter many such eye-openers in the coming chapters.

Just close your eyes for a while and reopen them with positive approach. Now you would see a beautiful young lady there in front of her dressing table. This happened with a simple change in perception.

Life gives you its beauty in all its forms, but our ignorance of appreciating it leads to unhappiness and negativity. If we try to understand things with a fresh perspective each breakdown can become a breakthrough, and each possibility of failure can become a possibility of success. Negativity has an equally forceful potential to be positive, we just have to learn to perceive it differently.

fresh perspective

Change your perception from the skull to beauty!

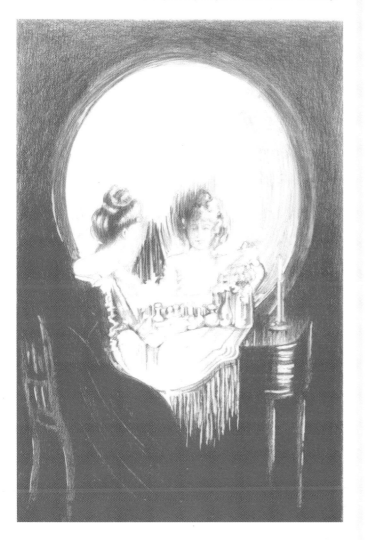

Our Unseen Anatomy

The second path of sensing is through the energy field that surrounds and permeates our body. This field is called our aura.

Aura is our energy link between the body and the universal life force. This is a very well organized network within and around our body, which associates us to the matrix of dynamism. This network consists of the prana nadis and the vital centers called the chakras. According to the science of Yoga we all have seven major chakras and numerous minor chakras.

These chakras are situated along the spine, vertically. They are one above the other. They are energy centers which spin like a wheel and open like a flower. They are related to health, well-being, psychic abilities and overall growth - physical, mental and spiritual. They are the blue print of our being and are situated at the reproductive center, navel, solar plexus, heart, throat, brow and crown of head. Our eastern tradition has an unbroken metaphysical understanding of the human being as a whole, interacting with its surrounding. These chakras are (as shown in figure) expressed with symbolic images. Even in these symbolic images, shapes, forms and colors are given much importance. Here the petals, geometrical shape and respective color of a specific chakra forms the basic symbolic image apart from others like animal, god or goddess, mantra, etc.

Inner pole anatomy

Our prana nadi emerging from chakras in auric body and higher link of sun and moon through the eye.

Geometrical forms of our seven Subtle Energy Centers

These chakras collect energy from the universe to nourish our prime organs. If there is any blockage in the intricate pathway of the chakra, it stops functioning appropriately. As a result of this disturbance our physical health, mood or thoughts can be affected. Each chakra has a definite important role to play.

Chakras are formed at the spots where the divine light intersects. They are similar to the eyes as light; colors, shapes and forms too influence them. These chakras are again linked to the five elements, ether and the consciousness. (See the figure of "How life began".)

Out of these seven chakras, the first five from below upwards are represented by one or the other physical link. The sixth and the seventh do not have any such physical links. They are representations of our superphysical senses - instinct and enlightenment or self-realization.

Thus, good seeing with better perception of new dimension can lead to a life worth living. Today, we are least concerned with what we see and its effects on our health, happiness and prosperity. We can successfully deal with many problems in our daily routine if only we pay more attention to what we see and how we perceive. If you do not pay attention to these you lose much of which you are sometimes not even aware.

This book is purposefully designed with many illustrations, simple step-by-step instructions and many practical experiments to help you understand about shapes and forms that influence us physically, mentally and spiritually throughout our lives. Here is a small effort in a simple way. It is like a pebble in the lake of your knowledge, yet, potent enough to produce ripples. If you resonate with these new ripples you will able to enter into the mystical state of bliss and awareness.

Start Experiencing

Sit comfortably in a calm and peaceful place. In the silence of 'not doing' start knowing what you feel and what is being offered by your surrounding. Let the inner chatter quiet down. Rest is automatic.

How Life began.

Pure consciousness

Cosmic Vibrations

Ether

Air   Fire

Substances with no consciousness

Water

Earth

Creatures with consciousness

Humans   Plants

Animals

BLESSINGS

"Dhara, you are the second person I have met in my life sharing my birthday. I am very happy about that. May Almighty bestow upon you the best of good luck. Love and blessings from me, my dear."

Mataji Narayani
Spiritual Guide and Divine Healer

Mystic Properties

Temples and churches set the
standard for a classic proportion.
They possess the mystical properties
and abilities to transform
supra-mental powers in us.

2

"Secret behind the excellent manifestation in nature is the divine proportion and its precise program at the core level".

Prof. Dr. Jiten Bhatt

Divine
Proportion

Shapes can change your life!

One morning an old friend of my father and his wife came to us for some advice. They told us that they were planning to take divorce. This was real shocking news because they had been so happy, for such a long time. We asked them what was the reason for such an extreme step and since when had this misunderstanding begun. They had no solid reasons, but they told that problems had started cropping up about three years ago. On further discussion with them, we came to know that they had shifted to a new house about three years ago. Since then the husband complained that the wife had been very irritable and started having hypertension. On the other hand the wife said that the husband always remained out of the house and was uninterested about house matters.

We got interested in their problem and went to visit their house the next day. What we first noticed upon entering their house was that the marble pieces they had fitted were all cracked, but they told us that they had created this special unique effect by dropping the big marble piece on the floor and fitted it as it is with the cracks. According to them this was a new creation of some famous architect. The other thing we observed was that their furniture, walls, paintings were all in bright stimulating colours and irregular shapes. A modern art painting in the bedroom contained many sharp ending lines and shapes.

My father just suggested a few simple changes in their house like placing carpets in the much used rooms, changing the color of furniture and walls to more subdued shades and changing all the paintings to those with some nature and related ideas and with lot of green color in them. He also suggested a painting of a beautiful red rose in their bedroom along with some changes according to Feng Shui and Vastu. A few days later, to my sheer delight, I found them so happy and cheerful! And three months later they did not even remember their plan of divorce. Then I asked my father how this situation completely changed within such a short time!

He explained : What he noticed in their house was that the shape of the marble which was irregular and broken. When any thing broken such as broken glass, mirror, stones etc. are kept in the house, they lower the circulation of good and beneficial energy. So the placement of carpets was suggested to lessen the effect of broken marble throughout the house.

When you love, you create, everywhere is the divine; when you hate, you destroy, everywhere is the devil. It is your standpoint that is projected onto reality.

The sharp and stimulating colors in the paintings caused irritating emotions and high blood pressure. More of green color and a painting of the rose was suggested because green color is for peace and rose indicates love, harmony and co-ordination. Some minor changes in the interiors of the house were made to bring accord and harmony in the house.

This changed their life dramatically and filled with peace and prosperity.

Shape Awareness

Each shape brims with vibrant energy. We must find out its positive or negative effect.

We live in the world of shapes and forms, there are innumerable shapes around us and in us. Some of the everyday shapes we use are those of decorative objects, designs, and plants in our home. They influence our daily life. Their use and misuse can greatly affect us. We see the shapes but we are not aware of their importance.

We do not know how they enrich our lives and that they have some of their own properties which are useful to us. Minor sensible changes in shapes can bring for us significant changes.

'Shapes' is a very deep and interesting subject. We already have some elementary knowledge about shapes yet a far deeper meaning remains to be learnt. Let us learn how the shapes interact within us. Our ultimate aim is to generate balance and harmony 'inside' using shapes. To achieve this we must understand each step more cautiously and with an awareness to try and understand its unconventional meaning.

Secret's of Jiten

Out of many one fundamental principle of Vaastu is Vastu (object, body and articles) and its inter-relationship with each other.

Shapes and its proportion interact with us powerfully. Select all the shapes of your home decor thoughtfully.

The Shape Processor

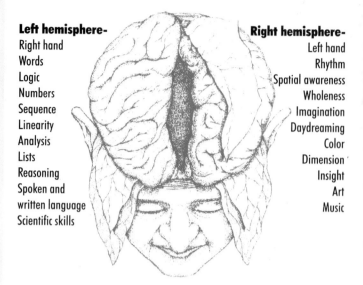

Left hemisphere-
Right hand
Words
Logic
Numbers
Sequence
Linearity
Analysis
Lists
Reasoning
Spoken and
written language
Scientific skills

Right hemisphere-
Left hand
Rhythm
Spatial awareness
Wholeness
Imagination
Daydreaming
Color
Dimension
Insight
Art
Music

The brain is one of our most intricate and most researched yet the most mysterious organs of our body. "An enchanted loom where millions of flashing shuttles weave a dissolving pattern, though always a meaningful one." said Sir Charles Sherrington. Keats defined it as "thoroughfare for all thoughts."

Our brain is a mushroom shaped structure with two similar hemispheres. They are connected to each other through nerve fibers, known as corpus callosum. This four inch long body of fibers which connects both the hemispheres and hence their special powers through it. It links information from both hemispheres.

Another important structure of our brain is our hypothalamus, which is quite near to and below the corpus callosum. Any disturbance here can cause serious psychological disturbances. It is one organ which virtually controls all our autonomous and involuntary functions like maintaining inner thermostat, regulating heart beats, food satiety, thirst, sleeping and waking patterns and many other biological rhythms by releasing hormones. It is our link between the mind and the body giving physical form to our thoughts and emotions. Indian philosophy says we possess the same number of minds as that of our brains. So we humans possess two minds as we have two brain hemispheres.

The corpus callosum and hypothalamus are two very important parts of our brain; we know that through science and research today. But the Egyptians have known this some 5,000 years ago. When in Egypt we found a representation of the brain stem in a symbolic form as a bird (Horus), sun disk (Ra) and corpus callosum (the Barque). They call this entire symbol as "the vault of heaven".

Brains and Minds

Lord Brahma, the Indian god of creation. He possesses four heads and so eight brain hemispheres. Thus he would possess eight minds too. This intriguing concept of 16 is yet to be discovered by us.

The two hemispheres of our brain are each dominant or specialized in certain distinct areas of intelligence and understanding, though they are both capable of working in all the areas. The right hemisphere controls the left hand and governs - rhythm, spatial awareness, gestalt (wholeness), imagination, daydreaming, color, dimension, insight, art and music. While the left hemisphere controls the right hand and governs - words, logic, numbers, sequence, linearity, analysis, lists, reasoning, spoken and written language and scientific skills.

The Chinese call our left hemisphere as crystalline brain as it accepts only systematic, logical, sequential and linear information of what it sees. They consider our right hemisphere as dragon brain as it accepts information, which is formless, may be three dimensioned or whole. It is the wholeness of the object that enters the right hemisphere whereas its rationality enters the left.

When we see a shape or symbol, both our hemispheres seek information from their own memories and understanding about that object. Transmitting and transforming that information through the corpus callosum they form a single clear image of that for our perception. The hypothalamus is also activated and it sends impulses for release of certain hormones, which arouse a distinct feeling or emotion about what we see. Any shape or form or symbol that we see but think is unimportant includes a series of definite processes in our brain and whole body, but we remain unaware of it. It leaves an impression on each and every cell of our body. Shapes and forms that we encounter daily in our surroundings influence us in a very significant manner by involving brain, mind, emotions, moods and physical existence. So let us make some simple effort in this direction to improve our input to the brain and mind, to receive better state of wellness in turn.

The Egyptian Vault of Heaven
5,000 years ago Egyptians understood the brain, its important parts and connection with heaven.

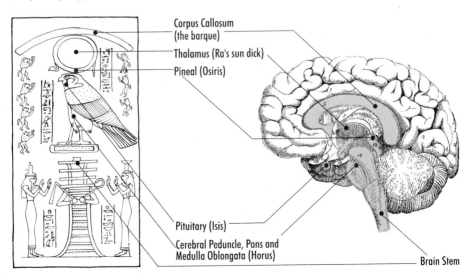

Corpus Callosum (the barque)
Thalamus (Ra's sun dick)
Pineal (Osiris)
Pituitary (Isis)
Cerebral Peduncle, Pons and Medulla Oblongata (Horus)
Brain Stem

"Nature! Out of the simplest matter it creates most diverse things, without the slightest effort with the greatest perfection and on everything it casts a sort of fine veil. Each of its creation has its own essence, each phenomenon has separate concept, but everything is a single whole" - Goethe.

Symmetry at the heart of everything

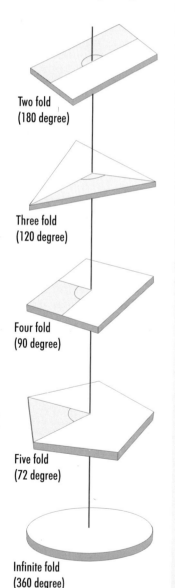

Two fold
(180 degree)

Three fold
(120 degree)

Four fold
(90 degree)

Five fold
(72 degree)

Infinite fold
(360 degree)

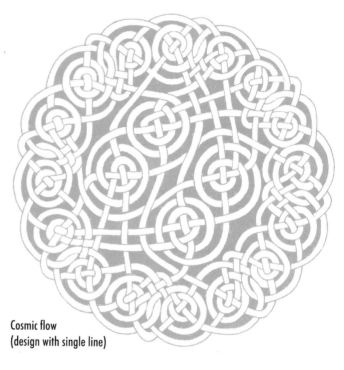

Cosmic flow
(design with single line)

Universal Symmetry

As a child and even today, I love flowers, leaves and trees, not knowing it is the symmetry in them which attracted me. Also, as a child, kaleidoscope was my most favorite toy. I could pass hours with it. Its changing patterns fascinated me. But now I understand the reason. The procession of unique but orderly images produced by it manifest dual aspects of symmetry, that is to say, its restraining power and its creative potentiality. It creates both these properties in our brain, activating it to function constructively. This constructively produces harmony and balance in the being, which is the basis of a happy and a successful life.

Symmetry is omnipresent

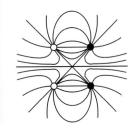

Symmetry is the basis of order which presents itself. Order is a state of regularity of arrangement or rhythmic progress. It is the basis of creation either of nature or of man. Symmetry is in the laws of physics, biology, astronomy and chemistry.

When we come upon objects containing symmetry we are instinctively impressed. This is not by its attractiveness and aesthetic value, but by the experience of its resonance with us.

It is not that regularity is synonymous with symmetry. Any other irregular pattern if repeated creates order.

Unseen vital pattern between ○positive pole and ●negative pole.

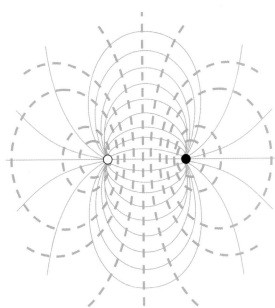

Symmetry is omnipresent . It is visible as well as invisible. Visible symmetry is in things surrounding us which we see and recognize. There is another form of symmetry which we experience but rarely or never ever recognize. This is the unseen or invisible symmetry such as that created by two poles of a magnet. A magnet for instance, creates beautiful symmetrical organisation of energy by producing lines of forces due to combination of two opposite poles. Earth as we know is a big magnet and the universe being a still bigger one, forming symmetry around and within it.

We exist in symmetry and symmetry exists in us. When we talk of symmetry, we are talking about congruity and rhythmic constancy of some kind or the other. Our way of seeing things, perceiving them and our cognitive process are deeply engrossed with principles of symmetry. Symmetry is not only a realm of material things, even colors and music constitute it. They are potent triggering factors for a fountain of feelings. The altering notes of differing pitches and volumes create harmony within themselves and a soothing effect in us. The combination of different shades of different colors, though seeming opposite, create balance. If we look to the other side, colors are nothing but wavelengths of magnetic field. These are invisible forces. Invisible forces can affect us to an extent where it can create feelings and emotions. Our mind and emotions control us creating harmony or disharmony. These basic principles were very wisely understood by our ancient cultures.

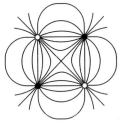

The invisible flow of energy between positive and negative poles

Knowing their exact effect on us, they designed certain patterns which were used in rituals to enhance quality of life. These designs were picked up from nature and their understanding of nature and its forces. Their understanding of the human mind and how it can be tackled and controlled, was much more superior and far more advanced than what we have invented through science. We have practically forgotten our ancient science and culture. So we need to revive them to live a harmonious and fruitful life.

Symmetry can exist in numerous ways. For simplification, it is presented in five basic patterns -

(1) Bilateral symmetry

(2) Rotational symmetry

(3) Spiral symmetry

(4) Branching symmetry

(5) Divine order

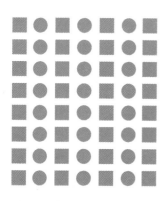

Eye reads, brain arranges automatically

As we read normally from left to right we can see square ■ , round ● and so on. But the brain makes its sequence of all squares and rounds.

Bilateral symmetry in nature

Bilateral symmetry

This type of symmetry is seen in objects in which one half is similar to the other half. It is perhaps the most clear and straight forward type of symmetry we see. We do not have to look further for an example of this than the left and right morphology of our bodies . When we look around, we see many objects and organisms sharing this kind of "mirrored" symmetry. Some of them are, as shown in the figures - a centipede, a leaf, a butterfly and a deer. Now look around yourself you will find many more such objects just around you. The list of such bilateral objects is endless.

In bilateral symmetry, it is the congruence and periodicity of object that involves us. It is perfectly in order, and hence predictable. Here elements on one side of an imagined line have their equivalent on the other side, hence producing balance .

This bilateral symmetry is the basis of all other kinds of symmetries. Being the most simplest form, it is most abundantly found in nature and used by us.

Rotational Symmetry

It is an equally congruent form of ' translation ' as bilateral symmetry. It involves movement of a different kind wherein objects pivot on a central point.

Here the element repeats itself turning around a center. It requires equivalence in arrangement of elements as well as the elements themselves. In a flower there is a order in which the petals are distributed radially. Each of these plants bearing flowers have their special coded response to the environment which is unique to its own species. Among the peculiarities of flowers one of the most astonishing is that the number of the petals in most cases conforms to the geometrical laws pertaining to circles. A starfish has no left or right in its world. It has a symmetry of a different type. It has its limbs radially directed with its body as a center.

Looking at a horizontally cut citrus fruit you will find the most evident form of rotational or radial symmetry. Here each compartment is rotationally symmetrical to the next. If we consider an atom, practically, the smallest unit of matter, we can see that electrons rotate around its nucleus. These electrons rotate around in seven concentric circles forming a good example of rotational symmetry, where every electron with every movement is creating balance in the atom as, a whole. When we come to rotational symmetry how can we forget planets in our solar system? Their rotational patterns and the paths followed by them create waves of cosmic energy of a certain wavelength. These waves reach the earth and affect us in a particular manner. These planets form an excellent example of rotational symmetry.

Rotational symmetry in nature

Spiral symmetry in DNA

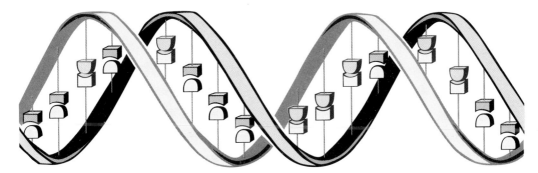

⚠ Spiral symmetry

Spirals or helices are found everywhere in nature. These spirals appear to be associated with dynamic systems. Hence they are very prevalent in animate organisms. Spirals are symbols of continuous movement. They constitute or are in turn constituted by continuous movement of energy.

Spiral symmetry in nature

The DNA (Deoxyribo Nucleic Acid) is the base of our existence and in general, of all species. This DNA is the main constituent of chromosomes of all living organisms . These chromosomes are responsible for species differentiation and individualizing their characteristics. The DNA is a helical structure having two chains forming the helix. Here the energy has transformed into the helical form supposed to be the symbol of continuous movement. Another example is the shell or the conch which is formed due to the water currents around it. The continuous movement around it forms its spiral shape. How can we forget our galaxy? Our galaxies are classic examples of spirals and energy movement. The galaxies form spirals due to the progression of cosmic energy into and around it.

⚠ Branching symmetry

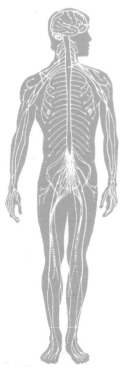

One of the most remarkable features in nature is the branching system. Rhythmicity in the natural world is one of the manifestations of order. Branching pattern may seem to us like anarchy or disorder but, actually that is what we think and see. Our mind perceives it in an entirely different manner. Branching teaches us propagation with rhythmicity and this is how our mind perceives it. Branching is an orderly process of division. It is abundantly found in nature all around us. If we take a look around in the environment where we live, we see numerous such examples. One of the most commonly encountered is the tree which has divided into many branches. This distinctive system is a part of its genetic inheritance.

Another example is the river which starts as a single spring of water. It widens and divides into numerous tributaries all through its way up to the delta. At the delta it forms a very fine network of such tributaries. In case we do not want to look around, we can always look inside. Our body also contains an excellent example of branching symmetry, that is , its nervous system. Branching, though not identical, is in order hence producing balance and as a result, harmony. Anything producing balance and harmony in nature is symmetrical.

Branching symmetry of nerves in the human body.

Divine Order

This is yet another kind of symmetry which is universal yet, not fully understood. We know very well that our solar system emerged from the Big Bang, millions of years ago. This Bang produced certain ripples of electromagnetic force throughout the universe. Evolution of Earth as well as other planets was due to this electromagnetic field around us known as the cosmos.

There is this cosmic order according to which energy flows. Today, we are not able to understand the rhythmicity and pattern of this balanced flow. So, we feel it is chaos. But is this actually chaos? Is this a disorder? No, we live into it harmoniously. How can anything bringing about harmony be a disorder? It is because we cannot understand the hierarchy of successive evolution of events, that we name it 'Uncertain'.

Cabbage slice:
Beautiful example of order / disorder.

Order and disorder are mere relative terms, inseparable in absolute means. Disorder can occur where order existed and order can occur where there is disorder . Order and disorder create balance and equilibrium. Actually there is nothing in nature which is in disorder. Many natural phenomena which seemed wilful and unpredictable are now found to contain profound mysterious regularities.

The symmetry and asymmetry constitute the foundation of relativity, quantum mechanics, solid-state physics, and atomic, sub-atomic and particle physics. This mystic cycle of symmetry and asymmetry and the balance of these two natural forms of life is very well understood by an ancient Chinese philosophy-Taoism . They named this impercieved realm of divine order, as Dragon, which we misunderstand as disorder. They believed in Dragon energy, the divine order as a very potent factor for existence. For them order of nature was an order of constant change in the restless energy. They believed that this vital energy flows everywhere - in the cosmos as well as in us . This vital energy flows rhythmically throughout the universe. This all-pervasive essential force seems to us as virtually beyond determination. It is this energy which gives life to nature and movement to water. This transmission of vital energy flowing is indeed a symmetry which is omnipresent and omnipotent. When we will understand this highest form of symmetry which is beyond logic, we will experience the ultimate happiness, that is, Bliss.

It only takes a change of perception to change your world including your body. Symmetry is not only order and regularity but rhythmicity and balance. When we think in terms of rhythmicity and balance we change our perception of things within and around us, creating harmony. Harmony leads us to a happier and satisfactory life.

Marble:
Yin-Yang divine force in nature.

In Chinese mythology paths of concentrated energy were symbolised by the dragon.

Five vibrant shapes of China

There are hundreds of shapes around us. It is impossible to study all of them. For all practical purposes, let us understand the five basic shapes related to the five elements.

1. Triangle, Pointed, Conical or Pyramidal (Fire element)

2. Square, Flat or Block like (Earth element)

3. Round, Curve, Spherical or Dome (Metal element)

4. Wave, Smooth ups and downs, Spiral or like ripples (Water element)

5. Long, Rectangle or tall, like Pillar (Wood element)

Other shapes are permutations and combinations of these shapes. For health and prosperity, we can use the properties of these shapes in home and office. Try redesigning your surroundings with vibrant shapes and see the results.

Fire

QUALITIES :
Intelligence, spirit and life, wisdom, reason, etiquette.

MATERIALS :
Animal products, shiny fabrics, things generating light & heat,

INTERIORS :
Kitchens, stoves, fire places.
SHAPES : Pointed, slanted, sharp angled, buildings where animals are kept.

IDEAL USES :
Libraries, religious schools, businesses involving fashion designing, furnaces, chemicals, veterinary clinics.

Earth

QUALITIES :
Sympathy, honesty, faith, reliability.

MATERIALS :
Clay, bricks, concrete, tiles, marble, porcelain, crystal, sand.

INTERIORS :
Storage areas, lounges, garages, inner court yards.

SHAPES :
Flat, low, box-like, square, construction of bricks, clay or concrete.

IDEAL USES :
Hospitals, jails, government buildings, tombs, vaults, banks, business involving mining, tunneling, ceramics, agriculture and civil engineering.

Metal

QUALITIES :
Morality, ethics, righteousness, practical thinking.

MATERIALS :
Aluminum, iron, steel, copper, mirrors, wires, transparent films.

INTERIORS :
Workshops, kitchens, metal sinks & stoves.

SHAPES :
Roads and highways, gently rounded hilltops, round, curved, domed roofs, arches, castles.

IDEAL USES :
Businesses dealing with finance, metal jewelry, hardware, knives and swords, commercial and manufacturing buildings.

Water

QUALITIES :
Communication, transmission of ideas, wisdom, socialization.

MATERIALS :
Glass, buildings that are distinguished by major uses of glass.

INTERIORS :
Bathrooms, laundries, kitchens, wine cellars, swimming pools, ponds, fountains.

SHAPES :
Irregular shapes and construction features that seem to be 'thrown together' rather than designed.

IDEAL USES :
Art galleries, museums, concert halls, ad agencies, media business involving publishing, computers, electrical engineering, oil refineries, bottling companies, sailing, boats.

Wood

QUALITIES :
Creation, nourishment, upward growth, love of humanity, flexible thinking, balance between family and career.

MATERIALS :
All types of wood, fibers, vegetables, fruits, herbs, flowers and plants.

INTERIORS :
Children's room, bed rooms, dining rooms.

SHAPES : Tall, columnar, oblong, rectangular shapes of religious structures, sky scrapers and high towers.

IDEAL USES :
Creativity, nourishment, growth, nurseries, hot houses, hospitals, healing centers, restaurants, wooden goods dealers.

 fresh prespective

From dark to light!

Can you make this light bulb glow? Yes. Stare at the center of the bulb for about 30 second. Now shift your gaze to the dot in the blank space to the right of the bulb. After a few seconds, you will see the bulb glow.

Secret's of Jiten

Water can be a divine medicine, try it when all others fail.

Aspiring Shapes

Down the ages, shapes have played a great role in our lives. In our ancient texts also, the origin and importance of shapes are explained in depth. They have shown us how different shapes can be useful to us in our daily life. e.g. if you store water in a round vessel and then bathe with that water, it gives you relaxation. Whereas if you bathe with water stored in triangle vessel it gives you strength. The outermost shape in the picture below is 'Bhadra Shape' for welfare and prosperity. Our sages already had the complete information about shapes and their effects. But, today due to our preoccupation with other things, and our relative "unawareness" we have lost this precious art. We very well know the importance of holy water in churches and in the water reservoir in front of temples. We must relearn this lesson in order to live a more fruitful life.

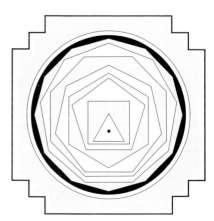

"Bhadra" shape for all-round prosperity and wellness.

Shape your Water
Effect of various 'Kundas' (Water Reservoirs)

Richness & Strength

Safeguard & Protection

Wish fulfilment & Progress

Joy & Pleasure

Love & Relationship

Balance & Harmony

Vitality & Wellness

Removes negativity

Peace & Relaxation

Seeing is a deeper process, eye is the first step and thousand other are in the mind.

#1. Shape Awareness

Find the five - pointed star in the mosaic below.

#2. Illusory Figure

See pyramid (not drawn) in below two figures.

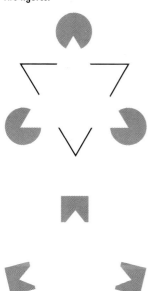

#3. Judge the Proportion

Is the distance from A to B shorter than from B to C ?

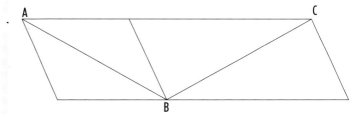

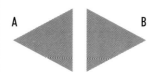

#4. Father - Mother

Find the invible mother in the visble father!

#5. Extended Vision

See the object for a while, the direction of the staircase changes as your perception changes

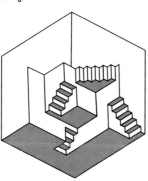

#6. Impossible Figure

Is it four steps or one?

#7. Apparant Movement

When you move this book in slightly circular motion, and glaze at the figure below movement is visible.

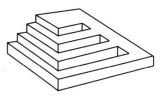

#8. Shape Distortion

Is this a perfect square?

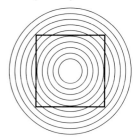

The Great Pyramid

In the Arabian Nights the
Great Pyramid was reputed to have
magic qualities and contain
extraordinary treasures.

"*Pyramid is a microprocessor of cosmic energy.*
It is an instrument between the energy circuit of Sun, Earth and Moon".

Prof. Dr. Jiten Bhatt

Decoding
Pyramid

The Pyramid has puzzled and fascinated mankind since ages. Its history, its size, its engineering and its era have always been a mystery. But most astonishing of all is its function. Why was it built? Why was it only of that shape? How does it work?

What is the Pyramid? A message left by the Gods? The store house of earth's past and future? A mechanism for concentrating unseen psychic energies? A royal tomb? A treasure house? An astronomical observatory? What ever it is, it has always been tantalizing and dazzling to us.

There are numerous questions arising in our mind and a picture of an enormous size in our eyes as we talk about Pyramids. They have always left us baffled with their astonishing way of working, their power of preserving and their energies.

A few years ago, examining the body of an Egyptian princess Mene whose body had lain for millenia in Pyramid, researchers determined that her skin cells were still capable of life, though, the princess was dead for almost 3000 years! Amazing, Isn't it?

Visible is equally supported by invisible.

Unsolved Mysteries

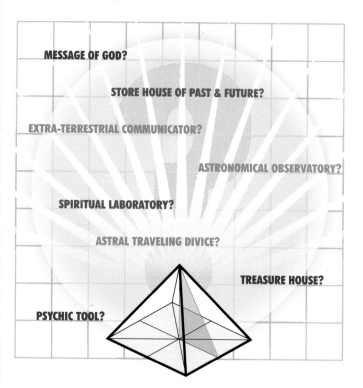

MESSAGE OF GOD?

STORE HOUSE OF PAST & FUTURE?

EXTRA-TERRESTRIAL COMMUNICATOR?

ASTRONOMICAL OBSERVATORY?

SPIRITUAL LABORATORY?

ASTRAL TRAVELING DIVICE?

TREASURE HOUSE?

PSYCHIC TOOL?

Since centuries the Pyramids of Egypt have been a constant inspiration for numerous exciting theories about their purpose and method of construction. Even their enigmatic hieroglyphic texts have mystified many. Everybody from poets to artists to archeologists to travelers have had many interesting things to say about them.

But a mystery is nothing but the lack of clarity about that matter. A mystery is like a tree where our eyes can see the upper part of it but not its roots, which are present below the surface. Similarly, science has given us the outer evident fragment of the pyramids. But still the inner formula has to be found out. It is because we are too much involved in searching for materialistic evidences like what stone was used and where did they get it? In spite of being non-archeological people we are so obsessed with all these minor details, which may be of least importance to us. We have to try and see the whole concept of the Pyramids and the real formula behind their construction. We should be able to use that for our purposes and in today's life style.

Pyramids have immense power, which the ancient Egyptians experimented and used for proposes we are not much aware of. We think they were built for restoring mummies. But evidence now shows they were built later, upon the mastabas , where all mummies or sarcophagus were found. No mummy was found inside the pyramid structure. They were all found from mastabas below the pyramid. This suggests that the Pyramids, though built on the mastabas, were constructed for purposes more than mere restoring the mummies of their Pharaohs.

Let us see the example of our own Taj Mahal. We know it is a tomb built by a Mughal emperor, Shah Jahan for his beautiful wife, Mumtaz Mahal. But very few of us may be aware of the fact that it was actually built by some Hindu King for his two queens. He built two such similar palaces for each of his queens on the two opposite banks of river Yamuna. One of them was white, which Shah Jahan reconstructed as Taj Mahal and the other was black, whose remains were recently excavated. Thus the fact can be quite different from what it appears to be now.

Pyramid is well supported by Earth and Cosmic powers

Imagine that our civilization is completely demolished today. Someone discovers the remains of our civilization some 4000-5000 years from today and finds a washing machine or a computer. From the excavation evidence they relate it to be the only use of electricity. To them and their civilization this would be a great archeological finding to the way we lived. But the truth still would be that we initially used electricity for lighting lamps, but later on used it for everything from alarm clocks to toasters to computers. To know about a civilization we should understand their era, needs, and the minds of people then. We cannot relate it to a part of materialistic evidence obtained today. Similarly a powerful mystic tool like Pyramid has to be understood in a more detailed and internal, non-materialistic path. We will learn more about the use of this powerful concept of pyramid energy in the chapter on PyraVastu.

Try This!

Can you Mix Pyramid & Vastu

Each eye is shown a different picture (one seeing only pyramid and the other eye only Vastu Purush). If you cross eyes slightly and try to see your nose also see the book. You will notice the two figures are blended, and the Vastu Purush seems to be in the Pyramid!

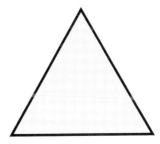

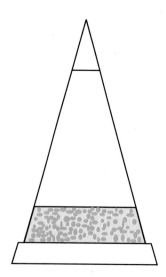

mer 'pyramid'

'Any gods who shall cause this pyramid and this construction of the king to be good and sturdy, it is they who will be vital, it is they who will be respected, it is they who will be impressive, it is they who will be in control... it is they who will take possession of the crown.'

Pyramid Texts 1650.

The Map on right is of Egypt, showing nine genuine pyramids and one first basic pyramid for experiment.

Exploring Egypt

Since the pyramids are enveloped in such a maze of hypothesis about themselves, they have fascinated me since childhood. It was last year that daddy and me went to Egypt. It was actually my first visit to the pyramids of Egypt. When we reached Cairo, the capital of Egypt, it seemed just as any other city of India to me. People around did not seem very different except for their language and attire. I saw how well day-to-day activities blended in and around the city in presence of such great historical wonders. These huge pyramids can be seen from the upper floors of all houses, buildings and monuments of Cairo. "Misr" as the local people call Cairo, indeed has a unique pervasive sense of timelessness about it.

The experience next day was truly life defining for me. Visiting the pyramids is undoubtedly an amazing experience. The huge mountains of stones built around 3rd century B.C., exude such an aura of mystery and omnipotence that they exceeded our imagination beyond reasonable boundaries. We spent the whole day visiting the inside of all pyramids at Giza. The next week swept by in visiting various pyramids and in experimenting and researching there. No book or person including me can exactly describe you this awe-inspiring experience of this land of pyramids where magic meets mystery. Let us explore this land and see its Pyramid-related history.

The Egyptians call the pyramids 'mer' which is probably derived from 'm' meaning instrument or device and 'er' meaning ascension or moving to the higher position.

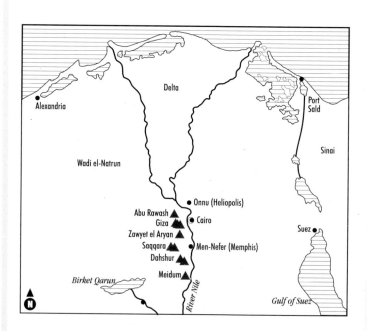

Pharaoh Zoser built the first pyramid in the 3rd century B.C. He built the Step Pyramid at Saqqara Necropolis. It was built on the suggestion of Imhotep, Pharaoh Zoser's high priest, a great architect, and scholar of medicine and healing sciences. He is considered by many to be the father of medicine. The Egyptian building techniques then progressed to many intermediate pyramids like those at Meidum and the Bent pyramid at Dahshur. It was during 2478 to 2413 B.C. that the Egyptian pyramid architecture was at its peak and the pyramids of Khafre, Menkaure and Khufu were constructed.

Secret's of Jiten

The real meaning of pyramid is the instrument (yantra) to lift us from all angles.

The Pyramids were built from large blocks of limestone and were covered by the smooth Tura limestone. They were crowned by capstones known as the pyamidion. These capstones were the exact miniature of the whole pyramid and were sometimes covered with thin sheets of an alloy of gold and silver. Thus the Pyramids were also considered being symbolic materialization of the Sun's rays.

The techniques they used to lift the blocks of limestone, some weighing around 2.5 tons and more than ten meters high, are still unknown. It is hypothesized that they must have used specially prepared ramps or slopes either straight or spiraling around the pyramid. It is thought that they must have dragged these stones on wooden logs or sledges. The knowledge of the ancient Egyptian in fields of mathematics, astronomy, and architecture seems quite advanced for their era, enabling them to build pyramids with such astonishing perfection and accuracy.

Hypothetical construction of a pyramid with the use of spiral ramps.

Previously we thought that slaves who must have been forced to work under inhuman conditions built pyramids. We thought it must have been due to the command of their cruel and megalomaniac Pharaohs. But modern archeology proves it wrong. They say skilled artisans, astrologists and workers who were paid regular wages and provided with food and houses built pyramids. These artisans had their own special methods of finding the accurate dimensions and measurements to built the pyramids. Farmers did manual labor in summers when Nile River was flooded and they could not work on their farms. They considered their Pharaohs as gods as they were so kind-hearted. They built these structures for some higher and nobler cause, not for mere personal use.

The technique used to determine true North by using the merkhet, a gauge that measured the position of a circumpolar star when it rose and set.

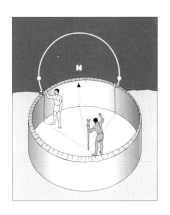

Do you know than not know O Asclepius, that Egypt is the copy of heaven, or rather, the place where, here below are mediated and projected all operations which govern and activate the heavenly forces, even more than that, if the whole truth is to be told our land is the temple of the entire world.

Hermes Tristmegistus to Asclepius,
Corpus Hermeticum.

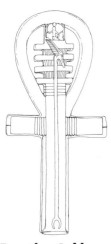

Egyptian Ankh

This represented the power of the Sun God. Ancient Egyptians believed that carrying it or wearing it brought good luck.

Land where magic meets mystery

Above are the two Egyptian deities or Neter- Ra and Tehuti (Thoth). Ra is the falcon headed Sun God of ancient Egypt. He was believed to be the creator of all life and source of energy for all living beings. He is still worshipped by people of certain cults. The other God is Tehuti (Thoth) who is the god of Magic and Occult Wisdom. It is said that he brings the thirst for the Cosmic Truth. He is the originator of all arts and sciences: mathematics, writing, astronomy, geometry and medicine. Egyptians refer to their gods as Neter, which mean the ones, who exist eternally.

The circular zodiac detail shown in this carving proves the depth of understanding of Egyptian masters. This picture shows 36 deacons, 10 day week and 12 arm represents 12 months of the year.

Secret Wisdom

Egyptian Gods and Goddesses represented aspects of the natural world. Like the numerous Gods and Goddesses of India, they too had different names for one god according to their forms or guises. To visualize this abstract quality of the Egyptian wisdom, high intuitive and intellectual abilities are required.

The Pyramids, their carvings, well decorated tombs and temples and their deep understanding of the laws of nature reflect immense knowledge and awareness the possessed. The myths, gods, spiritual beliefs and symbolization show their esoteric insight and depth of wisdom. The great Egyptian masters may have intentionally represented all this knowledge in the symbolic form. They would have done so to pass their wisdom only to those capable of understanding their symbols, thus, intending to use their knowledge, magic and mesmerism only for the benefit of humanity. The Egyptians not only possessed such deep knowledge in fields of writing, magic, mathematics, geometry, astronomy, and medicine but they also knew how to preserve it. Their pictures, paintings, sculptures, monuments, jewelry and preserved bodies or mummies were extremely well preserved for later generations to gain from it.

The figure on right shows, Hawk - headed man holding a spear shows angle dividing seven stars of the Great Bear into four and three.

▲ Symbolic Expressions

Ancient Egypt was one of the oldest civilizations to have developed a symbolic expression. They call this language as Medu-Netru. It uses symbols from nature which possess a geometrical value, sound, volume, energy and a feeling about it. It connects one mentally, emotionally and spiritually to that symbol. Let us understand this with the example of their god of time, Sebek or the Crocodile God. A crocodile is directly connected to the aspect of time because of its biological cycle and anatomical evidence. A crocodile comes up on the land in daytime and slips beneath the waters during night. This shows that crocodile is a solar animal, which is directly connected to the Sun. Therefore it symbolizes the concept of duality or day and night in 24 hours. A female crocodile carries her eggs for 60 days and breeds them for 60 days. It has 60 teeth, 60 vertebrae and lives for about 60 years.

Sixty is our fundamental unit of measurement of time. 60 seconds constitute a minute and 60 minutes constitute an hour. Thus a crocodile aptly symbolizes the concept of time.

Sebek, the Crocodile God. He represented Time for the ancient Egyptians.

Scarab: the Egyptians call this beetle-like insect, Khefru. Ancient Egyptians understood the beginning of life, with the ball of sun being pushed. The Khefru pushes a ball of dirt on earth, when it walks. Thus, the scarab meant reflector of light, truth and regeneration to the ancient Egyptians. Even today, Scarab amulets, rings, pendants and other pieces of jewelry made from precious stones are worn in Egypt for protection.

Can you believe this!

I am the Time.
My each cell is the hidden formula of time, surrender to me.

Symbolic Language

Try these charts to write your name or to send a secret message.

God with the arms supporting the sky, indicates

10,00,000

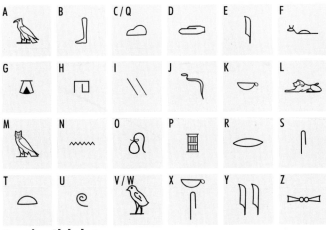

Egyptian Alphabets

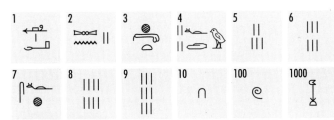

Egyptian Numbers

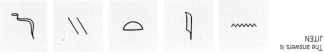

Can you decode this!

The answers is
JITEN

The Egyptian Hieroglyphics

Hieroglyph is the sacred written language of the ancient Egyptians. They had developed this unique and highly evolved form of writing or expressing which even included grammar. Their decorative form of writing was not only applied on the temple, tombs, mastabas and pyramids but also in form of scriptures on the papyrus. They had developed alphabet, numbers and certain complex group of hieroglyphs, which had different meanings when written together. Their pronunciations were entirely different than those used by us when speaking English.

Let us learn a little about this mysterious script and see whether we can write our names and other simple details or names of our friends and members of family. You can also inscribe them on a pendant in gold or silver, which is a very common practice in Egypt.

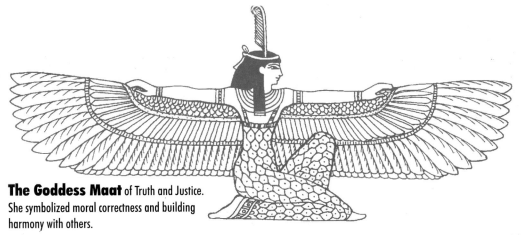

The Goddess Maat of Truth and Justice. She symbolized moral correctness and building harmony with others.

▲ Giza Power Plant

A visit at the Giza plateau is like instant attunement with the Pharaonic times. The necropolis of Giza was once connected with the Nile through canals and basins, which washed the valley temples of the Pyramids. It was Khufu who built the first Pyramid in this plateau, then known as Rosetau. He was followed by his two successors, Khafre and Menkaure. Thus making Giza one of the most powerful pyramid sites.

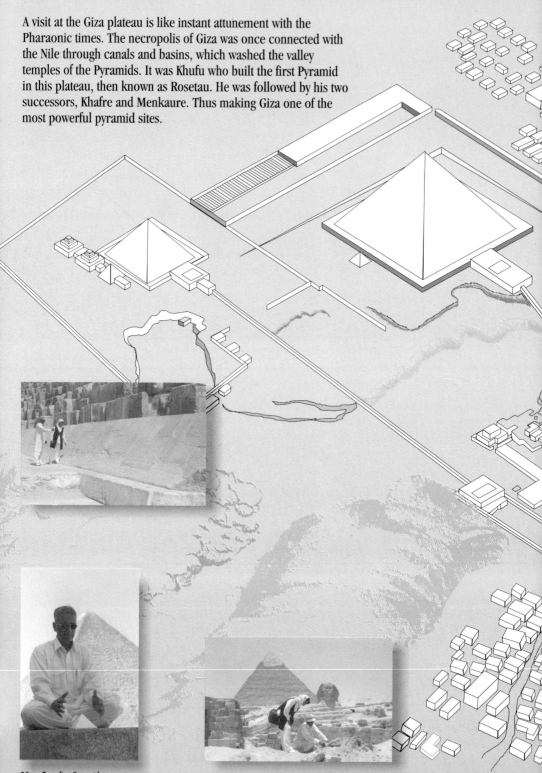

Facts and Figures

Pyramids are amazing structures. Their cause is a mystery, yet their existence is an undoubted fact.

◆The base of The Great Pyramid is slightly more than 13 acres and it is levelled to a fraction of an inch.

◆More than 2,600,000 blocks of granite and limestone weighing from 2 to 70 tons each are used.

◆They are so accurately put together that the joints are never more than 1/5th of an inch wide.

◆The pyramids contain more solid masonry than all the temples built in India.

◆The largest stone known measures 27 feet in length, 5 feet in breadth and 7 feet in width and weighs over 70 tons.

◆The stones used for construction of the Great Pyramid could be used for making 30 Empire State buildings.

◆The stones in the structure would be enough for a wall of 3ft height and 1ft width to be built from Delhi to Kolkota, Kolkota to Chennai, Chennai to Mumbai and Mumbai to Delhi.

◆During exploratory flight of Mariner-9 to planet Mars, massive pyramidal structures of about base of 3 miles and height of 4,800 feet were photographed and according to reports at N.A.S.A. they are not the ones created naturally but seem to be made with measurements and accuracy.

◆The Great Pyramid is so perfectly oriented towards true north, that it is only 3 minutes off. The best modern effort of ours in creating the structure in true north is at the Paris Observatory which is 6 minutes off.

◆If you multiply the weight of the Great Pyramid (about 5,300, 000 tons) with 1,000, 000, 000, 000,000 you get the approximate weight of the earth.

The great seal of the United States.
Mystic Pyramid symbol is the secret of their control and power.

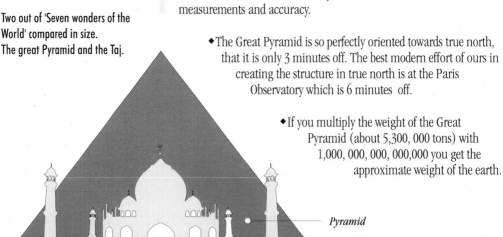

Two out of 'Seven wonders of the World' compared in size.
The great Pyramid and the Taj.

Pyramid
Taj
Man

 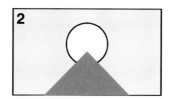 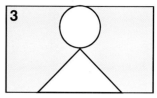

In early spring, when the sun rises just high enough above the apex of the Great Pyramid, the whole shadow on the north face vanishes at the strike of noon.

More Facts

- The average height of all land above sea level is given to be 455 feet and amazingly the height of Pyramid is also 454.5 feet.(without the capstone)

- The lime stones used in the building of Pyramid were brought from about a distance of 500 miles because there is no evidence of limestone quarry anywhere nearer than that.

- 2,600,00 are estimated to be used in making of The Great Pyramid. It was built in 20 years ie. 7300 workdays. This means 365 stones were arranged daily or 30 stones every hour for 12 hours a day. It seems absolutely impossible to put and arrange accurately the stones weighing 2-70 tons in just 2 minutes even with our modern equipment.

Secret's of Jiten

The Pyramids were built in the center of the World. They knew the importance of Brahmasthala according to Vastu 5000 years back.

The vital center is most important. This is to be selected for some special purpose (more in PyraVastu page 129).

Lower Egypt is the geographical center of ther land surface of the whole world.

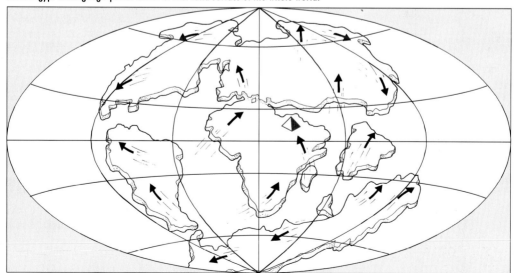

World's First Pyramid

Zoser (Saqqara)
Base: 121 x 109 m
Height: 60 m
Volume: 3,30,400 cu.m

Important Nine

The major Pyramids were built during the 3rd and the 4th dynasty. These huge structures represent much more than an advanced cultural development. The accuracy of their masonry is comparable to the modern day technologies we possess with help of computers. Only these ten pyramids are considered as genuine and they are located within 80 km (50 miles) of each other. The first Pyramid or the Step Pyramid was built on a mastaba where Pharaoh Zoser's identification was left. The remaining nine are considered to be of more importance. There were no identification marks left on them by the Pharaohs who built them. The number nine is of great importance for the Pyramids as Egyptians considered nine as the number of Neteru (gods) who created this universe. This group of nine deities was known as Ennead. The ancient Egyptian texts refer to the Ennead as a single powerful divine entity.

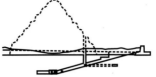

Sekhemket (Saqqara)
Base: 120 x 120 m
Height: 7 m (unfinished)
Volume: 33,600 cu.m

Khaba (Zawiyet el-Aryan)
Base: 84 x 84 m
Height: 20 m (unfinished)
Volume: 47,040 cu.m

Sneferu (Meidum)
Base: 144 x 144 m
Height: 92 m
Volume: 6,38,733 cu.m

Bent Pyramid (Dahshur)
Base: 188 x 188 m
Height: 105 m
Volume: 12,37,040 cu.m

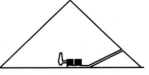

Red Pyramid (Dahshur)
Base: 220 x 220 m
Height: 105 m
Volume: 16,94,000 cu.m

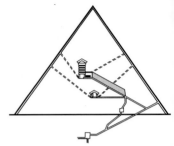

Khufu (Giza), Great Pyramid
Base: 230 x 230 m
Height: 146.42 m
Volume: 25,83,280 cu.m

Gedefre (Abu Rawash)
Base: 106 x 106 m
Height: 67 m
Volume: 1,31,043 cu.m

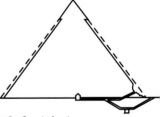

Khafre (Giza)
Base: 215 x 215 m
Height: 143 m
Volume: 22,11,090 cu.m

Menkaure (Giza)
Base: 102 x 104 m
Height: 65 m
Volume: 2,35,180 cu.m

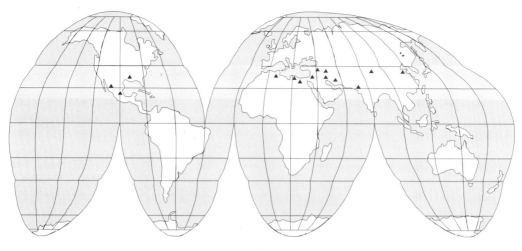

World - map showing the common latitude - (red) band of ancient civilizations

Types of pyramid

Toltec-Maya city in ancient America

Ziggurat at Tchaga-Zanbil, Elam

Barabudur, Java

Tenochtitlan, Aztecs, in the Lake Texcoco

⌂ Pyramids all Around

Egypt is well known for its Pyramids and their mysteries, but Egypt is not the only place where Pyramids are found. They are seen all over the world at different places, though they were discovered late.

The great Pyramid of Egypt is widely known because it is the largest and also mathematically and geometrically most perfect. It has no missing features as in some other Pyramids.

Pyramids were discovered in many parts of the world, notably in Mexico, the Himalayan valleys, South America, China, Siberia, Central America, Cambodia, Africa, France, England and the United States. Besides the Great Pyramid there are 130 other minor and major Pyramids in Egypt.

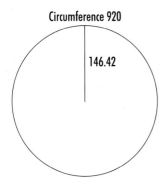

Circumference 920

146.42

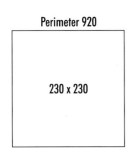

Perimeter 920

230 x 230

Trangle area:
146.42 x 230 / 2 = 16838

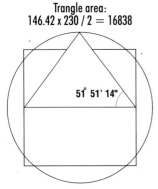

51° 51' 14"

Pyramid generation mathematics

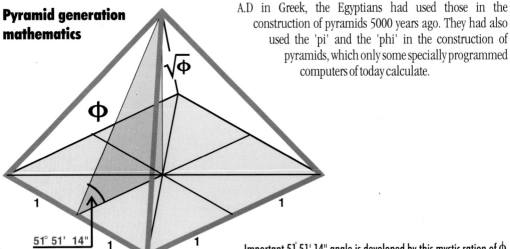

√φ

φ

1

1

51° 51' 14"   1

1

Important 51° 51' 14" angle is developed by this mystic ration of φ

Mystic Geometry

The 15th century was the time of great geographical discoveries. Between the 17th and the 18th centuries people in the West grew quite curious about the shape of the Earth, its size and many other such queries.

Egyptians already knew all this about 5000 years ago. But nobody was aware of their knowledge which was hidden amidst the hot sands of the Sahara desert. Since none could correctly understand and interpret their language, it remained a secret until the 19th century.

To the ancient Egyptians, numbers were of great significance. They had hidden meanings for numbers and were not available to common men of that time. Only the priest and highly learned people had access to their meanings. It is an intuitivist thought by some that the pyramids contain all necessary information to ensure the continuation of the world. The Egyptians had a highly evolved method of measuring weights and distance. Our modern mathematics still uses some of those principles like 360-degree circle, 60-second minute, 60-minute hour and many others. They had also a very advanced knowledge of the movements of the Earth plates. When built, the pyramids were in the center of the world and the Great Pyramid of Giza was considered to be the Prime Meridian or the starting point for calculation of time. It was considered that the pyramids were a part of the global co-ordinate system. Even today they are situated almost in the center of the world. Although we believe that the irrational numbers were not discovered before the 3rd century A.D in Greek, the Egyptians had used those in the construction of pyramids 5000 years ago. They had also used the 'pi' and the 'phi' in the construction of pyramids, which only some specially programmed computers of today calculate.

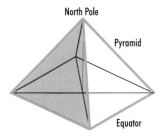

∧ Magic Ratio (φ) 'PHI

The measurement of the earth is not possible without the knowledge of · 'pi' (π) (geometrical constant used to calculate the circumference of a circle).

They calculated the circumference of the earth by careful observation of the movements of the planets and stars. We can see this knowledge in the making of the Pyramids. It is an encapsulation of the knowledge of that time. Egyptian scale of measurement is based on the earth's dimensions. The standard British inch was derived from a unit of measurement used by the ancient Egyptians. The Pyramid, incorporated in its dimensions a value of 3.14159+ for pi, an amazingly accurate value when compared to Taylor's 3.144. The Pyramid's base-length, when divided into units of 25 inches, gives 365.2. This figure represents the number of days in a year! The Gregorian Calendar and the concept of a day of 24 hours has come from ancient Egypt.

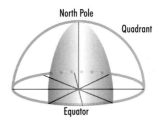

Pyramid geometry is directly related with the spherical shape of the earth.

Another more important ratio is (φ) , 'PHI' is an unending ratio as 'PI'. This mystical number is as old as history and well connected with life-force. The leaf distribution in plants is represented by a curious system of numbers known as a summation series, also called the fibonacci series.

This series is obtained by adding together the two proceeding terms. Thus : 1, 2, 3, 5, 8, 13, 21, 34, 55, 89, 144, 233, 377, 610, 987, 1597, 2584, 4181, 6765 ...etc.

This ratio of 'PHI' or 1.618033989.... is obtained by dividing any one term of the summation series by its predecessor.

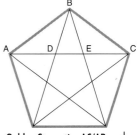

Golden Star ratio: AC/AB = φ

'PHI' is also known as the 'SACRED CUT'. This magic ratio was used by all ancient great Masters. This is considered to be the most perfect aesthetic proportion of division.

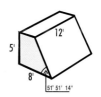

Due to huge structure each stone requires very high accuracy.

Occult power of pyramid is developed because of its perfect tunning with the nature's law and mathematical ratios. In occult language when circle becomes square and a square is transformed into infinite point, the pyramid is generated. Also our body is divided by the same ratio. Due to this harmonious occult language between man and the pyramid we get amazing results.

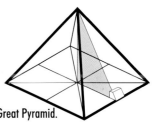

Relation of the casting stones to the slope of the Great Pyramid.

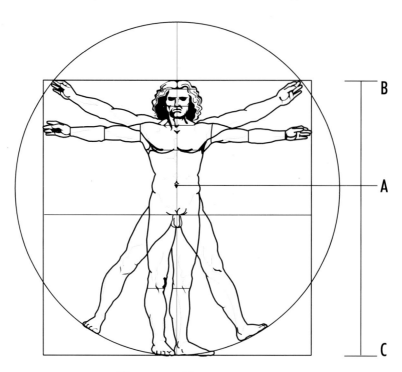

Human body ratio: AC/AB or BC/AC = 1.618 i.e. same as of pyramid

B

A

C

Human Geometry

The geometry of the human body is indicative of the highest mysteries of the cosmos. The circle may be formed from a person lying on his back, with a compass placed at the navel. The square is formed from the measurement of the height from head to toe and the width of the outstretched arms. Man is a microcosm, the perfect image of the universe.
In the above drawing by Leonardo da Vinci, ca.1510. we can see the golden section as a basis of measurements on the human body. The sacred proportion appears throughout nature and is the governing ratio in the Great Pyramid

Occult Experience

Alexander the Great visited this mysterious King's chamber and experienced some unexplainable feeling and so did many others. But I never believed those stories until I visited the King's chamber myself. When we went into that chamber, meditation just happened. There was something very different, a feeling and an experience that cannot be expressed in words. Something clicked inside, yet nothing drastic occurred there as said in the stories. This unique effect is the result of the perfect proportioning of the King's chamber and the whole Great Pyramid.

Figure showing dimensional accuracy of the King's chamber is the Great Pyramid

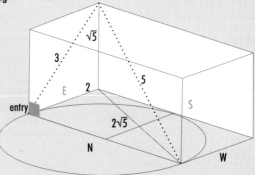

Two
Powerful Shapes

As we already know, shapes are two or three dimensional. Now let us study more about the three dimensional shapes and their properties.

The unmanifested energy is continuously transformed into shapes. Shapes are working boundaries of different energies for some purpose. We see thousands of different shapes and also shapes which are constantly changing from one to another. They are undergoing an everlasting evolution. 'Shape' is the basis of universal happening . Our single life is too short to study and understand it. Here we will make a joint effort to study a few important shapes that we encounter in our daily lives.

Sphere is the most stable shape of the universe and it can be in the form of soap bubble, hot air balloon, pebbles on river bank or sea shore, playing balls and marbles, beads of a necklace, earth and planets, our super computer-brain, eyes and many more. Geometrically the distance of the surface of the sphere from its center is equidistant. This is a very important shape in 'shape-energetics'. These type of shapes are static yin,

feminine, calming down, having controlling and pacifying property, and condensed form of any energy.

Pointed shapes with different bases, like Conical, Pyramidal, Diamond, or like spikes, points or pricks coming out, the shapes like that of the sun, pollen or viruses, are all dynamic shapes, having yang, male, father, motivating, activating and emitting properties.

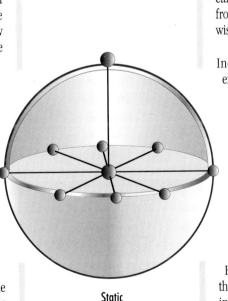

Dynamic

Static

In the mind power instrument pyramidal shape and dome (half of the sphere) is very popular. We can see hundreds of examples from our life and from ancient wisdom.

Indian temples are unique examples of the combination of both 'energy shapes'. The dome, yin shape is found in the front and the Pyramidal, yang shape is found at the back. Many researchers have put great efforts to find out the secret energetics of Pyramid, many hypothesis and theories have come out of this work. From all this, one thing is sure that the Pyramid is the shape-instrument that resonates with the cosmic energy emanating from the sun and outer space, to the earth.

Cosmic Connection

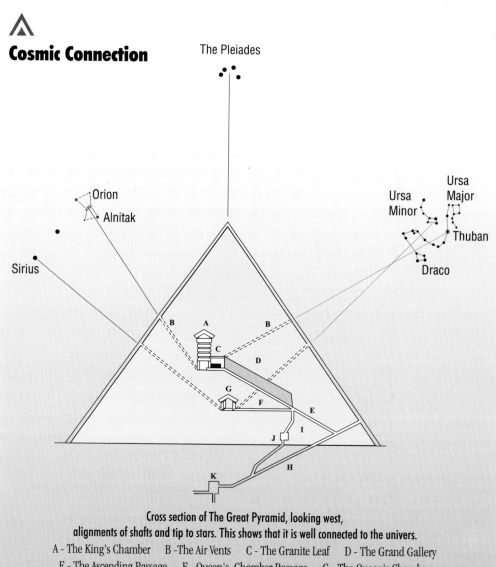

Cross section of The Great Pyramid, looking west,
alignments of shafts and tip to stars. This shows that it is well connected to the univers.

A - The King's Chamber   B -The Air Vents   C - The Granite Leaf   D - The Grand Gallery
E - The Ascending Passage   F - Queen's Chamber Passage   G - The Queen's Chamber
H - The Descending Passage   I - The 'Well Shaft'   J - The 'Grotto'
K - The 'Pit'   L - Outline of the Pyramid

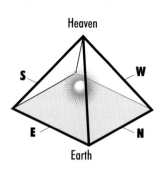

Six Interactions

The pyramid interacts with the universal energy is in six directions -
energy from four sides, top (heaven) and bottom (earth). In this earth
is represented by the square base and the apex represents the sky.
Interaction with four sides are made with triangular face. Pyramid is
microprocessor of all universal energy. It works with showering energy
from the sun, moon and planets and ascending energy of earth.
Meeting of all six energies is at 'Mid' the center.

◭ Pyramid Chakra

Man is a smaller version of the universe. As per the sacred geometry of the ancient Egyptians, the space inside the Pyramid is the whole universe in itself. It is constructed keeping in mind the 'human architecture'.

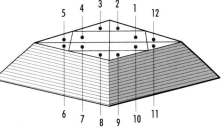

Also, in Indian cosmology the concept of 'Purusha' - the man is central. In India, temples are built according to the spiritual human anatomy. According to our ancient literature of 'Upanishadas', the human being has five basic vital elements. They believe that man is the reflection of Nature - our Universe and so, the architecture should reflect the Man. The Man is controlled by the five elements and seven energy chakras. Thus, the beautiful co-relation of universe-man-architecture creates a link between the essentiality of our five elements and seven energy centers. This perfect miniature universe of pyramid can bring balance and harmony in a particle, cell or matter.

Cross section of pyramid at the center of gravity is connected with 12 aspects of life.

1. Physical appearance
2. Inheritance, wealth
3. Brothers, Sisters
4. Mother, prosperity
5. Intellect, children, love
6. Enemies, diseases
7. Marriage and business partner
8. Death, losses
9. Good luck, journeys
10. Father, prestige
11. Personal gains
12. Expenditures and bondage

The pyramid is directly related to the seven energy centers and five elements of our body.

Hidden -Power Center

Simple meaning of Pyramid is Pyra+Mid, Pyra means fire and Mid means center.
In ancient days scholars use to put whole formula in a single word or sentence.
So it can't be that simple, let's explore this Pyra+Mid formula!

Pyra + Mid

Fire is known as 'Agni' in Sanskrit. It has many other meanings too in Sanskrit. The deeper
meaning of fire in relation to life force, body or a cell is initiation or firing, triggering or
motivating activity at the genetic code or the center of our floppy disk.
The Egyptian masters had already understood the deeper meaning of 'fire' and had devised the
Pyramid according to that purpose. According to them, 'Pyramid' is divided in to two parts -
'PYRA' and 'MID'
'PYRA' means fire, the Initiator at the center core or nuclei. 'MID' means in the middle. Center is
very important, the 'Master Key' to unlock the secrets within.

Though only very little is known about Pyramids today, they are a scientifically designed
instruments with holistic approach.
The complete detailed knowledge of stars, galaxy, sun, planets, earth's dimensions, amount of
land and water on earth, rotating speed of magnetic field, gravity, wind, time, space and energy,
life force and the aspect of body, mind and spirit is seen in the making of the Pyramid. Its perfect
creation owes itself to this deeper knowledge.

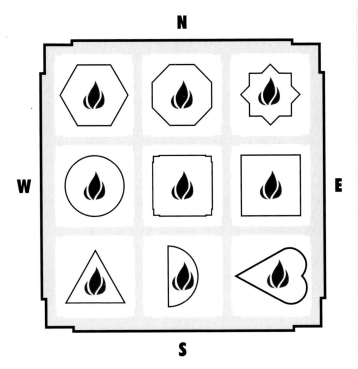

N

W

E

S

Different shapes used for desired results.

Pyramidal Fire

Sun is the 'source of origin' of all creation on our planet. Our inner momentum is guided by the Sun. It is the essential element of life and it is our super soul.

Science and religion both believe in the power of the Sun. In many religions, Fire is worshipped as God. It is the vibrant form or a communicating terminal of the Sun. Importance of holy fire is seen alike in India and abroad. In India people believe in Sun as their father and earth as their mother. Mother Earth is surrounded by a layer of atmosphere or a subtle body of Earth. Due to our unawareness about this holistic concept, we are spoiling the vital etheric body of earth by chemicals, noise, air pollution and by nuclear radiations. These disturbances directly affect us physiologically and pyschologically.

In Vedic times, our ancestors had evolved a wonderful method of Yagna (Holy Fire). Yagna is the subtle process of healing, revitalizing, harmonizing or purifying the auric body of Mother Earth and ourselves with the help of Pyramidal fire.

Performing Yagna

Let us learn, step-by- step the simple method of performing this holy fire (Yagna) which can bring health and happiness in our life. Now-a-days many people, here and abroad, practice the performance of holy fire and those who regularly practice this process of holy fire are called 'Agnihotra'.

Exactly at sunrise and sunset after uttering the first Mantra as given below add the first portion of the offering to the FIRE. Then utter the second Mantra and add the remaining portion of the offering to the FIRE. Try to sit near the fire as long as you can immediately after each Yagna to experience the peace.

Success & Prosperity

Marriage & Children

Well-being

Enemy destruction

Peace

Neutralisation of bad effects

Annihilation of disease

Rain

Total health

Yagna

At Sunrise :
Sgryaya Swaha, Suryaya Idam Na Mama
(Add the first portion of the offering to 'FIRE')
Prajapataye Swaha, Prajapataya Idam Na Mama
(Add the remaining portion of the offering to 'FIRE') This completes
morning Yagna.

At Sunset :
Agnaye Swaha, Agnaye Idam Na Mama
(Add the first portion of the offering to 'FIRE')
Prajapataye Swaha, Prajapataya Idam Na Mama
(Add the remaining portion of the offering to 'FIRE') This completes
Evening Yagna.

Note :
1. The sunrise and sunset timing are to be found out for the place
(where one is performing Yagna) from the local almanac or from the
nearby weather station.
2. A pinch of rice grains and two three drops of cow's ghee together
forms the offering to be made to the FIRE.

How to perform Yagna?

Yagna requires a variety of specific materials.
Container :
For Yagna a copper Pyramid of prescribed size is required.

Rice :
Unbroken pieces of unpolished rice should be used for Yagna

Ghee :
Ghee should be prepared from the butter of cow's pure milk.

Dried Cow Dung :
Cow dung is a medicinal substance.
Dried cow dung cakes should be used.

'FIRE' preparation :
Take a few pieces of dry cow dung and keep one small flat piece in the
bottom touching the Pyramid. Arrange the other pieces on the four
sides of the Pyramid in such a way as to allow free air movement so
that everything is completely burned. Light the fire by using camphor
or 'GUGUL' or 'DHOOP' or apply ghee in sufficient quantity to the
pieces of cow dung. One should not use kerosene or cooking gas or such
other material for lighting the fire.

Effect of various Agni in
Kundas (holy-fire vessels)

Make your own Pyramid!

If you are interested in performing Pyramid experiments you can make one of your own Pyramids. A step-by-step method to prepare one is given below.

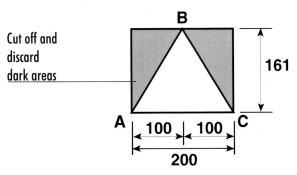

Cut off and discard dark areas

B

161

A | **100** | **100** | **C**

200

**Fig. 1 Basic Pattern for side
(You will need 4 of these)**

The simplest Pyramid to prepare is the one that is made of four identical triangles taped together at the side. The efficiency of Pyramid improves if it has a flat base hinged to the bottom of one of the sides. It is possible to make Pyramids as high as you like, provided you keep the proportions constant. You can select and make any size given in the table.

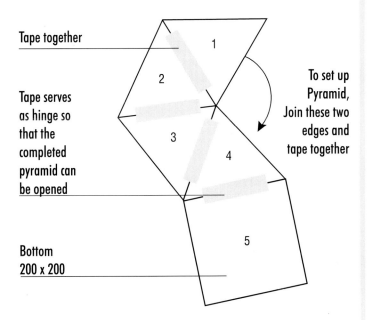

Tape together

Tape serves as hinge so that the completed pyramid can be opened

Bottom
200 x 200

1

2

3

4

5

To set up Pyramid, Join these two edges and tape together

Fig. 2

To start with -

1) Take a hard cardboard or a mount board.

2) Measure four rectangles each measuring 200mm base and 161 mm height. Cut them.

3) Put them on a table with the base-side facing you.

4) Draw one centre line on it, 100 mm from both sides.

5) Now connect the line from A to B and B to C as shown in figure 1.

6) Using sharp scissors, blade or cutter cut along AB and BC.

7) Now you will have four Pyramid faces of the same dimensions as that of the Great Pyramid.

8) Put the Pyramid faces on the table and tape them together with a masking or cellulose tape, as shown in figure 2.

9) Cut a square piece of the hard cardboard or mount board with 200 mm each side and join this to the base of any one of the Pyramid faces as shown in figure 2.

10) Join all the sides of the Pyramid to complete the model.

11) Do not join the base piece in all directions, to allow you to place the required experimenting material inside.
As per the experiments done by researchers, maximum energy concentration in the Pyramid is at its 1/3 rd height from the bottom in the central axis passing from the apex. In the original Pyramid also the King's Chamber is located at 1/3 rd height. So, to get optimum results we will prepare one such platform for our model Pyramid.

12) Now, with the same cardboard make a square platform such that it is 1/3 rd the height of your Pyramid. That will be of approximately 42 mm height and 50 X 50 mm base, as shown in figure 3.

13) Orient your model Pyramid perfectly to the north-south magnetic pole axis of the earth to obtain accurate results.

14) Lastly, stick a spotless white paper on all sides of your model.

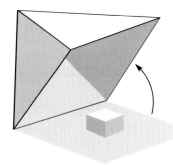

Pyramid with platform

And, that is your basic experimental Pyramid model ready. For making some Pyramids larger than this , a table for reference is given below. For optimum results always insist on accuracy of measurement and perfect magnetic north-south axis orientation.

Base (in mm)	Side (in mm)	Height* (in mm)	Platform height (in mm)
100	95.14	63.66	21.22
200	190.28	127.32	42.44
300	285.42	190.98	63.66
400	380.56	254.64	84.88
500	475.70	318.30	106.10

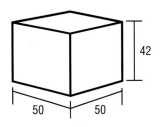

Fig. 3 Platform

* NOTE - Height given in the table is that obtained after construction of your Pyramid.

Orientation of Pyramid
As shown in the figure no. 4, any one base line of Pyramid must be aligned parallel to the north-south axis. For accurate results buy one magnetic compass from a scientific apparatus supplier.

Placement of your Pyramid
Your Pyramid is precious for you and hence keep it properly. There are some small instructions that have to be followed for getting positive results.

1) Your Pyramid must be kept in a clean, airy place.

2) There should be no filth in its surroundings.

3) Electric wires, electric and electronic gadgets must be kept at a distance. But if your purpose is for computers and electronic appliances, then you can place the Pyramid on them.

4) Its apex should always be pointing upwards.

5) There should be some space above its apex and around.

Fig. No. 4 Orientation

S

W

E

N

Baseline

Material of Pyramid

Spotless white is the most ideal color for any material used in making Pyramid. So white art card, white plastic or acrylic are the ideal materials to be used. In natural material use white colored 'deodar' or silver wood.

Plywood is not very advisable because inside its layer, inferior quality of material is used with adhesives and chemicals. In short, apply white colour inside and outside your Pyramid made with any material.

The power of Pyramid can be enhanced by fixing copper, silver or gold at the apex of Pyramid. The best examples of this are found at the apex of temples, gurudwaras, mosques and churches.

Scientific Experimenting

For comparative scientific data collection you need control box of the same volume as that of the Pyramid.

Overloading

Many times it is found that desired results are not obtained. One common reason for this is the overloading of the material inside. The maximum volume of material inside must be less than 1/5th the volume of the Pyramid.

For example, when experimenting with a medium sized apple you need minimum of 500 X 500 mm Pyramid. Whereas for sharpening of razor blade you can use a Pyramid with base of 100 X 100 mm.

As an allopathic doctor I was doubtful about 'Pyramid Power'. But when I started using 'Pyramid 9x9' in my practice, miraculous results were achieved.

Dr. Pir Mohammed Rahmany
Well experienced medical practitioner, now specialist in Pyramid & Magnet Therapy

EXPERT'S OPINION

Start Experimenting

As pyramids are the most interesting ancient mysteries, thousands of scientists, researchers and miracle lovers try to explore them. Due to its magical properties amazing results are obtained, you to a can unfold some.

Since the publication of

'Psychic Discoveries behind the Iron Curtain', a number of experiments have been made by scientists, including our own researchers with models of different sizes, materials and research objects.

You need not be an expert to experiment with Pyramids. So, you too can go ahead and venture into the unexplained nature of working of the Pyramid.

At Razor's Edge

Karel Drbal Czech, radio engineer built a small Pyramid and put a razor blade into it. After some days he took the blade for shaving and to his astonishment it had re-sharpened. He kept the blade in the Pyramid between the shaves and for next 50 mornings he

Sharpen blade

Dry Cell charging

shaved with that magically blade - before that he could only have five shaves from a blade. Isn't it amazing ! But then how does it work? The Pyramid shape creates two-folded magnetic energy field which apparently combines with the dehydration process. All matter has moisture molecules within. The vibratory field set-up of Pyramid causes dehydration in matter molecules, resulting in vacancy within the molecule structure which in turn allow flow of molecule to ride in the magnetic field of the blade's edge, causing "sharpening" of the edge. Pyramid-treated blade edges just "round off" gradually but they never cause painful tugging or pulling of facial hair.

This re-sharpening phenomena also works for larger blades such as knives, scissors and other cutlery. However, it takes longer time due to larger mass involved. And yes, don't forget to align the blade's edge in North - South axis as shown in the figure.

Re-Charge Dry Battery

Today, the use of dry cells has increased extensively. Machines, electronic gadgets, toys etc. run on them

In almost every other tool, dry cells are used. Their increased utility makes them expensive. The re-charging apparatus is also costly. If you are on the look-out for something priceless, which also has many other advantages, then Pyramid is your answer.

Place your used dry cell under the Pyramid for about a week, aligned in north-south axis. If you have larger cells you would need longer time or a larger Pyramid.

Pyramid Milk

Milk, one of the best source of nutrients for kids and adults alike, is no doubt the most easily and abundantly available. Milk, when treated under the Pyramid for about 20 minutes, energizes and forms a very good tonic for all. More potent and energized milk can provide better health and strength than the normal milk.

You need not put any other flavourings and additional for more strength and energy because the milk itself has sufficient reserves and it enhances absolutely under Pyramid energy. But if you like flavoured milk, you can go for it. Remember to put the milk in the Pyramid 'before' adding artificial flavours.

Your kids too will like Pyramid milk and it will act as the best tonic for them. So wouldn't you like to give your family more energized strength and vitality?

Try Coffee

Leave a cup of coffee under the Pyramid for 20 - 30 minutes. Ah! what a change! You will find that its bitterness disappears and it has a mellower taste. A tin of fresh ground or instant coffee, should be left under the Pyramid overnight before making the coffee

Better satisfaction and taste

You can also try this with other drinks like fresh juices, wines and liquors. Pyramid makes them taste fresher and better. Especially the "tinny" flavour of canned drinks disappears on treatment with Pyramid.

So, isn't this a quick and interesting way to demonstrate Pyramid energy to your friends?

Natural Polish

Are you fed-up wearing dull jewellery and you don't have time to give them for polishing every now and then? Then Pyramid can help you here.

Place your Jewellery (preferably new) under the Pyramid after its first use and continue this after every use and your precious possessions will remain shiny for a longer time.

Not only jewellery, your coin collection, metallic antiques and other metal items will retain their shine and lustre for a longer time, if kept under the Pyramid.

Frozen Foods

Treat the food with Pyramid energy before freezing it. It will retain the fresh taste longer and resist the deterioration in texture often seen in frozen foods. Also keep the frozen food in the Pyramid for de-freezing which will give better taste and high edibility.

Meats

Place fresh or frozen meat under the Pyramid for about an hour, it will taste better and mellower. It is especially wonderful for improving the taste and diminishing the strong flavour of liver. Your meat will become tender and energized when kept under Pyramid.

Natural Foods

Honey, spices, herbs, sugar, eggs and dairy products have effective energizing in the

Pyramids, since they become more flavoured. The herbs and honey turn to surprising tonics and their effects in curing and healing are enhanced.

Bread & Chapatis

Breads in their original packing without any additional ingredients and preservatives, kept in the Pyramid for more than 7 weeks, unrefrigerated, showed no discernible loss of freshness. Now, whenever you buy breads or make chapatis keep them under Pyramid. They will remain fresh for longer time and you have additional benefits of cosmic energy too!

Fruits & Vegetables

Place your fresh fruit and vegetables under the Pyramid for about an hour before placing them in the fridge. They will retain their natural flavour and juiciness. If you are able to keep them under Pyramid all

Natural preserver

the time, they will last indefinitely, simply drying-up instead of rotting.

Dehydrating Foods

Extensive research it has revealed that Pyramid energy discourages, and in some cases, completely stops, the bacterial growth. But Pyramid encourages the dehydration process. Fruits, vegetables, and meat retain more of their fresh texture and flavour by Pyramid dehydrating.

Pets Like It!

Animals seem much more sensitive to Pyramid vibrations than people. Isn't it strange ? Try giving your pets a choice and you will be astonished to find that almost without fail they choose Pyramid energized water or food.

Pets seem to be more active, sporty and enthusiastic when kept under Pyramid or when given Pyramid charged food or drinks. It also heals their wounds more rapidly and keeps them healthy and lively throughout.

So, why don't you place a Pyramid above your pet's bed, provide it with Pyramid energized food and check it out for yourself ?

Sprout Tonic!

Pyramid sprouts are the richest source of easily available and digestable natural vitamins, minerals and enzymes, than any other natural food. They are rich in vitamins A, B-complex, C,D,E,G,K and minerals such as calcium, magnesium, phosphorous, chlorine, potassium and sodium. These minerals and vitamins are natural in form and so they are easily digested. They also supply us all eight essential amino-acids.

Weight control is also very easy when dieting on sprouts. Diet of well chosen sprouts when on, for losing weight, one does not end up looking drawn or flabby. Skin and muscles become firm and the whole body undergoes a slow process of 'rejuvenation'. One can live on sprout food for years together without any nutritional deficiency.

Pyramid sprouts are anti-constipative, anti-gas, enzyme-rich healing food which retards ageing and keeps the person beautiful, healthy and young. The sprouts are totally free from cholesterol, saturated fat and uric acid, ammonical salt etc.

Sprouts are very useful for our body and they also can be mixed and blended with many other accompaniments- 1. Raw and uncooked 2. As paste mixed with flour of chapati, paratha, etc 3. With salads 4. With green sauce 5. With honey 6. With fruits 7. With vegetables 8. With eggs 9. With soaked dry fruits 10. With upma and poha as dressing and many others.

Pyramid sprouts are excellent for people of all ages. From children to aged ones, every one can benefit from sprouts.

Sprouts act as the best natural tonic for children. When the paste of sprouts is kept under Pyramid overnight and then applied to skin, it rejuvenates the skin which appears younger, facial spots on skin vanish and it appears absolutely beautiful. The Pyramid helps in energizing the fabulous and marvellous working of the sprouts.

You can try making Pyramid sprouts for yourself. Take it daily and look at your rejuvenation with your own eyes! Here is a look at the vitamin-mineral content of some of the pulses and cereals used by us every day.

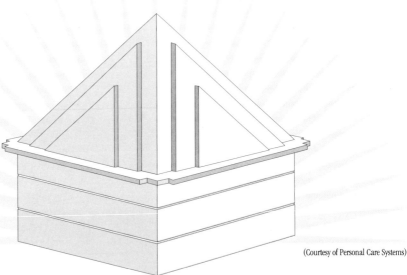

(Courtesy of Personal Care Systems)

Sprout Pyramid
This pyramid sprout maker is your powerful source of natural vitamins.

Daily Reference Chart

All our regualar food are full of rich vital elements, but what we need is the knowledge to get maximum beneifit out of each.

WHEAT

Vitamins : B1, B2, B3, B5, B6 and E

Minerals : Potassium, Zinc, Calcium, Sodium, Magnesium, Sulphur and Phosphorus.

WATER CRESS

Vitamins : A, B1, B2, B3, C, and D

Minerals : Potassium, Calcium, Iodine, Iron and Phosphorus.

METHI

Vitamins : A, B1, B2, B3, B5, and D

Minerals : Iron, Phosphorus. Sodium and Potassium.

MOONG

Vitamins : A, B1, B2, B3, and C,

Minerals : Calcium, Phosphorus, Iron, Sodium, and Potassium.

MATH BEAN

Vitamins : B2 and B3,

Minerals : Calcium, Phosphorus, Iron, Potassium, Copper, Sulphur and Magnesium,

KABULI CHANA

Vitamins : A, B1, B2, B3, C, D, E,

Minerals : Phosphorus, Zinc, Potassium, and Magnesium,

Also contains large quantity of essential amino acids.

ALFALFA

Vitamins : A, C, and D.

Minerals : Very liberal amount

Also contains all eight aminoacids and chlorophyll and fibers.

SOYA BEAN

Vitamins : A, B1, B2, B3, and C

Minerals : Calcium, Phosphorus and Iron

What's More...

In addition to all these, sprouts also contain a liberal amount of Protein, Carbohydrate, Water, very less Fat and some Calories

⋀ Flowers Forever!

Flowers, the messengers of love, beauty and joy, have always been a part of your special occasions and you have always wanted to preserve them as they are. But, you've never been able to.

With the Pyramid almost always you will be able to preserve your choicest flowers for longer. Keep your flowers under the Pyramid and then they will retain their beauty, color and fragrance for a longer time (about 30%), although they would dehydrate.

You can make your own flower medicine too with Pyramid energy. Take a bowl of pure water and place the flower of your choice in it and leave it over night in the pyramid. Drink the water in the morning which will act as your personal flower medicine.

Long lasting freshness

Flowers too can be eternal and medicinal with Pyramid energy.

⋀ Tobacco, Cigarette and Gutkha

Pyramid can charge a single cigarette or gutkha satchel in 20 minutes, a pack in 2 hours and a carton overnight. But, what does it charge in cigarette or gutkha or pipe ? What are its effects and how does it help?

The Pyramid charges and treats the tobacco in them. It removes all artificial flavours but enhances the taste and feel of the tobacco and other natural flavourings (if any). It lessens the toxic effects in the gutkhas, pipes and cigarettes.

A Pyramid charged cigarette will never give you that sharp "bite" effect and would give you a new feeling with less negative drift.

Counter balance negativity

So, Pyramid also provides a new dimension for tobacco lovers.

Sound Sleep

Are you suffering from sleeplessness or sleepiness ? Then, look at how the Pyramid can help you here.

Place some Pyramids under your bed or just place some under your pillow and mattress or hang one above your head while you go to sleep. You will find that though you sleep comparatively for lesser time, you will feel much more relaxed, more fresh and more energetic. So now with Pyramid you have a cozy way to get rid of sleep problems.

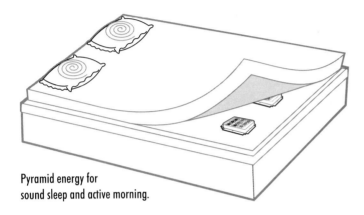

Pyramid energy for
sound sleep and active morning.

Top view of your bed

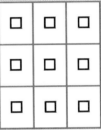

Nine Pyramid Yantra
under the mattress

Kayakalp

Who does not like to have a newer younger, more beautiful and nicer look? Then what you need is only Kayakalp or rejuvenation with the help of Pyramid energy.

Cosmetics and cosmetology is a rapidly evolving and changing field. The beautification of the body is desired by most people. Training in this area starts with the young and continues throughout life. The storage of these cosmetics is a very expensive process because their life is short.

With Pyramid, the shelf-life of cosmetics are prolonged. Not only that, Pyramid charged cosmetics like creams, lotions, oils, cleansing milks, herbs etc. give better results. Pyramid-water is also very effective for gaining of fresh, cleaner, radiant look. When Pyramid water is applied on face it feels as if thousands of needles are lightly massaging the facial muscles.

You can also put in your hand lotions, herbal cosmetics, soaps, toothpaste etc. and see that their efficiency is increased.

In the cycle of day and night we get two golden chances to change our life. One just before sleep and another just after arising. Utilize them properly.

When trying bleaching or coloring and perming hair, hang a Pyramid above or treat the chemicals required in the Pyramid before applying. This reduces the time taken with effective Pyramid energizing. Hair grooming aids will also benefit since hair is protein and water, and both respond very well to Pyramid energy.

The Pyramid's possible effect on our living cells still remains an open question, waiting for a careful study in laboratories by scientists and researchers.

Secret's of Jiten

Pain is not our enemy but a true friend, it warns us well before the disasters.

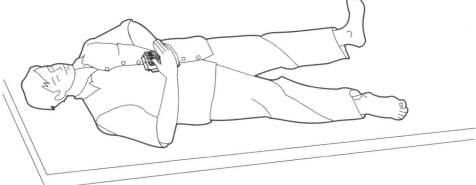

▲ Healing Phenomena

The Pyramid, indeed does generate a force field that contributes to healing, but it may not apply to some persons for some mystical reasons.

Pyramid works on all seven levels of human systems - physical, etheric, astral, lower mind, higher mind, soul and spirit.

The Pyramid provides us the energy of rejuvenating the tissues, relieving aches and pains and other minor disorders in just an hour or half . It can also help in diseases like psoriasis, insomnia, fractures, high or low blood pressure etc., but it takes time.

Pyramid healing power has immense effects not only on humans but also on animals, plants and other living beings.

Pyramid Energy can aid healing quickly. The pain relief is seen in just a few minutes. It is faster than the usual time. But understanding of this shortened length of healing time by Pyramid, is still a mystery. When water or medicine or herb is given without Pyramid charging, it is found that it does not work as efficiently. Hence, Pyramid actually works and is not simply a placebo.

▲ Reduce Pain

Pain causes great mental, physical and emotional disturbance, no matter however minor it is.

Pyramid can provide you with help here too. Place your painkilling tablets, creams and lotions under the Pyramid and their application to the injured area will bring relief comparatively faster. You can try another simpler way to deal with pain. Just apply Pyramid charged water packs, or dip that part in to it for about 30 minutes and see your pain vanish.

Heal Fast!
Use powers of Pyramid in complement to usual medical care.

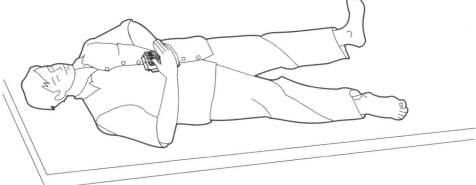

Open Pyramid

For meditation, distance reiki, chanting,. etc. This can open new doors to occult wisdom.

Deeper Meditation

People of every age and background are experiencing deep rest and peace in meditation and many believe, this energy - force within can be directed creatively.

Pyramid biofeedback testing has showed higher Beta activity. Even when the subject's eyes were open, several bursts of theta waves occurred between alpha patterns. This showed accelerated and deeper meditative states which are easily possible within a Pyramid environment.

The eight most frequently reported reactions in Pyramids are -
1. Tingling sensation
2. Feeling of warmth
3. Sense of weightlessness
4. Freedom from tension and feeling of relaxation
5. "Dropping away" of external sights, sounds and stimuli
6. Different colors, graphic visions and dreams
7. Time distortion
8. Deeper, more satisfying Meditation

▲ Attention Children!

Extensive experimentation has been done using children because they have not yet screened out the sensations which adults consider useless. They have been calm and relaxed and they did not complain of any disturbing or uneasy feelings. Hyperkinetic children treated under Pyramid for about 30-45 minutes daily showed creativity, steady-mindedness and were able to study for a longer time.

▲ Chocolates, Candies or Sweets

Natural home-made chocolates and candies without artificial flavorings when placed under the Pyramid acquire a sweeter and a nicer taste. But the artificial flavored candies when placed under Pyramids, lose their flavors and only seem to be pieces of sugar. Artificially flavored sweets and candies will also possess Pyramid energy but the harmful artificial flavors will vanish.

Children enjoy being under the open pyramid. Also helps in enchncing creativity and I.Q.

For children I always use ' Mind Power Pyramid' with Reiki for memory improvement. Also accelerates brain development in mentally challenged children.

Dr. V. Sukumaran
Child Health Consultant
Grand Master/ Founder, New Life Reiki

EXPERT'S OPINION

⋀ Mentally Challenged Children

Mentally disturbed children have always intrigued inventors.

Pyramid researches have shown that they can have special benefits from Pyramid treatments.

These children if kept under Pyramid or if allowed to sit under Pyramid for 30-45 minutes every morning and evening, seem to become more calm and composed. Sometimes they even show traces of normality.

Though there is no claim of evidence, Pyramid therapy has been used by many specialists as an healing aid to patients.

⋀ Exam Stress

Pyramids can become a very handy tool and most beneficial source for improvement of memory, boosting confidence and lessening stress.

Exam and test times are stressful and tension-filled periods for children. You can help them during this time or in their overall study period, by just placing the Pyramid under their seats, on their study-table or hang one above their head or just let him/her meditate under the Pyramid or sit placing Pyramid on head for 10 minutes in the morning and evening.

You can also give your child a pyramid locket which can be put around his /her neck giving constant pyramid energy to your child. Such a pyramid-locket can be worn around the neck every day or during exams which gives your child a stress and tension-free environment for studying and writing in exams.

In case of a hard subject you can place a wish under the pyramid (instructions for pyramid Yantra wish machine is given in chapter of 'Yantra'). Also you can place a pyramid on books of those subjects that your child finds difficult. While placing the pyramid make a wish that your child comes through with flying colors in that subject too. Pyramid energy will help strengthen your and your child's positive efforts. Keep the pyramid placed on the books until he / she takes to read that book and replace it on the book thereafter. Give your child a helping hand to stand and see him rise tall.

So why not give your child the gift he/she will always cherish?

Memory Pyramid As on this child's head is for concentration and memory power.

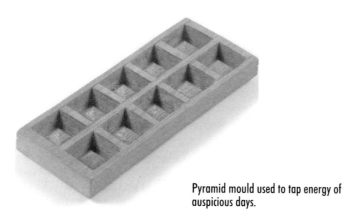

Pyramid mould used to tap energy of auspicious days.

The interaction of the medicine with your body will improve and the reactions will lessen. So now you can charge your own medicines and be less tense about its side-effects. Doesn't it ease your daily routine with no extra efforts ?

Capture Luck

In India, even today in many places the Pyramid is used to collect beneficial showering on these auspicious day. There are special Pyramid moulds created for this purpose.

On an auspicious day, jaggery is melted and set in a mould. This provides them with the benefits of Pyramid energy along with the special energy of the auspicious day.

This 1000 year old custom can help us to capture blessing or a boon descending from heaven. This energy is useful for enhancing luck and removing negative blocks and for good health.

Infant Care

Pyramids will help you understand your infants more efficiently and nicely. For us, understanding and interpreting their way of expressing is always confusing.

If your infant cries a lot without visible reason hang a Pyramid above its cradle or bed and you will find him happy and playing. Also do feed him with Pyramid milk, juices and water for more benefits (in case of infants who drink bottled milk.)

Beyond Medicines !

Do you take some medicines daily ? Are you afraid of the side effects ?

Put your medicine in the Pyramid overnight (preferably) before taking it. And always keep it under Pyramid for further charging. Your medicine can be anything - a herb, a household remedy, an ayurvedic medicine, an allopathic drug, a homeopathic dose, auto urine, batch flower remedy, flower oils, etc. This process of keeping your medicine atleast overnight will improve the effect of the medicine and decrease its side-effects (if any).

Pyramid-treated medicine.

Gem, Crystal & Pyramids

There is a belief that gems, stones and minerals can heal an ailing body or mind and ward off evil, illness and misfortune. They also play a key part in electromagnetic influences in all matter.

Researchers have shown that Pyramid treated stones, gems and minerals give off definite heat and pulsating vibrations. Reports also tell about the increased frequency and intensity of certain occasionally occurring crystals.

Pyramid Water

Water is the nectar on earth, the most important essential of life. When it is treated with Pyramid, it can become our best "natural tonic."

Human beings can stay without food for 5 weeks, but without water only for 5 days in moderate climate.

Pyramid treated water not only acts as a tonic to the body but it has numerous other advantages too. When Pyramid treated water is applied to injured parts, instant relief has been reported and the same has also been reported for insect bites and rashes.

Pyramid water when applied to face for about 5 to 6 weeks, the skin becomes smoother and younger looking. When this water is used in cooking, the food becomes more tasty and appetising. Cooking time also lessens.

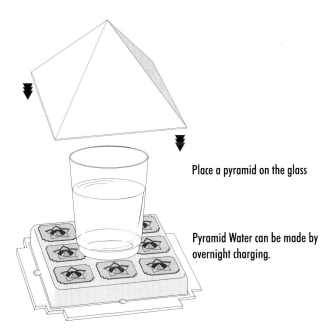

Place a pyramid on the glass

Pyramid Water can be made by overnight charging.

In an experiment, a piece of decayed meat was taken and divided into two. One was kept in plain water while the other in Pyramid water. After one week, the meat in plain water had decayed further emitting unbearable smell while that in Pyramid water had sedimented with no trace of foul smell and the water was clear.

It is also found that taking a glass of Pyramid water daily acts as an aid to the digestive system. An upset stomach quickly heals and elimination process also improves leading to better health. It is also reported that the water left inside the Pyramid somehow retains its oxygen.

The human being is nothing but a water baby.
Newborn baby has 77% water
Children have 59% water
Adults have 45-65% water

83%	of water is present in	blood
82%	of water is present in	kidneys
75%	of water is present in	muscles
74%	of water is present in	brain
69%	of water is present in	liver
22%	of water is present in	bones

Holy Water

There are many places in the world whose waters are considered "holy". The places where these waters are found have special energies. But have you noticed the shape of "kund" where the holy waters are found?

They are of the shape of a step Pyramid 'inverted' with exact specifications of dimensions and size. So, next time you go there just see it for yourself.

Pyramid water can prove to be a boon for your health, your pets, aquariums etc. Try some of the experiments with yourself and your family. Though we make no tall claims, it is assured that you will get startling results !

Pyramid Poultry

Happy, healthy and calm animals produce better quality products over a longer period of time, increasing the economic conditions of the farmer and health conditions of the community.

The use of pure water, food and habitat will enormously benefit farming communities from all over the world! More so, when all these are Pyramid energized.

Seeds and Plants

In two pots we planted the same quantity and quality of seeds. One was kept under the Pyramid and other was kept outside the Pyramid. Both of them were given same amount of sunlight, air, water and manure. Surprisingly, the plant under the Pyramid showed more rapid and healthy growth while that of the other plant was comparatively less and at half the rate.

The hybrid seeds of flowers and vegetables have become very expensive and you cannot be afford to waste them. So, for a greater yield of flowers, vegetables etc. at home or in farms, keep the seeds under the Pyramid for about a week till they become Pyramid potentialized and then sow them to obtain maximum and qualitative yield.

Keep the Pyramids over the green-house or besides the plant or water the plant with Pyramid-energized water for better growth of your plants.

For storing your grains for a longer time, place them in the Pyramid for about a week or decide the period depending on the quantity of the grains and then store them. Pyramid takes away even the least water content of the grain

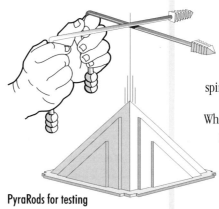

PyraRods for testing pyramid energy

Pyramid Energy Test

Do you want to know the energy of Pyramid? There are only a few ways of obtaining information about the Pyramid energy,. One of it is by 'Kirlian photography' and other by 'Biosensor technique'. But these two instruments are expensive and also involve a lengthy process. You also have a built-in system in our body by which you can check Pyramid energy.

Energy Levels and Pyramid

The energy surrounding all matter is known as "AURA". If we check this aura by the 'Kirlian photography' or if we see it, it is seen as a band of colours emanating from the body. If we check this aura by feeling it with our hands or by some instrument such as a pendulum or a L-Rod we can feel it. This energy field makes a shell around us. The size of this shell depends on how healthy we are - physically, mentally, emotionally and spiritually.

When one is subjected to the pyramid , this field of aura intensifies and expands. Expanded aura gives one better energy and health. Get yourself photographed by a Kirlian camera without pyramid and later with pyramid. Now check for the difference yourself.

You can also check the pyramid energy with help of a pendulum or a L-Rod dowsing. If your hands are sensitive enough to pick up the energy field try to check that with your hands.

Anybody can feel this energy change anywhere, anytime with help of any of these techniques. You can also experience yourself. Just by sitting outside the pyramid and inside it and you would instinctively feel nice inside the pyramid. Check it out!

What is Dowsing?

"Dowsing is a way of using the body's own reflexes to help you interpret the world around you".

Tom Graves,
(The Dowsers Workbook)

What does Dowsing need?

Dowsing requires just a simple pointed bob 'plumbob' or any other pointed object which can be suspended to a string. Dowsing needs no expensive, complicated apparatus. The most important thing required is a conscious and receptive 'you'.

How can Dowsing help you?

Dowsing is thousands of years old. It is a well-established practice used all over the world.

Dowsing can help you find out your own suitable-
1   Food
2   Medicines
3   Flowers and Vegetables
4   Plants
5   Lottery Numbers
6   Sacred Stones, Gems and Crystals
7   Business and Life Patterns
8   Pets and Soul Mates
9   City and House

Dowsing can also help you locate-
1   Your lost belongings
2   Water/Minerals/Oil, etc. and many other things you would like to venture and find out.

Dowsing can be fun and an interesting way to a newer life. All it needs is practice and a desire to learn.

There are some simple experiments you can do with your own Dowsing instrument which can be a home-made or professional pendulum, L-rod, Y-rod, bobber or an aurameter. You can thus check Pyramid energy all by yourself.

Hold your pendulum about 1 ft. exactly over the apex of Pyramid and slowly bring down the

pendulum allowing it to be free for movement and you will see that it starts rotating spirally just about 6-7 inches or more above the Pyramid depending on your sensitivity. The Dowsing shows spiral, circular, rotating movement over Pyramid indicating its energy flow.
Dowsing is a helpful art and one can learn it very well.

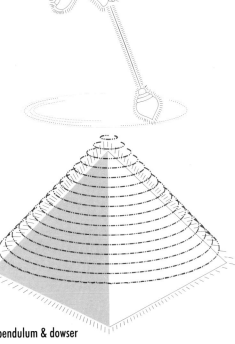

Auric field of Pyramid, pendulum & dowser

Pyramid Therapy

Recovery is a phase after disease or operation which takes time. When time actually seems to hang on to your hands. Pyramid can help you to pass this time faster, in a more constructive and pleasant way, because the energy generated by the Pyramids adds an extra pep to life, banishing dullness and lethargy. It also speeds up the healing process and can have great applications in hospitals and clinics of all kind. It also works wonders with children.

Save Petrol

Petrol, the fuel with ever rising cost, can also be Pyramid-charged. But, why? When you charge your petrol with Pyramid energy, it will give you more mileage. To experiment with this fix your Pyramid above the fuel tank and you will see fabulous results in a few days.

You can also place the Pyramid on the dashboard of your four-wheeler or under the seat of your two-wheeler or on the engine for better efficiency of the vehicle and to lessen the chances of accidents.

Computer and Pyramids

Computers today, are very much prone to viruses and other problems. Everyone wants to have a solution to this. Researches have shown and many have reported that their computers show a better efficiency and working capacity with Pyramid application rather than without it.

Electronic gadgets have also been noticed to work more effectively after the placing of Pyramids on them. Operating your remote control, move away from the television or v.c.r. till the spot where its range completes. Place the Pyramid on it for about 5 minutes and operate again from that spot and you will see that it works. Isn't this a quicker way to examine the Pyramid-power?

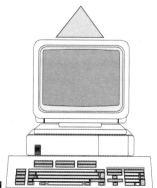

Pyramid safe guard

Positive Health

A great deal of research is being done to discover more about ions. Negative ions are considered to be beneficial to human beings in many ways.

In research done by N.A.S.A. about the positive and negative ions and their effect on our body are as follows.

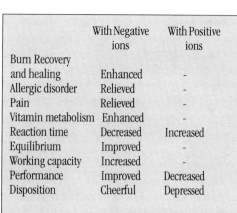

	With Negative ions	With Positive ions
Burn Recovery and healing	Enhanced	-
Allergic disorder	Relieved	-
Pain	Relieved	-
Vitamin metabolism	Enhanced	-
Reaction time	Decreased	Increased
Equilibrium	Improved	-
Working capacity	Increased	-
Performance	Improved	Decreased
Disposition	Cheerful	Depressed

The report of Dr. Edward Podolsky shows that positive ions irritate people with asthma, rheumatism, neuritis, gout and sinusitis, whereas negative ions help ease the discomfort of these disorders.

The Pyramid brings about negative ionization in the room and lessens the positive ions which makes air seem more fresh and perky. The person feels energetic and cheerful. So use the new researched Pyramid power.

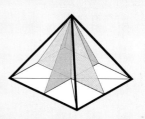

▲ Money Multiplier

Here we will learn how we can maximize our potential to become rich and prosperous with the help of a currency note and Pyramid Yantra. We will mentally enhance our positive powers and cross all the negative hurdles.

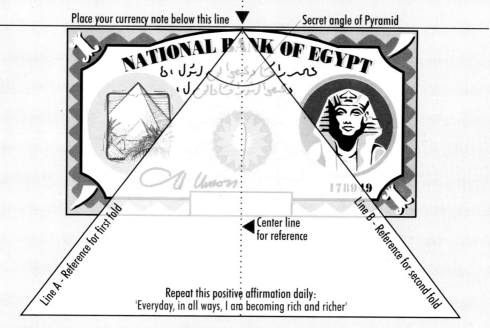

Place your currency note below this line ▼   Secret angle of Pyramid

NATIONAL BANK OF EGYPT

Line A - Reference for first fold

Line B - Reference for second fold

◀ Center line for reference

Repeat this positive affirmation daily:
'Everyday, in all ways, I am becoming rich and richer'

Step 1 Take a new currency note of the smallest value, like a rupee note for India, a dollar note in US, a pound in UK or any other currency prevalent in your country. Make one fold exactly from the center of the note. This is for your reference, which helps you put the note in the center of the pyramid section in the figure. Now open the fold and place the note on the figure shown above. Ensure that the center line of your fold coincides with that of the line shown in the figure.

Step 2 Now carefully make two folds one after the other on the reference lines A and B, as shown in the figure.

Step 3 Now give the final touch. Give your note a proper shape by folding all the additional angles at the lower seam. Fix the angles with a glue to make a perfect cross section of the pyramid.

Your Money Multiplier is now ready for exercise. It is now necessary to energize it with "Prana" or the power to execute. Everyday in the morning put this shaped note in your left hand and place right hand on it. Repeat the affirmation given in the figure, religiously and positively for 15 times verbally. Do this regularly for 30 days. You will see that things have started to change around you, enriching you and your purpose.

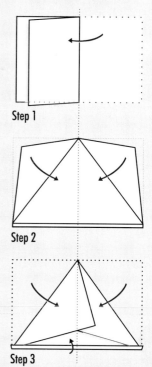

Step 1

Step 2

Step 3

"When you fix your heart on one point then nothing is impossible for you."

-Lord Buddha

Let us enter an experience that is completely new and amazing, and which will be help you live more fruitfully. "Wish machine" will definitely shape your destiny. It will harmonize others and you with the surrounding making life more lively.

What is a 'Wish Machine'?

Ever since the Pyramid was discovered as a source of mystical energy, it has been tried for making dreams and wishes come true. Pyramid is always linked to mysticism and symbolized as an occult wisdom. The best universal examples of Pyramidal Wish Machine are temples and churches, all around the world. There are several ways of making your wishes and dreams come true but Pyramid-Yantra is one of the most personal, effective, easy and safe ways of doing so.

Pyramid Wish Machine

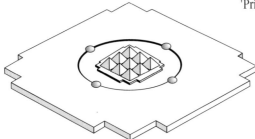

You have two roles in life. One is social where you have to pay attention to your family, friends and society.

The other is the private individual life where you heed to only 'I'.

There is always a wish you have dearly cherished.

In individual life you may have many wishes which you have always wanted but which are secret even from your family and friends. Wish machine can become a handy tool for your own personal use. providing you with 'Privacy' and also fulfilling your wishes.

How is it used?

There are many simple ways of using 'Wish-Machine'. The most simple way to go about it is -

Pyramid wish-machine is a new way to make your dreams and wishes come true.

Just place your wish under a well-oriented Pyramid on a piece of paper and see your dreams being fulfilled.

◆ Write your wish clearly, briefly and positively on a plain, white, square, piece of paper about 70 X 70 mm, with red ink.

◆ Make two folds of this piece and place it under the cosmic-dome of your wish machine and then place the Pyramid above.

◆ Sit calmly in a quiet place and hold the wish machine in the left hand and place the right hand above.

- Now repeat your wish for 2 minutes and then place your wish-machine in a safe place.

- Continue this process twice daily until your wish is fulfilled.

Can I make my wish stronger?

Yes, of course. There are some ways of doing so.

- Every direction has it own properties and benefits.
If you hold the wish-machine and sit facing that direction you get its benefits.
East is for - Love, peace, harmony, spiritualism, happiness, name and fame.
West is for - Health, freedom from disease, physical fitness and relationship.
North is for - Money, material, land, building, possession, treasure, jewellery, promotion, business and luxury.
South is for - Protection from enemy, defence and safeguard from evil effects.
You have to analyse your wish and find out which direction it applies to. Then hold the wish machine in your hand. Sit facing the required direction and imagine those forces helping you.

- You can write down the wish as if it were already accomplished and you are happy with it.

- If you can, draw yourself in the desired circumstances along with written wish.

- Place your photograph, hair sample, blood drop on blotting paper or any other personal object with the written wish.

- If you want to further enhance the effect, take the wish machine to your temple, church or spiritual place. Sit and charge with your thought power.

- The blessing of gurus or saints can also help you further.

- The most powerful way is to visualize yourself as a light and penetrate through the Pyramid to your wish and imagine yourself in the circumstances you wish. Then imagine bringing that wish to the outside world as you come back. Do this twice a day with due faith and single-mindedness for best results.

- If your wish is related to your family or group, sitting together and charging unitedly with thought power will also help.

Does this Really Work?
Isn't this a Superstition?

Within certain limits it does work, and thousands of people have used this technique to obtain positive results.

What is the Difference between Other Techniques and this?

In other techniques you just use your own power and positive thoughts, whereas here you have the boundless Pyramid power working hand-in-hand with you. Its shape and cosmic geometry will help you all the way to your goal and the directions will direct you to a proper channel for improving your thought pattern. One more advantage is that once you have installed this wish machine it works on its own and needs comparatively less of your time to nourish it with positive thoughts.

It is a superstition if you think Pyramid can bring about changes in conditions and circumstances all by itself. It is not a superstition when used with certain changes in rigid thoughts and ideas. If you believe in it with faith, it certainly strengthens the effect of your experiences.

Then even the mystical Pyramid energy is on your side to aid you to go ahead successfully.

How Does It work?

The explanation of the working of wish-machine is not yet discovered by science, but it is explained by an 'assumption - presumption' theory which is like a hypothesis.

Today we are very much aware and we know about telepathy and that there is a unique super physical link between us and the objects in our contact. Whenever we think of something, it goes out in form of cosmic telepathic vibrations. Other people receive it on a subconscious level, but don't react to it until and unless it is in harmony with their own conceptual thinking.

The Pyramid wish machine works on the power of Pyramid. Your visualization, reinforcement and intense will.

Once you install your wish machine there is always a relation between you and your wish machine which will allows you to operate the machine from a distance. For example, sitting in the office just close your eyes, visualize the machine and repeat the wish as many times as you like.

You are what you think and imagine yourself to be, your thoughts make you. The Pyramid can provide you with a favorable condition and help you with its mystical powerful energies.

Do's and Don't's

✓ Do start with the name of the God or any other higher energy you believe in.

✓ Do make sure that your wish is reasonable enough for your subconscious to accept.

✓ Do keep your wish machine away from children and others to avoid disturbance in alignment.

✓ Do keep it in a proper and safe place away from electricity and electric and electronic gadgets for. e.g. in puja room.

✓ Do maintain a best positive attitude towards the accomplishment of your aim.

✓ Do give your wish a careful thought, foresee the consequences which may arise, and if you would be comfortable and able to cope with those consequences.

Secret's of Jiten

Believe, believe, believe in the magical forces of nature!
Believe with all your heart, mind and soul!
Believe that you have a special place and play a special part in this magical world!

× Don't put too many wishes together at one time, make more than one wish machine in case of many wishes and there should be a distance of at least one foot between them.

× Don't write anything you or your subconscious does not believe in.

× Don't be tempted to harm or exploit anyone because the wish machine will operate through you and that would cause trouble to yourself.

Get your emotions, feelings, dreams, goals, wishes and aspirations be fulfilled with least of your help. What you only need is faith, self-confidence, an attitude to accept new opportunities, perfect visualization and a positive attitude towards the zest of life. You will then find your life more meaningful, energetic, enthusiastic and joyful, the world for you would be a better and nicer place than before, with a lot more hope.

This tool will surely help you to lead a successful and productive life.

Is there a special day or time to install?

Don't wait, the best time is right now!
But you can see the calendar for good days or ask an astrologer for the same or follow the Pyra Rhythm time table given below.

Best day in each month is your birth date or single digit match with the date.
For example;
if your birth day is on 25th, so your lucky dates are 25, 16 or 7.
Same way second lucky date is single digit of the birth date total.
Example;
if your birth date is 25-06-1983 then 2+5+0+6+1+9+8+3=34, 3+4=7.
So again the dates are 7, 16 and 25.
(This may not be same in your case.)

Pyra Rhythm

Below chart shows Fa [ ] Maa [ ] rhythm during the day. All pyramids should be programmed during the Fa period, but not preferred in Maa duration.
Example: If you want to program on Monday then positive time is 6 to 7:30 am, 9 to 10:30 am or between 1:30 to 6 pm.

Pyra Rythm chart

⌂ The Lab Confirms

Yesterday's mysteries are today's science and the mysteries today will become science of tomorrow.

It's our global duty to contribute for a better environmental condition. Each one of us must perform some experiment which are eco-friendly.

Start with simple ones, as per your interest. Perform them in a systematic, well-documented, repeatable method under controlled conditions.

If you get results we have a small request, please contribute to the PyraNet by sending your findings- write to; Dr. Dhara Bhatt, PO Box 808, Vadodara 390010, India. Your valuable contribution will definitely help in a noble cause of wellness for all of us.

Many experiments as well as people report changes in mental, physical and emotional states as a result of Pyramid exposure. The presence of unusual energy fields have been monitored in solids, liquids, plants, insects, animals, and above all in humans, by a variety of techniques, with different people and research objects.

Experiments conducted in various conditions along with different equipment and persons have led to many astonishing discoveries about Pyramid energy.

An unusual experiment on skin temperatures, showed that females increased their temperature on sitting in the Pyramid while males reduced their temperatures.

Experiments were conducted using Kirlian photography technique, to see the difference in the aura of persons before and after sitting under the Pyramid for 15 minutes. They revealed some very interesting differences. The later pictures were brighter and showed more energy field - aura, the edge of corona was less frayed, the dendrites were sharper, and the pattern was unbroken. The brighter the aura greater the amount of energy and balance.

The laboratory test of my blood samples were taken after sitting under the Pyramid for three months for an hour daily. The report after three months indicated some changes. The Pyramid works to brings the processes of the body into balance. The tests speak for themselves anyway

Before

After

Aura picture taken before sitting in Pyramid and after sitting for 15 minutes in Pyramid

Report of Dr. Dhara Bhatt

PARAMETER	BEFORE 10/02'	AFTER 2/03'	NORMAL RANGE
RBC	4.29	4.98	4.2 - 5.4 M/ul
WBC	6.20	9.10	$4.5 \times 10^3 - 10.5 \times 10^3$
Hgb	11.90	13.00	11.5 - 16.5 g/ 100 cc
HcT	34.10	39.10	37 - 47 %
MCV	79.49	78.51	76 - 98 fL
MCH	27.74	26.10	27 - 35 pg
MCHC	34.90	33.25	31 - 35 gm/dl
Differential Count			
POLY	69	70	50 - 70 %
LYMPHO	26	24	20 - 40 %
EOSINO	4	4	01 - 05 %
MONO	1	2	01 - 06 %

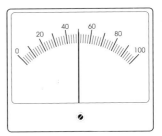

Before

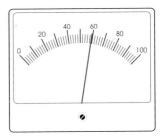

After

Many other medical experiments were carried out regarding blood samples, temperature, plants, animals, insects, non-living objects and on humans which showed many astonishing and amazing facts.

You too can try experimenting and make your own discoveries.

Bioforce Meter
Reading shows increase in energy flow after the pyramidal treatment.

" My experience with Pyramid Power is very good. Pyramid Water is the best medicine. "

Dr. A.K. Bhattacharya
Master of Tridosha Homeopathy, Telepathy & Bio-Magnet.

EXPERT'S OPINION

Vastu Purusha

Symbolization of cosmic energies in man-made boundaries with the power of five heads, 100 hands, 16 legs, 3 tails and 360 hairs.

4

"Vastu shastra is a holistic science of creating harmony of subtle energies of the supreme being, planets, earth and man made or natural objects with us. Knowledge of Vastu Shastra helps us bring out our best to fulfill our dreams and desires."

Prof. Dr. Jiten Bhatt

Understanding
Vastu

What is Vastu?

Vastu Vidya is one of our very ancient Indian architectural sciences. It was basically designed to guide construction of houses, work places, temples, and other buildings. It gives us the knowledge of devising better living and working conditions, which are in harmony with the laws of Nature. A house designed according to Vastu should be one, which, not only protects us from extreme weather conditions, but also provides us a sense of well-being and comfort.

Vastu deals with all aspects of construction like selection of land, building materials, technology used to build, placement of rooms, doors or windows and many others. It is the knowledge of everything used in the process of construction and it's surrounding. This Indian science is one step ahead of today's architectural science. It deals not only with the construction and the interaction of physical properties but also with it's subtle energy and radiations. It is the knowledge of interaction of a living being at all levels of existence. It teaches us the inner and outer functions of Man and material. So Vastu is the only subject which directly deals with all our needs of material, physical, emotional, mental, spiritual and environmental harmony. This subject is very interesting, wide and has a deep effect on our lives.

Let us understand it this way-each cell in our body is a complete unit in it, but to understand the human body we have to understand each system consisting of numerous organs and cells.

Similarly, Vastu is also a complete and holistic science. For applying it we need to understand the material as well as the subtle and spiritual laws around us. The ancient texts of Vastu Vidya state that one must have the prior knowledge of the four Vedas and their four *Upavedas*, before starting to practice Vastu.

We should have a multi-dimensional approach in order to obtain optimum results. We should have the knowledge of the science of life and death, anatomy of the human body, mind and spirit, cosmology, astrology, time, shapes and forms, yantra and the concept of space. We should learn to communicate with material or objects apparently appearing to be non-living. For this communication we must understand divine proportions and secret formulas of harmony, music, aesthetics, interior designing, symmetry and the mystic geometry of all things in existence.

Can you believe this!

For perfect Vastu you need deep knowledge of 365 subjects.

Decide the Goal

Even before putting an effort we must decide our goal and define our requirements. To reach any destination a faster way is through a "Super track". Vastu Vidya suggests a symbolic formula to achieve a quick and obstacle free journey. It tells us to focus and imagine Lord Ganesha. He is also known by many other names, like "Vinayaka" or the leader who leads us through every tough path, and "Vighnaharta" or the one who removes all the obstacles. He has two wives or partners Riddhi, who gives prosperity and Siddhi, who provides all-round success.

Lord Ganesha is like a pass to this "Super track" of Vastu. Vastu and all Indian arts and sciences consider him to be the initiator of all good deeds. Just visualize his image or create his symbol before any auspicious deed. He invokes trouble-freeness. Never forget to remember the Guru who gave you the knowledge or showed you this path. He is said to be the link between your knowledge and your goal. Remind yourself of the God or Goddess you believe in and imagine the divine energy showering upon you.

Positive Affirmation

"I will open my mind and trust my own power within. I surrender all negativity to almighty, miracles will start to manifest in my life. I am prepared for it".

The above affirmation is a master-key to personal Vastu. Write it down or repeat it verbally for 15 times in one sitting.

Rules of the "Super track"

The most important rule is to know how to navigate through this track. All you have to do is to surrender yourself to the Almighty. Be free and flow along with the divine wind. This is that force which automatically takes us towards our goal without any effort from our side. Time taken to reach is directly related to the resistance offered by us. The more we resist the longer it will take to reach. Be positive about where the divine flow takes you, rest assured it will never lead you incorrectly.

Perfect Learning

To gain the best knowledge we must go the best of universities or teachers. Similarly, here too you have to learn from the best. But this field does not require any physical presence of a teacher. You have to learn with your own imagination and understanding. Indian texts say, that to learn any holistic path we must go to Goddess *Saraswati*. She is the source of complete knowledge of the four Man / Units. It is said only with her blessings we can understand the complete totality of existence. Imagine Mother *Saraswati* and remove any negativity that prevails in you. Pray to her to remove all rigid thoughts and ideas. She will lead you to Truth with her divine light.

The Mother Saraswati
Giver of knowledge and wisdom

⋀
Prepare yourself for Infinite Help

We rarely realize that there is so much to receive from our surroundings. We believe we all are individuals and live independently. We have to come out of this illusion and connect with the world around. We are all interconnected with each other and the things around us. We are a part of this network, which includes living as well as non-living beings. This network is so well designed that we have the freedom to function independently yet remain it. Science understands this network as the Hologram.

Four Man Principle

Universal Man supports the Global Man, Global Man supports the Man. Similarly, Man supports the Vastu man and Vastu man supports the Brahmasthala and Brahmasthala supports the Brahma-bindu (the ultimate vital center).

This network is very well explained in Vastu Vidya in form of the "Four Purush" or Men "Four Unit" theory. It says that the whole is represented in a part and the part is identical to the whole. These four men are -1. Vastu Purush, which we will discuss in this chapter later. 2. The Man, about whom we already know quite much like his anatomy, physiology etc. 3. The Global man - it connects us to all living beings on this planet. He consists of all human beings, animals, birds, trees, insects and others, which are made from cell or cells and are capable of producing similar living beings. 4. The Universal man - he connects us to everything in this world as well as that in the cosmos. He tells us to understand that there is nothing existing, which is dead. Even non-living objects are capable of communication. They also have a complete system within themselves as we do but it is very different from that of ours. Hence we feel them to be more rigid or "Jad". It is just that they are more devoted to their assigned functions by the Universal Man.

This concept links us with everything from stars and planets to fire, earth, water, ether, space, plants, flowers, medicine, animals and even to bacteria and viruses. It teaches us to live in harmony with everything around and within us. Thus, Vastu Vidya is the art and science of learning to create harmony in all our inner and outer functions and at all the four levels of the four Units / Men.

Universal man
Global man
Man
Vastu man
Vital Center

The Fundamentals of Action

System of Vastu is designed on the universal factors of time and space. It is like understanding the heart and mind of the Universal Man or "Purush". Each functional element goes through the three-phased cycle. These three phases are construction, maintenance and destruction. Similarly in the Universal Unit there are these three phases. In Vastu they are symbolized as "Brahma"- the one who creates, "Vishnu"- the one prevents and maintains and "Mahesh"- the one who destroys and reconstructs. These three phases are continuously functioning in synchronicity. Any object formed is bound to sustain before it is destroyed. Similarly each object or being,

Lord Vishwakarma

The son of Brahma who looks after the execution of all creation on Earth. He is the originator of Vastu.

which is destroyed, will reconstruct before it is created and sustained. Destruction constitutes of two different semi-phases - the actual destruction or death and the resurrection or reconstruction. If we see it through the concept of time; it is the cycle of past, present and future.

Roots of Vastu

We already know that all things are created from the part of Universal Man called "Brahma". It is stated in Vastu that he had a daughter - *Saraswati* and a son- *Vishwakarma*. His daughter is given the departments of Knowledge, Learning and Wisdom. His son looks after the execution of all Creation and Constructions especially on the Earth. Hence for us he is the originator of Vastu.

The Life Cycle

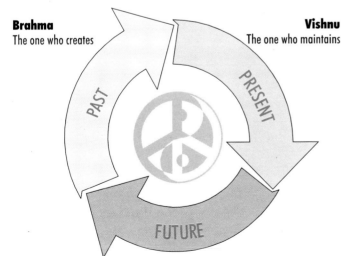

Brahma
The one who creates

Vishnu
The one who maintains

PAST

PRESENT

FUTURE

Mahesh
The one who destroys and reconstructs

Secret's of Jiten

The ultimate formula of Vastu is to understand the motivating force behind the process of a seed becoming the tree and the tree becoming a seed.

Energetic's of Vastu

At this stage it is very important for us to know the fundamentals of energy, which is the base of Vastu. Energy is the intrinsic capacity of any matter or form to perform an action. It has infinite potential to create or destroy. Our body is an ideal mode to study energy and its capacities. Our energy is divided into- Physical energy and Mind energy. Physical energy gives us all the strength, momentum, vitality, stamina or ability of action. Without this we become weak, tired and fatigued. We know very well that even when we are sick we still are the same person but just the lack of energy makes us feel so much different. Our whole body requires a lot of energy for maintaining its numerous functions.

Mental energy gives us the motivation, desire, zeal, passion or that initial spark

to start an action and continue it. Without this mind energy we would be lethargic, lazy or negative. The stimulation or depletion of this energy is directly responsible for all stages of existence like health and disease, joy and sorrow or prosperity and poverty. Energy is the origin of all change. We now know that mind energy is more potent than physical energy.

Now we can truly understand and appreciate the concept of symbols. The symbols are the initiators of these mental sparks. The correct knowledge about their use can lead us to reach our goals easily and quickly. In energetic's of Vastu too, the concept of Hologram is applied. A part represents the whole. Hence we can apply Vastu to any physical objects like table, bed, room, house, farm, temple, vehicle, building, township, city, country or continent. This can also be applied to levels other than the physical like mental, emotional or spiritual. Vastu has its own anatomy, which we will understand later, when understanding of Vastu Purush and the laws of Vastu.

Behind every result the motivating energy of mind is more responsible than the physical energy of the body.

Power Generation Formula

We know very well why a river flows from higher to lower level or why the apple falls to the ground or why don't we fall into the sky when the Earth rotates. It is due to the gravitational force of the Earth. In Vastu Vidya two opposite forces symbolize it.

One of them is the "Brahma" who is the nourishing force in any seed, physical or abstract. It gives the seed all the necessary energy to grow into an enormous tree. The second equal yet opposite force is called the "Ananta" or the infinite force. It is the inherent property in any seed to generate millions like it. This axis between "Brahma" and "Ananta" is the central axis. This dynamism is the basic power formula behind true Vastu. This generates the central axis between Earth and Heaven.

Earth rotates from West to East, and so we receive immense energy from the East, which is known as "Ishwara". The West is known as "Varuna". This axis between the East and West or "Ishwara" and "Varuna" is known as the second power axis. Similarly, the third power axis is that of the magnetic flow from the North or "Kubera" to the South or "Yama". In Vastu it is known as the axis of the journey of life and death or from material to subtle. There are two auxiliary axis. One is North-East to South-West, represented by Soma and Nirtti and the other is North-West to South-East, represented by Vayu and Agni.

Uplifting force to heaven - The Brahma

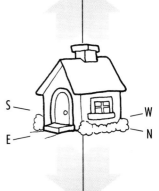

Energy representation of nine houses

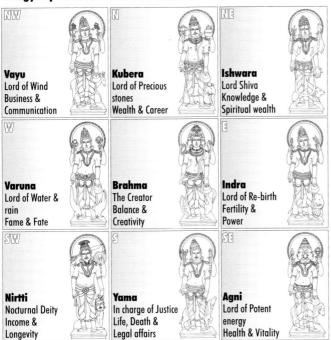

NW	N	NE
Vayu Lord of Wind Business & Communication	**Kubera** Lord of Precious stones Wealth & Career	**Ishwara** Lord Shiva Knowledge & Spiritual wealth
W		E
Varuna Lord of Water & rain Fame & Fate	**Brahma** The Creator Balance & Creativity	**Indra** Lord of Re-birth Fertility & Power
SW	S	SE
Nirtti Nocturnal Deity Income & Longevity	**Yama** In charge of Justice Life, Death & Legal affairs	**Agni** Lord of Potent energy Health & Vitality

Materializing force of the earth - The Ananta

Cosmic Connection

In Vastu Vidya this connection is explained in two ways. One way is Space and the other is Time. We already know the connection between the Man and the other Units. In the Universal Man, object and its relationship is studied. Secondly the concept of Time is considered essential. Results depend on the various permutations and combinations of both the concepts. The objects in relation of the Universal Man are the nine planets. In Vastu all these planets are very important and each of them is allotted a direction and a separate purpose. In Vastu Vidya Earth is the centre whereas in the Navagraha theory the Sun is considered the center.

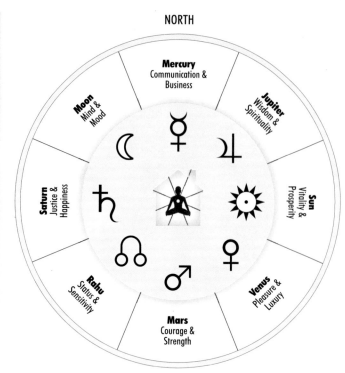

NORTH

Mercury Communication & Business

Jupiter Wisdom & Spirituality

Sun Vitality & Prosperity

Venus Pleasure & Luxury

Mars Courage & Strength

Rahu Status & Sensitivity

Saturn Justice & Happiness

Moon Mind & Mood

Location of planets according to Vastu and its influence.

MINA PISCES PURVABHADRAPADA	MESHA ARIES ASHVINI	VRISHABHA TAURUS KAITTIKA	MITHUNA GEMINI MRIGSIRAS
KUMBHA AQUARIUS DHANISHTHA			KARKATA CANCER PUNARVASU
MAKARA CAPRICORN UTTARASHADA			SIMHA LEO MAGHA
DHANUS SAGITTARIUS MULA	VRISHCHIKA SCORPIO VISHAKHA	TULA LIBRA CHITRA	KANYA VIRGO UTTARAPHALGUNI

The other connections or relations of the Time with the Space are understood by Kaal Purush or the Zodiac theory. It very well connects the movement of time and space. Each part of the Kaal Purush is associated with each zodiac sign.

The relationship of *Kaal Purusha* with zodiac signs and *Nakshatra*.

Five Energy Interlink

Our whole manifestation is finely knit with the five basic energies. These five energies also play a vital role in Vastu. We must be very careful with the placement of these five energies and their harmony with the environment.
We have already seen the process of the growth of tree from a seed. The seed requires all the five elements for growth. Firstly it requires soil then water, heat or fire, air and space for expansion. For any growth or expansion this basic principle remains the same. Let us understand the interaction and its interlink from the chart below.

In this example we will start with the heat element, considering the Sun to be the source of all evolution in our universe. As we have learnt in our school, heat evaporates the water converting it into vapour. Vapour goes into the air becoming clouds (space). The clouds strike the mountains and become water and this cycle goes on.
In Vastu Vidya these five elements have a vital role to play.

The chart below shows division of five elements.

Five Elements	Earth	Water	Fire	Air	Space
Energy	Gravitational	Rain	Solar	Wind	Sound
Functions	Smell	Taste	Sight	Touch	Hearing
Sense organs	Nose	Tongue	Eyes	Skin	Ear
Shape	Square	Crescent	Triangle	Hexagon	Point

The chart below shows that each element is further divided into the five elements into our body.

Five Elements	Earth	Water	Fire	Air	Space
Ether	Ego	Citta	Intellect	Mind	Antahkaran
Air	Apana	Prana	Udana	Samana	Vyana
Fire	Nose	Tongue	Eyes	Skin	Ear
Water	Rectum	Genitals	Feet	Hands	Speech
Earth	Smell	Flavour	Form	Touch	Sound
Functions	Smelling/Excreting	Eating/Enjoyment	Sight/Walking	Touch/Action	Hearing/Speaking
Symbol	Vajra	Lotus	Swastik	Six points	Point
Dosha	Kapha	Kapha	Pitta	Vaata	Vaata
Guna	Tamas	Tamas	Sattwa	Rajas	Sattwa
Physical attribute	Roughness	Liquidity	Heat	Movement	Resistance

Conclusion: In this Vastu world there are two ends. One is the Universal man or unit, which is beyond our control. We cannot change its rules of functioning. The other end is the Vastu man or unit. This is very much under our control and works as per our wish. With proper knowledge of the Vastu man we can definitely create a better world for ourselves.
We have just understood one important part or phase of Vastu. But still the other remains to be comprehended. This second end or phase is the TIME. All modern Vastu texts overlook this extremely vital end. So let us try to understand this time factor.

⋀
Time Vastu

This concept of Time Vastu is totally new to our existing perception of Vastu Vidya. Prof. Dr. Jiten Bhatt has always given us new dimensions to think and work upon. This is also one of his latest visions in the field of Vastu.

According to him, Time is a cardinal part of all things in existence. Time is one of the fundamental concepts of the universe. This invisible flow is perpetually in the heart of everything from an atom to the Sun. It invariably follows a cycle or path and is directly connected to all creation and demolition. Everybody and everything has a Time cycle of its own. This is also applicable for us, the Vastu man to the Universal man.

We know that the cycle of time is one of the important components of our lives- the cycle of life and death. Also, other apparent cycle we know is the moon phase of 30 days. Similarly, a year is also divided into two phases. One is the *Dakshinayana*, a six month dark or south half of the year. The other is *Uttarayana*, which also is a six month period known as the bright or north half of the year. The *Uttarayana* is the day time of the Global man or unit.

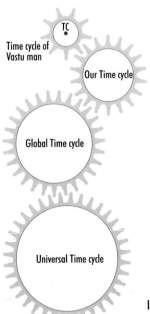

Rotation of Vastu man. He it rotates in the eight directions in a year. This is called Chara Vastu.

In the same manner, the Universal man also follows a time cycle, which is divided into four parts. These four parts are - *Sata yuga* or the Golden age, *Treta yuga* or the Silver age, *Dwaapara yuga* or the Copper age and the *Kal yuga* or the Iron age.

Vastu has three cycles. One is the Nitya Vastu, which means daily Vastu. This Vastu changes every three hours. Second is the Chara Vastu, or the yearly Vastu. We know that the Vastu purush changes the direction of his head eight times in a year. The Vastu we are usually aware is the Sthira Vastu. It is the deep rooted or the stable Vastu. Here we treat our house or plot considering the head of the Vastu Purush in North-East direction.

TC

Time cycle of Vastu man

Our Time cycle

Global Time cycle

Universal Time cycle

In Time Vastu the universal time is beyond our control. It is only the Sthira time that can be directed as per our wish. The Sthira Time is the time right now. This moment of 'right now' is an extremely minute yet steady part of time. The sum of all these moments is our life. So this present moment is very important in Time Vastu. This moment is called the Time centre or 'TC'. It is the 'TC' which propels our personal Vastu towards a brighter tomorrow.

In Vastu there are only two important core centers from where we can solve all our Vastu problems. These two are the Time center 'TC' and the Pyra center 'PC' or the space center (See page 129). Thus, TC is the only internal key to change Vastu.

In this matrix of time, we have only one point in our hand and it is Time Center (TC).

Let's Start

We know Vastu Shastra, literally means 'the science of building' Vastu is not merely calculations and physical dimensions. It is deeply related to Indian philosophy, religion and cosmic energy. It is the micro-built environment of man which deals with permutations and combinations of the 9 Grahas (planets),12 Raashis (sun signs), 12 Houses and 27 *Nakshatras* (constellations) Vastu Shastra is an age old science of architecture developed in India. It is a 'Vedanga', a branch of 'Sthapatya veda' which in turn is the part of 'Yajur Veda'. Hence, Vastu is a science discovered by our great saints and sages to lead human beings to a more happy and prosperous life.

Vastu Shastra is a very deep and complicated subject. The gist of it can be given as under-

Ideal Proportions

Proportions for house and buildings
A:B are 1:1, 1:1.25, 1:1.5

Slope of the plot

It is one of the most important factors in deciding positive and negative energies. The slope must be from west to east and from south to north.

Shape of the plot

(i) Square - This shape with all angles of 90° is considered to be auspicious, prosperous, giving success in all fields and promoting overall growth.

(ii) Rectangle - This shape with all four angles of 90° is also considered to be lucky, prosperous and promoting overall growth.

(iii) Circular - Such a plot is very beneficial for growth of wealth and knowledge. But rectangular or square buildings should not be constructed on it.

(iv) Hexagonal - Residence on such plot is good, it enhances growth, progress and prosperity.

(v) Oval - Such a plot is inauspicious, harmful and brings losses.

(vi) Triangular - Such a plot causes loss due to fire, penalty and government harassment.

(vii) Parallelogram - This shape of the plot is not good. It causes financial losses, quarrels in family and unhappy life to the dweller.

(viii) Star - Such a plot causes quarrels, litigations and destruction of peace.

(ix) Trident - Such a shape of plot causes loss of peace and quarrels in the house.

(x) Mridanga - Such a shape of the plot can cause death of wife.

(xi) Semi-circular - This shape of plot brings poverty to the resider.

(xii) Wheel-shaped - This shape is not good for living. It brings poverty in the house.

(xiii) Bhadrasan - Residence on such shape of plot is auspicious and fetches all round happiness to dwellers.

(xiv) Gau Mukhakar - This shape of plot is very auspicious for construction of houses but it is not suitable for commercial purposes.

(xv) Singh Mukhakar - Such shape of plot is beneficial for commercial purposes but it is not suitable for houses.

Sun and Moon

When the plot is divided diagonally equal in two parts the part on the North-East is the 'Sun' part whereas that on the South-West side is the 'Moon' part. The sun side should be lower, brighter and lighter and moon side should be higher, darker and heavier.

Five Elements

The whole world including our body is made up of 5 essential elements i.e. earth, water, fire, air and space. Vastu is nothing but the science of balancing of the above five elements in proportion, to keep the residents of the house, in perfect harmony for right decisions, peace and happiness.

Eight Directions

There are four main directions but even the four sub-directions are equally important. These sectors help us in the designing of the house and placement of kitchen, Puja room, dining room etc. because every direction has its own importance in Vastu-Shastra.

WN	N	NE
W		E
WS	S	SE

Nine Energies

The plot is divided into nine parts according to the grids on it. Each section or part represents one of the nine planetary energies.

4	9	2
3	5	7
8	1	6

The plot is distributed into 9 x 9 grids making 81 houses.

Papa   **The North, The God Kuber (Wealth)**   Charaki

24 Vayu	26 Nag	27 Mukhya	28 Nhallat	29 Kuber	30 Shail	31 Aditi	32 Diti	1 Ish Shiki
24 Pap	36	42 Rudra	43 Prithvi -dhara	43 Prithvi -dhara	43 Prithvi -dhara	44 Apavarsa	33	2 Parjanya
23 Shesh	36 Ruddras	42	43 Prithvi -dhara	43 Prithvi -dhara	43 Prithvi -dhara	44	33 Apa	3 Jayant
22 Asur	41 Maitra	41 Maitra	45 Brama	45 Brama	45 Brama	37 Aryama	37 Aryama	4 Indra
21 Varun	41 Maitra	41 Maitra	45 Brama	45 Brama	45 Brama	37 Aryama	37 Aryama	5 Surya
20 Pushya	41 Maitra	41 Maitra	45 Brama	45 Brama	45 Brama	37 Aryama	37 Aryama	6 Satya
19 Sugriv	35 Jay	40	39 Vivas- -vat	39 Vivas- -vat	39 Vivas- -vat	38	34 Savitra	7 Bhrush
18 Nandi	35	40 Indra	39 Vivas- -vat	39 Vivas- -vat	39 Vivas- -vat	38 Savita	34	8 Aakash
17 Pitru	16 Mriga	15 Nhrig Raj	14 Gundh- -arv	13 Yama	12 Gruhk- -shat	11 Vitaya	10 Pusha	9 Anil

The West, The God Varun (Rains)

The East, The God Indra (Prosperity)

Putana   **The South, The God Yama (Death, Justice)**   Vidarika

Creation of Vastu-Purush

According to a story in *Matsya - Puran*, Vastu-Purusha was created from a sweat drop of Lord-Shiva. Vastu-Purusha was cruel, horrifying and devoured everything on his way. When he was granted the boon of eating anything from the three worlds by Lord Shiva. All deities were terrified. So they collectively caught hold of the Vastu-Purusha and threw him to the ground with face downwards, head in north-east and feet in south-west. 45 deities held his body, 13 from within and 32 from outside his body area. The names and relative positions of all 45 deities is given in the chart.

N

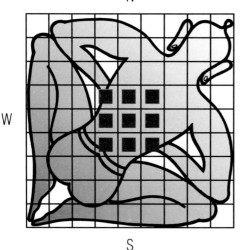

W   E

S

Marma Points

Below are the vital points situated on the eight important energy lines. These are the highly sensitive points affecting us physically, emotionally or spiritually.
We must take care of these Marma points. So that they are not hurt by any heavy or sharp objets like pillars or nails.

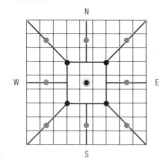

Importance of Brahmasthala

Brahmasthala is the center of the square plot. The center of any object or place is very important. The nucleus of cell, the fulcrum of the lever etc. are some examples of important center points. Brahmasthala is therefore an important factor to be considered in Vastu, while constructing a house or any other building. The energy lines running through the center are also equally important. In ancient times, people knew the importance of Brahmasthala and so temples, deities, courtyards, holy *tulsi* plants etc. were located in the center of village, house or palaces. Every morning for charging the center a pooja of *Tulsi* was done. This central part or Brahmasthala is located in the central nine squares of the 81 grid plan of Vastu *Mandala*. It is located around the navel of Vastu-Purush.

In Vastu, it is believed that if the Brahamasthala is 'hurt' by fixing of nails, pillars, pegs, heavy objects etc. then the owner will be in trouble. So Brahmasthala, being one of the very important parts in a building, has to be safe-guarded.

Importance of Geometric Shape

Extension at North - East
Good for growth, Excessive Wealth

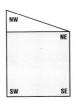

Extension at North - West
Unhappiness, More Enemies, Loss in Business, Theft

Reduction at North - East
Loss of financial growth, Health and Peace

Reduction at North - West
Good for Growth, Prosperity.

Extension at North - East
Good for growth, Prosperity

Extension at South - West
Ill Health, Mental unhappiness, Accidental injury, No Prosperity

Reduction at North - East
Unhappiness, Enmity, Loss of wealth

Reduction at North - West
Ill health, Mental Unhappiness, Accidental injury

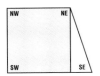

Extension at South - East
Quarrel and Litigation, Illness, Financial loss

Extension at North - West
Mental upset, Defection, Poverty and Loss of Vehicles

Reduction at South - East
Good for growth

Reduction at South - West
Mental unrest, Ill Health, Financial Loss & Loss of Position or reputation

Extension at South - East
Litigation, Unwanted expenses, Bad for children and women

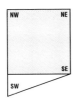

Extension at South - West
Financial loss, Defection and Accidents

Reduction at South - East
Financial loss, Loss of reputation, and possibility of suicides

Reduction at South - West
Destruction, worries, Litigation, Unwanted Expenses

Importance of Roads

(i) Roads on all four sides.
If there are parallel roads on all four sides of the plot, persons living in such a plot will gain progress, wealth, health and prosperity.

(ii) Roads on N, E and W.
This is also an auspicious plot and here the progress is very rapid, people living here lead a happy life and business flourishes well.

(iii)Roads on S, E and W
Persons staying on such a plot become well known. Here women play an important part in business and make special progress.

(iv) Roads on N, W and S.
People living in such a plot are happy and prosperous, but they are not interested in social work.

(v) Roads on N, E and S.
People living in this plot live happily but such plots are considered to be of medium category.

(vi)Roads on N and W.
People living on such plots will gain wealth.

(vii) Roads on N and E.
People living on such plots become well known. They get new opportunities or new business and become prosperous.

(viii) Roads on S and W. Such a plot is very suitable for business class people because business flourishes on such plots.

(ix) Roads on S and E.

Persons living on such plots spend lot on entertainment but then too live a happy and enjoyable life.

(x) Roads on N and S.

People living on such plots lead a prosperous life. But, instead of happiness in house, they have jealousy, clashes and enmity.

(xi) Roads on W and E

Such plots are good and they give prosperity to the residents.

(xii) Road on N

Brings wealth and prosperity.

(xiii) Road on S

Business of female oriented articles and their requirements, hospitals, entertainment and bars can flourish well here.

(xiiv) Road on W

These plots are of medium category but are good for business.

(xv) Road on E

These plots are very auspicious. Residents of these plots gain fame and prosperity.

(xvi) Road Endings

When the plot has a road ending in it, it is not very good. But if it is from north-east (from N and E) north-west (only from W) and south-east (only from S) it is auspicious. All other endings are inauspicious, which is shown in the figure.

(xvii) Junction or "T" Road

Plot with such a juction on any of its side, is considered to be poor Vastu quality.

Results of different gate locations

EAST SIDE
1 Fire Hazard 2 Good for women 3 Prosperity 4 Favour from Helpful People 5 Restlessness and Anger 6 False allegation 7 Harshness and Sadness 8 Theft 9 Damage to Male Child and/or wealth.

SOUTH SIDE
9 Damage to Male Child and/or wealth 10 Slave like condition manifest 11 Meanmindedness 12 Prosperity or Human Growth 13 Inauspicious 14 Ungratefulness or fear 15 Financial Loss 16 Damage to the capabilities of son 17 Trouble to Son, Unwanted Expenses.

The width of a door should be "half" of the height of the door

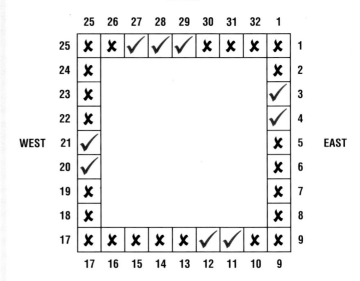

Gate Locations

Door must be with central opening.
The door frame must be rectangular. If arch is required it must be with the extra frame .

WEST SIDE
17 Trouble to Son, Unwanted Expenses 18 Enmity 19 Financial Loss 20 Financial and Human Growth 21 Financial and Human Growth 22 Government harassment 23 Financial Loss 24 Sickness 25 Tragical Death, Accidental Injury, Imprisonment

NORTH SIDE
25 Tragical Death, Accidental Injury, Imprisonment 26 Enmity 27 Happiness 28 Financial Gain, Human Growth 29 All Type of Gains 30 Enmity with Son 31 Problems for Females 32 Failure 1Loss due to Fire

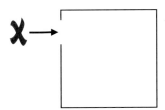

Secret's of Jiten

Majority of diseases enter through mouth and evil sprits through door, protect both for well-being.

Dwara Veda (Obstacles at the front door)

Obstacles at the entrance of home causes problems to its residents : Tree - harms children, Well - causes mental disorders, Temple - hampers growth, Staircase - unhappiness, Road / Street - reduces longevity, Corner of another building - causes various tensions, Pillar - problems on female members, Muddy pit / Gutter - brings worries and hardships, Water drainage - causes expenses to exceed income, Lift - drains health and wealth, Loud speaker / Constant sound - brings bad omen, Factory / Machine - troubles and pain, High wall / Building - hinders progress, Electric / Telephone pole - causes serious diseases.

Placement of the Building

The placement of the house should be towards South-West. North-East should remain open according to Sun-Moon principle or symmetrically in the centre of the plot.

Staircase

The staircase should be provided in the West or North sides of a building.
The turning should be in clockwise (right hand) direction while climbing up, as shown.

Diagonal Plot

Diagonal Plot or Building is not advisable.

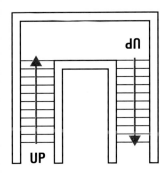

Home Chart

The placement of the different rooms in the house can give us different effects. Some of the suggested placements as per Vastu are given here.

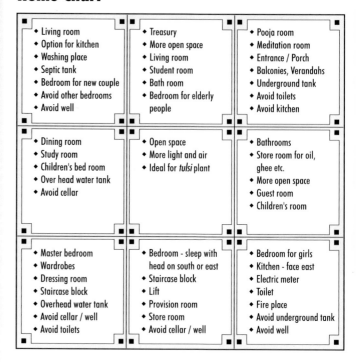

- ◆ Living room
- ◆ Option for kitchen
- ◆ Washing place
- ◆ Septic tank
- ◆ Bedroom for new couple
- ◆ Avoid other bedrooms
- ◆ Avoid well

- ◆ Treasury
- ◆ More open space
- ◆ Living room
- ◆ Student room
- ◆ Bath room
- ◆ Bedroom for elderly people

- ◆ Pooja room
- ◆ Meditation room
- ◆ Entrance / Porch
- ◆ Balconies, Verandahs
- ◆ Underground tank
- ◆ Avoid toilets
- ◆ Avoid kitchen

- ◆ Dining room
- ◆ Study room
- ◆ Children's bed room
- ◆ Over head water tank
- ◆ Avoid cellar

- ◆ Open space
- ◆ More light and air
- ◆ Ideal for *tulsi* plant

- ◆ Bathrooms
- ◆ Store room for oil, ghee etc.
- ◆ More open space
- ◆ Guest room
- ◆ Children's room

- ◆ Master bedroom
- ◆ Wardrobes
- ◆ Dressing room
- ◆ Staircase block
- ◆ Overhead water tank
- ◆ Avoid cellar / well
- ◆ Avoid toilets

- ◆ Bedroom - sleep with head on south or east
- ◆ Staircase block
- ◆ Lift
- ◆ Provision room
- ◆ Store room
- ◆ Avoid cellar / well

- ◆ Bedroom for girls
- ◆ Kitchen - face east
- ◆ Electric meter
- ◆ Toilet
- ◆ Fire place
- ◆ Avoid underground tank
- ◆ Avoid well

Office Chart

Suggested placements in an office as per Vastu.

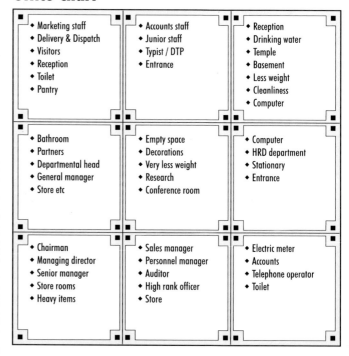

- ◆ Marketing staff
- ◆ Delivery & Dispatch
- ◆ Visitors
- ◆ Reception
- ◆ Toilet
- ◆ Pantry

- ◆ Accounts staff
- ◆ Junior staff
- ◆ Typist / DTP
- ◆ Entrance

- ◆ Reception
- ◆ Drinking water
- ◆ Temple
- ◆ Basement
- ◆ Less weight
- ◆ Cleanliness
- ◆ Computer

- ◆ Bathroom
- ◆ Partners
- ◆ Departmental head
- ◆ General manager
- ◆ Store etc

- ◆ Empty space
- ◆ Decorations
- ◆ Very less weight
- ◆ Research
- ◆ Conference room

- ◆ Computer
- ◆ HRD department
- ◆ Stationary
- ◆ Entrance

- ◆ Chairman
- ◆ Managing director
- ◆ Senior manager
- ◆ Store rooms
- ◆ Heavy items

- ◆ Sales manager
- ◆ Personnel manager
- ◆ Auditor
- ◆ High rank officer
- ◆ Store

- ◆ Electric meter
- ◆ Accounts
- ◆ Telephone operator
- ◆ Toilet

Shop & Commercial complex Chart

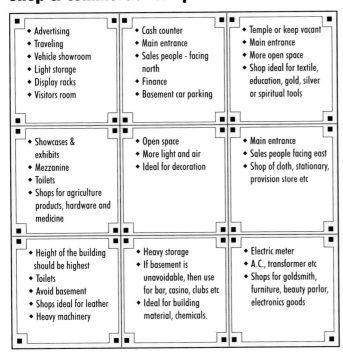

• Advertising • Traveling • Vehicle showroom • Light storage • Display racks • Visitors room	• Cash counter • Main entrance • Sales people - facing north • Finance • Basement car parking	• Temple or keep vacant • Main entrance • More open space • Shop ideal for textile, education, gold, silver or spiritual tools
• Showcases & exhibits • Mezzanine • Toilets • Shops for agriculture products, hardware and medicine	• Open space • More light and air • Ideal for decoration	• Main entrance • Sales people facing east • Shop of cloth, stationary, provision store etc
• Height of the building should be highest • Toilets • Avoid basement • Shops ideal for leather • Heavy machinery	• Heavy storage • If basement is unavoidable, then use for bar, casino, clubs etc • Ideal for building material, chemicals.	• Electric meter • A.C., transformer etc • Shops for goldsmith, furniture, beauty parlor, electronics goods

Some of the suggested placements as per Vastu for shop and commercial complex.

Factory Chart

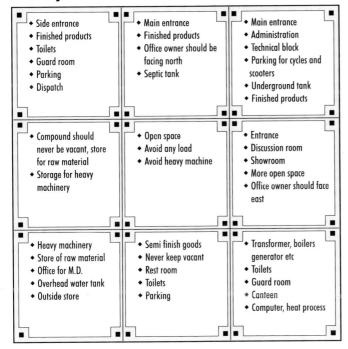

• Side entrance • Finished products • Toilets • Guard room • Parking • Dispatch	• Main entrance • Finished products • Office owner should be facing north • Septic tank	• Main entrance • Administration • Technical block • Parking for cycles and scooters • Underground tank • Finished products
• Compound should never be vacant, store for raw material • Storage for heavy machinery	• Open space • Avoid any load • Avoid heavy machine	• Entrance • Discussion room • Showroom • More open space • Office owner should face east
• Heavy machinery • Store of raw material • Office for M.D. • Overhead water tank • Outside store	• Semi finish goods • Never keep vacant • Rest room • Toilets • Parking	• Transformer, boilers generator etc • Toilets • Guard room • Canteen • Computer, heat process

Suggested placements in a factory as per Vastu.

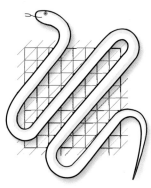

Energy Grid concept of Vastu Vidya is symbolized by snake, vertical, horizontal and cross grid.
One must activate the plot before use. A Symbolic puja or activation of snake energy is necessary.

Snake head in Rashi

NW	Mina, Mesha, Vrishabha
NE	Mithuna, Karkat, Simha
SE	Kanya, Tula, Vrishchika
SW	Dhanus, Makara, Kumbha

The Two Paths

Once you read the chapter on Vastu, you will definitely find numerous drawbacks in your house or work place. Now the concern is about the solution. We have already studied the two paths of solving a problem- the Outer pole technique and the Inner pole technique.

If you consider using the Outer pole technique you will have to correct the defects by demolishing, breaking or physical alteration. But many times it is not possible for us to follow this path due to inconvenience, government regulations or other restrictions. Another path to achieve results is the Inner pole technique. It deals with the vital center within. Here any technique, which works on the root level, can be used. These techniques can be Tantra, Mantra or Yantra.

Tantra is the principle of the higher level or real understanding of the divine dance between the "Shiva" and "Shakti" or the Energy and the Matter. Mantra is the principle of the cosmic vibrations around us. Yantra is the principle of using an instrument, tool or vehicle to reach the core. All these techniques influence our core and transform the wrong interpretation of information to create balance.

In Vastu the first thing to do after purchasing a plot is a "Vastu pooja". It is an auspicious symbolic ceremony to transform the plot to become beneficial to us. This symbolic ceremony is performed to activate the vital energy of the plot which is in the form of a snake. This snake rotates through the four houses in a year. We should be very cautious while digging or starting a construction. The head of this snake energy must never be hurt. The plot must be harmonized with us. Also many yantras are placed at the tail, in layers in this pooja or ceremony.

So let us learn more about this powerful technique of yantra to create harmony in and around us.

Sri Yantra
The powerful symbolic toolsin "Tantric Sadhana" to uplift our consciousness to supreme consciousness.

Understanding Yantras

Yantras are two or three dimensional definitely calculated power diagrams.

Yantras are a potent and dynamic sacred geometric configuration and concepts. For a definite purpose, a specific configuration is generated and with help of our inbuilt power we use it to obtain results. These yantras start from a mystic point (the *bindu*), the core and unfold to concentric circuits.

The yantras, though of many different types, are mainly divided into 5 types -

1) *Bhoomi Prishth Yantra* - it is a made out of materials from earth and is further divided into -
    i) Raised Yantras including lines
    ii) Carved Yantras

2) *Meru Prishth Yantra* - These are in the shape of mountain. They are broad at the base and have pointed apex.

3) *Patal Yantra* - This is of the reverse shape of 'Meru Yantra', that is   their apex points downwards. They are carved.

4) *Meru Prastar Yantra* - These are the cut yantras.

5) *Ruram Prashth Yantra* - These are forged ones. Their bottom is rectangular whereas the top is like tortoise back.

All these yantras are sub-divided according to the five elements of the world - Earth, Air, Fire, Water and Ether. These yantras have been made for different purposes indicating their specific uses -

1) *Prithvi Tatva* (The Earth element) - These yantras bestow comforts, contentment, fulfil ambitions and attain success.

2) *Jal Tatva* - (The Water element) - These yantras bestow love, smoothness, affection, wisdom and removes restlessness.

3) *Agni Tatva* - (The Fire element) - These yantras bestow success, respect, victory and removes troubles.

4) *Vayu Tatva* - (The Air element) - These yantras are very powerful but, if not properly used, they can lead to difficulties, disrespect, also attracts the user to vices .

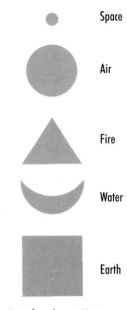

Space

Air

Fire

Water

Earth

Basic five element Yantra

Tibetan energy-balancing yantra.
Placed on the cross roads.

5) *Akasha Tatva* - (The Ether element) - These yantras bestow love, affection, education, success, spirituality and removes worries.

Although we have discussed only some yantras here, there are many yantras in all different countries and religious sects. 'Yantra' is a very vast and deep subject which has been studied by our ancestors throughout the world.

Hence, Yantra is a psychic tool of personal fulfilment. Though it is a complex symbolic construction with multiple layers of metaphysical meaning, it also aids Man to return to his original wholeness. Bliss (Paramanandam) and super consciousness (Parma Chaitanya)

⚠ Pyramid Yantra

Our temples, churches, gurudwaras, mosques and other religious places are the link between us and the heaven. When we feel the need of supernatural help, we visit these places. Not only that, we have also always taken our complaints, dreams, desires, aims and goals to them. We have made them our last hope. When we need miracles to happen, these are the only places we seek. Hence, they are the best examples of pyramid yantra as a Wish Machine. Let us know more about it.

All around the world there are many spiritual places with lots of different types and shapes. But as we see, basically all these shapes are divided only in two parts -
1)   Dome shaped
2)   Pyramidal and Conical Pointed shaped

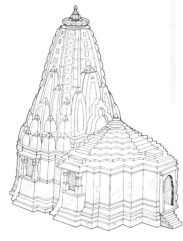

Spiritual yantras
for wish fulfilment

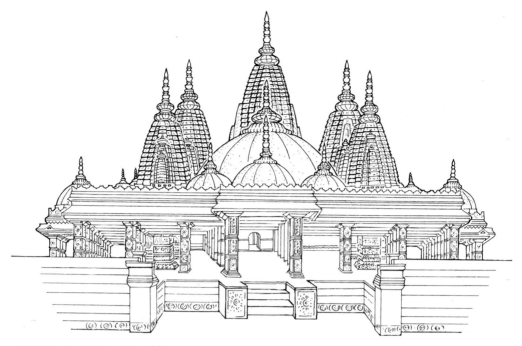

Indian Temple with Pyramids and Domes

In China and other South-East and East-Asian countries we can see beautiful pointed shapes in use. They can be seen in their temples and other architecture. In Islamic and Buddhist religions we can see powerful domed, rounded, curved shapes in mosque and other religious places. In India we have all together different structures, here in temples we have a pointed pyramidal shape at the back and a dome shape in front, i.e. equal importance is given to both the shapes.

To increase the power of shapes the multiplication phenomena is used. Two methods of multiplication are observed:

1)   **Vertical Multiplication**
2)   **Horizontal Multiplication**

⋀ Vertical Multiplication

This is done by multiplying or placing symmetrical shapes in a vertical plane. The best example of this is the 'Pagoda".

⌂ Horizontal Multiplication

In this method the same shape is repeated again and again horizontally on a plane. The best example of this is the 'Church'.

Nav Graha Yantra

In many cases both multiplications are seen together and this is called the projection technique. Here the basic shape is repeated by projecting it through the previous one and the best example here is of the temple *Shikhars*.

In Indian temples the story of multiplicity does not end just here. They have a whole pre-planned flow chart for preparing the temples. They start with the selection of location, the types of trees and quality of soil, also underwater currents and laylines are checked as per vastu science. After doing all this a pit is dug and a yantra called 'Vastu Purush Mandal' is put inside and covered. Then 'Nav Grah Yantra' is placed and covered, then the 'Sri Yantra' is placed and covered and above all this, the idol of god or goddess is placed. The chamber of God the temple has a pyramidal shape above to enhance the effect of all yantras. Then, after all this is completely constructed, the energization of temple is done which is called *Pranpratistha*.

As we know, Pyramid is the most basic shape because its mathematics is directly related with life force, which we have already discussed in the chapter Pyramid. Placing of Pyramid shape and multiplying it will give better results. Ancient texts and recent researches have shown that a Pyramid is divided into three parts-

1) The base - One of the important parts of Pyramid for inter-resonance.

2) Body - Necessary for energy circulation.

3) Apex or cap - Also a powerful part for interaction with cosmic energy. This is specially prepared from gems, precious stones and metals, crystals, granite etc.

All our religious places are powerful instruments for betterment of our lives and fulfilment of our aims and objectives. But today we have no time for specially going to those places and we need something similar which can

Base plan of the temple Three Yantras represent three *Shaktis*.

be handy and personal. Pyramid yantra can be very helpful to you here because it is smaller, handy, personalized and an easy to use device. So, you can work with your Pyramid yantra any time, anywhere - at your ease and privacy. Pyramid yantra is specially designed with all these principles.

Yantra Dynamics

Fundamental shapes used in different types of yantras are shown below-

1) The universe in its unmanifested form represented by the great seed point.
2) Expansion of universe is done by the integration of male and female energies, represented by triangles.
3) Harmony and balance is represented by the combination of two triangles.
4) Five element principle is shown by golden star, mainly used for health and vitality.
5) Each element is represented by 5 shapes
6) Manifestations of 9 represents 9 planets and 9 energies on grid of 9.
7) Different levels of manifestations of energy are represented by concentric circles.
8) Flow of energy in different directions is represented by 4, 8, 12 and 16 petals.
9) The rotational energy, clockwise or anticlock wise, is represented by 'swastika'.

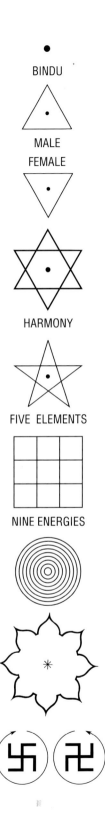

BINDU

MALE

FEMALE

HARMONY

FIVE ELEMENTS

NINE ENERGIES

Can you believe this!

"The nectar is the end result of churning. My essence is at the tail, catch me from the tail".
- *Vastu Man*

Let's see how you can use yantra. The most powerful and useful yantra is the Harmony Yantra. Harmony is the most important essence of relationship. Without it we may create mis-co-ordination and disturbances. When we are totally in harmony with what we are doing, we then attract harmonious people and situations towards us. To bring about this we have to be in harmony with-

1) Our mother nature
2) Our mind and body
3) Ourselves and the surrounding people and places.

All these three harmonies can make our life more enjoyable and lively.

But if you have disharmony with someone, say husband - wife, father - son, mother-in-law - daughter-in-law, or any other such relations then 'Harmony Yantra' can be very helpful to you.

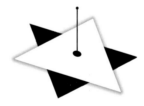

How To Make 'Harmony Yantra'

◆ Take a piece of white paper.

◆ Cut two triangles of same size, preferably equilateral.

◆ Write and place the yin energy name i.e.- wife, son or daughter-in-law, etc. in the triangle with one corner facing you and yang energy name on the triangle with base on your side, as shown in figure.

◆ Place the yang name triangle above the yin name triangle as shown in the figure.

◆ Put the pen, pencil or any other pointed object passing exactly from the center of both the triangle.

◆ Close your eyes, sit calmly and repeat your wish 100 times.

◆ Then put a pin in the center and leave the harmony yantra on a place without disturbance.

◆ Repeat your wish daily for one minute a day till it is fulfilled.
But if your problem is very acute you can try with Harmony 9x9 yantra (see page 212).

Real Voice

I have received numerous feedbacks on the various experiments performed by many people. Below are few of them from the many Experts who have sent me their valuable feedbacks.

"In my practice of Geobiology, Geomancy, Space healing, Vastu, Reiki and Feng Shui using pyramids designed by Prof. Dr. Jiten Bhatt, I have found astounding success".

Col. Subhash Chadha (Retd.)
Geomancy, Vastu and Feng Shui consultant

"In my 18 years of Vastu practice, to get result in negative lands like grave, tomb, burial ground, place of murder, accidental death was discouraging.
In many cases I was affected by this negative forces. But today with positive power of pyramids I have new dimension and confidence to make such places positive".

Dr. N. S. Pawar
Vastu, Pyramid analyst, Aura photography

"I have successfully used the wonderful - Dr. Bhatt's PyraVastu devices, based on the Power of Mind to remove Vastu defects for my numerous clients in India, USA, Canada, Singapore, Malaysia etc".

Pt. Gopal Sharma
Governer - All India Federation of Astrologers society.

"Triorigin principles have been able define neutro energy at the 1/3 height in pyramid, which is a miracle creator. I have personally experienced miracles of Multier 9x9 pyramids and Fortune plate etc developed by Dr. Bhatt".

Dr. Suman Motilal Shah
Authorised SU JOK Acupuncture lecturer and Reiki master

"Today's challenge to Vastu experts is to rectify the Vastu defects without physical altering, shifting and dismantling the building structure. Very easy and effective solution to this great problem is just follow the PyraVastu. Results are like miracles".

Ganesh Tamrakar
Vastu consultant

"I find Pyramid Yantra a powerful tool for Vaasthu correction without demolition. It has given amazing results. People love to adopt this, since it is cost effective and non-destructive. Especially they are very useful in correcting plots".

Er. Dr. K. A. Natesan
Vaastu consultant

" I always use Pyramid Yantra in my practice and I get lot of appreciation from my clients. I am very much thankful to this new system evolved after 5000 years by Dr. Jiten Bhatt".

Kunwar Nerender Singh
Vastu consultant, Advance Reiki healer

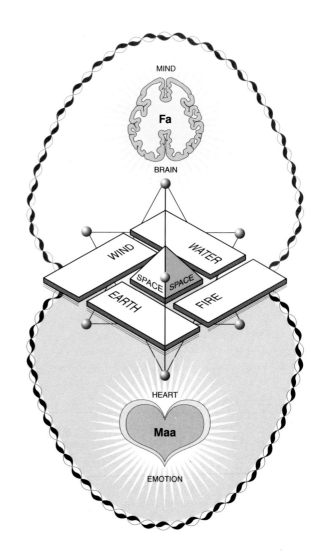

Better Solutions

Pyra Vastu is a practical art to harmonize - mind, body and spirit with the environment, by just placing pre-programmed 'Pyramid Yantra' at appropriate locations; to achieve health, happiness and prosperity.

PyraVastu is ideal for correcting Vastu and feng shui defects without physical-alteration, shifting or breaking home, shop or factory.

"PyraVastu is a powerful science of creating balance and harmony by core level corrections, with the help of pre-programmed Pyramid Yantra.
It is based on the essential principles of subtle anatomy and the laws of the universe.
Here we utilize our own hidden capabilities to achieve a better tomorrow."

Prof. Dr. Jiten Bhatt

Pyra-Vastu

Invention of PyraVastu

To have a home 'sweet-home' is our basic need. Peace, harmony, prosperity and health is what we desire there. Vastu and Feng Shui harmonize our spirit, home and environment. In spite of this, these arts are practically impossible to apply wholly. By using the core principles of Vastu, Feng Shui and other ancient sciences Prof. Dr. Jiten Bhatt has invented this new practical yet deep rooted spiritual method of PyraVastu.

Prof. Dr. Jiten Bhatt is a scientist having many multidimensional inventions on his name. He has an experience of 30 years in health, healing and other related fields. One of his most result-oriented inventions is this unique technique of Pynergy and PyraVastu. With this technique he has successfully benefitted thousands of people. We will here learn its secrets to solve day to day problems.

PyraVastu is complementary to Vastu and Feng Shui but its dynamic action starts exactly at the opposite end. It is just like using medicine and meditation for achieving health.

Vastu and Feng Shui is more like offering solutions for outer visible end, like thousands of branches and leaves. PyraVastu deals with the roots or vital force, behind all action within it. It is a totally innovative concept of subtle level correction with pyramid yantras based on mind over matter. It deals with our inbuilt power and ability of Mind-Body-Emotion. This powerful intention at the core level induces energy within us. Thus, subtle energy level correction is more powerful than that done by material or physical means. First principle in PyraVastu - is that of Mind over Matter.

Core Principle #1
Mind over Matter

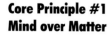

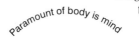

Mind is more powerful than body in the same way energy is more powerful than matter, yantra is more powerful than constructions and center is more powerful than yantra.

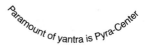

Pyramid Vastu Revolution

Pyravastu revolution is a new, dynamic and result-oriented system designed by Prof. Dr. Jiten Bhatt is not just the usage of pyramids in vastu. This is a totally new concept created for the first time in the world. It is a precise interactive permutation and combination of the vital force within and around us known as the "Pynergy". Pyravastu is the efficient management of this pynergy network to bring about a positive awareness in and around us. It helps us achieve better emotional, mental and physical state of wellness. Are you ready to join this advanced yet original revolution, which has benefited 2.5 million people in just 30 years?

Prof. Dr. Jiten Bhatt has made a deep study of Egyptian, Indian, Mexican, Chinese and other ancient concepts of Mind Power Tools (MPT, as he calls them). After years of research into these MPTs like pyramids, yantras, *Mandalas,* symbols and many others he invented this totally new revolutionary power tool - **"Pyramid Yantra"**. This pyramid yantra looks quite similar to the Egyptian pyramids but its working principle is very different and can be used for numerous specific purposes.

He designs this new system in such a practical way that anybody can implement it in their lives even for better solutions of day to day problems. Pyramid Yantra works at the core of all things and beings in existence and hence helps in creating balance and harmony at the core of all our problems. It is a very versatile MPT, which can aid where the materialistic sciences cannot offer much help.

This new MPT can be used in symbiosis with any other discipline of mental, physical and emotional wellness. It enhances the effect of any healthy living system like Yoga, Meditation, Healing, Astrology, Vastu, Feng Shui and many others.

"Are you ready?"
- Prof. Dr. Jiten Bhatt

Prof. Dr. Jiten Bhatt is actively working for developing such healthy solutions since 30 years. Mataji Narayani and Swami Ananda first introduced him to the field of healing sciences. Basically an engineer, he is was keenly interested in developing solutions for healthy living, which are highly effective yet simple to use and understand. He has dedicated his life to teach and train others who can become capable of carrying forward these solutions to this and the next generations.

He is the founder of many healing associations in India and is actively involved with such associations abroad. His lectures here and abroad have evoked awareness in thousands of people. He is the pioneer in India to introduce Holistic Healing as a subject in universities. He also is an honorary adviser to many hospitals and health care centers. You too can be a part of this positive revolution to optimise your health, happiness, peace and prosperity.

Base of PyraVastu - Tattvas

As we are working on subtle level we should know and understand the subtle anatomy very well. The Tattva diagram below defines the various sub-functions which are unfolded from the initial unity. It is through these functions that the flow of energy is channelized for us to experience the world. The pure Tattvas divide into two - Shiva & Shakti which interact with the three energies of will, knowledge and action, which are the prime movers of cosmic evolution. The next comes the psychical Tattva which is also called "Maya Shakti". It is divided into five limitations - Kalaa, Vidya, Raga, Kaal and Niyati. These five veil and obscure our perception of reality. Then next are the physical Tattvas which are divided into Purush and Prakriti (Fa & Maa), Male and Female. The Prakriti is divided into Sattva, Rajas and Tamas, which are further divided into 3 modes of mind, 5 sense organs, 5 action agents; 5 subtle and 5 gross elements.

Core Principle #2

Second core principle of PyraVastu are the Tattvas. PyraVastu deals more with FaMaa - powerful intention and pure love or in other words Mind and Emotions. Also the five subtle and gross elements and their inter-relationship play an important role.

Now let's explore the power of mind, dynamic action of love by understanding deeper meanings of FaMaa.

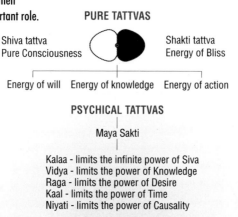

PURE TATTVAS

Shiva tattva
Pure Consciousness

Shakti tattva
Energy of Bliss

Energy of will   Energy of knowledge   Energy of action

PSYCHICAL TATTVAS

Maya Sakti

Kalaa - limits the infinite power of Siva
Vidya - limits the power of Knowledge
Raga - limits the power of Desire
Kaal - limits the power of Time
Niyati - limits the power of Causality

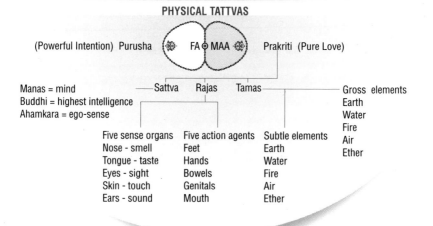

PHYSICAL TATTVAS

(Powerful Intention) Purusha ❀ FA ⊙ MAA ❀ Prakriti (Pure Love)

Manas = mind
Buddhi = highest intelligence
Ahamkara = ego-sense

Sattva   Rajas   Tamas

Gross elements
Earth
Water
Fire
Air
Ether

Five sense organs	Five action agents	Subtle elements
Nose - smell	Feet	Earth
Tongue - taste	Hands	Water
Eyes - sight	Bowels	Fire
Skin - touch	Genitals	Air
Ears - sound	Mouth	Ether

FaMaa - Fundamental law of PyraVastu

One of the most important principles is FaMaa. So we must throughly understand the fundamental law of FaMaa. Let's see a few examples - Sun & Moon though very different are the essence of nature for all creation on the earth. Father & Mother, where Fa emanates from Heavens controlling our destiny and Maa emerges from earth and controls our desires. Similarly male and female principle balances all life. Happiness and Sadness there is no happiness without sadness. it is like creating Fa within Maa and vice versa. Fa can be like a tree that is visible with Maa of equal potential as roots which are not visible. Hence Fa and Maa in spite of being opposite are complementary and co-operative to each other and are the fundamentals of all our actions field.

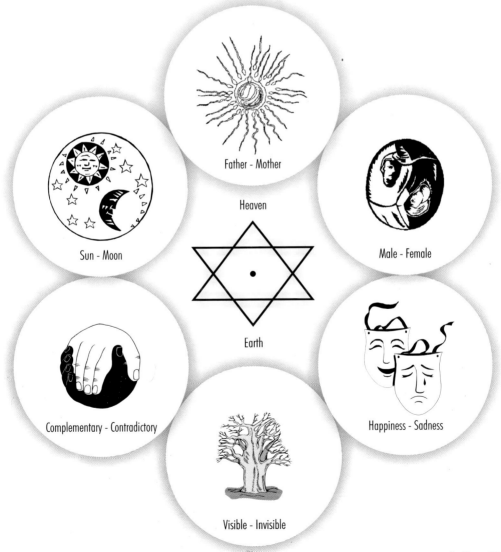

Father - Mother

Heaven

Sun - Moon

Male - Female

Earth

Complementary - Contradictory

Happiness - Sadness

Visible - Invisible

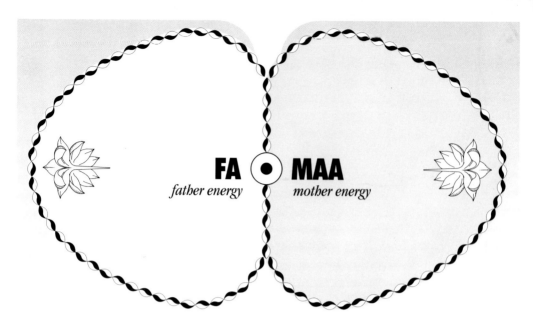

FA ⊙ **MAA**
father energy *mother energy*

Now we know the subtle anatomy, and understand that we are all working between the two powerful divine opposites - Shiva and Shakti. Here in PyraVastu, we deal with Man - his surroundings, how he is affected by them, what he can do and what he can achieve. Our journey of life begins from the divine union of a micro Fa (Sperm) and a micro Maa (Ovum). Hence it is due to Fa and Maa that we have our present miraculous body.

Everything in this universe including us is harmoniously divided into two divisions, Fa and Maa. On the level of divine we are divided into - Pure Consciousness and Bliss, on level of mind and emotions - Will and Love and on level of body - Nervous system and Circulatory system. Balance between Fa and Maa brings natural happiness, health and prosperity. We will see how to put this enormous power into practical use within us.

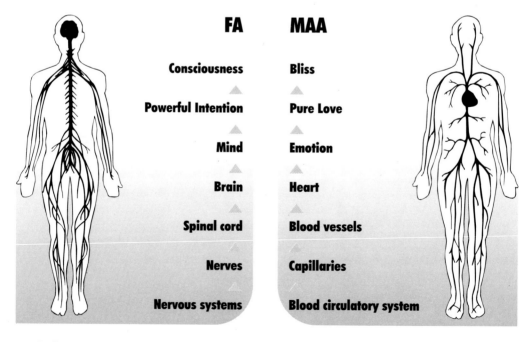

FA   **MAA**

Consciousness   Bliss

Powerful Intention   Pure Love

Mind   Emotion

Brain   Heart

Spinal cord   Blood vessels

Nerves   Capillaries

Nervous systems   Blood circulatory system

Enhance your mind and emotion power!

Mind power development is the basic need of growth and prosperity. Power of emotion is the nutrition for happiness. Any amount of learning on this mystic subject is less, but here we will explore three simple methods to enhance our mind and emotional power. Use the following 3-power steps every moment to change your life and get maximum benefits in PyraVastu.

Travel from visible to invisible, to explore infinite powers.

1. Believe in yourself

Faith evokes from the heart. Faith in your own abilities is a must. Without a humble but reasonable confidence in your own power you cannot be successful or happy. But with sound self-confidence you can succeed. A sense of inferiority and inadequacy interferes with the attainment of your hopes, and self-confidence leads to self-realisation and successful achievement of goals. Dynamics of faith will give more inner strength.

2. Remove negative blocks

This modern technique is referred to as ' auto-suggestion', used by many doctors and professionals the world over.
With whole hearted effort you can definitely remove the following negative blocks.

Here are some harmful formula phrases which we should avoid at all cost:
I can't, I shouldn't, I'm going to fail.
I'm not lucky, Nobody loves me.
I'll always be unhappy, I'm going to be ill .
I'm always wrong, I'm shy.
I was born under a bad sign.

Infinite power is within you.
Remove these negative blocks.

3. Positive affirmations

The power of positive thinking with dynamic power of faith will give you results beyond imagination.

So, think positive;
Every day, in all ways,
I am becoming stronger and
stronger, happy, healthy
and prosperous.

Explore the power of 'Manas Tattva' (Fa) and Prem Tattva (Maa) in any situation of life. This would definitely give you results.

FaMaa power programming

All work is done between two opposite ends or polarities - e.g. positive and negative in electricity and Fa Maa in living beings. These are our two inbuilt power generators. As the head and the heart are the farthest poles of reality, reason and love, logic and life. So is every thing else and hence all pyramid yantra require FaMaa programing.

FaMaa application before installing any pyramid yantra will orient millions of micro particles in the space of the instrument. They start to communicate harmoniously with each other and also with their centers as per our program, purpose or wish.

FaMaa programming

The figure shows the position of millions of space particles tuned to work in harmony with you after FaMaa programming.

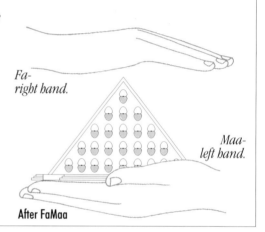

Fa- right hand.

Maa- left hand.

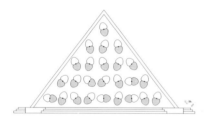

Before FaMaa

After FaMaa

Let's start Step-by-Step Programming:
1. Sit in a quiet, calm and comfortable place.
2. Rub your hands lightly for 1- 2 minutes.
3. Place the instrument on Maa (left) hand, then place the Fa (right) hand on top of it.
4. Close your eyes.
5. Create Maa awareness for 30 seconds by evoking pure love within yourself from heart.
6. Then create Fa awareness for 30 seconds by repeating your purpose with intense will from brain.
7. Repeat steps 5 and 6 alternatively for 3-5 minutes.
8. You can now place the FaMaa oriented instrument wherever needed, to fulfill your purpose.

Basically, FaMaa is the subtle method of powerful charging of your Pyramid Yantra. FaMaa can be created by remembering your Father and Mother or God and Goddess you believe in. You can also use healing techniques like Reiki, Pranic Healing, Meditation or by any other spiritual method.

Space Network!

Another important factor in PyraVastu is accurate space for the specific purpose. When matter dominates over spirit, it gives rise to the five elements. The five - foldedness of material nature provides the basis of our existence. The five elements - Earth, Water, Fire, Wind and Ether or Space govern us. Harmony between these elements in our body as well as in our surrounding environment brings about peace and balance within us. To bring about changes in these physical Tattvas, we have to use the five - element theory.

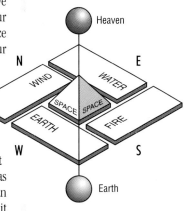

Five Elements and Central Axis

The modern scientific theory says that whatever is happening around us is based on the fundamental factor of TIME and SPACE. Each change and action in the universe is due to the mass and movement of subatomic particles. The space plays a vital role in this process as without space nothing grows or expands. Hence, space becomes an important element which is more potent than other elements when it comes to bringing about changes. Space is omnipresent and also a common link of resonating communication in the universe. Knowledge of this space network is a prime factor in PyraVastu.

When we make boundaries by any means - say physical i.e. by walls and roof, then that space is a bounded space. This bounded space works in two ways - one independently and other in harmony with the outer space. Its own working depends on the geometry of the boundary. Now if we know the property of the bounded space and a technique of using that space, then we can take advantage of the same. The power of pyramid yantra is based on the permutation, combination and interaction of such known multiple spaces. So multiple space is one of the most important factor in this technique of PyraVastu.

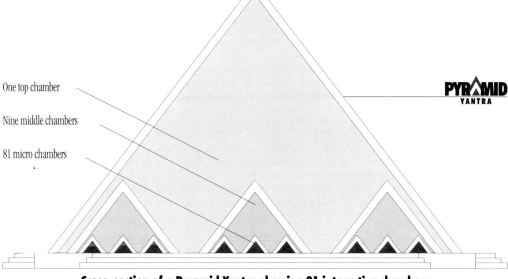

One top chamber

Nine middle chambers

81 micro chambers

PYRAMID
YANTRA

Cross-section of a Pyramid Yantra showing 91 interactive chambers

Power generation formula - 9x9

This secret law of 9x9 is used in many ways in the occult sciences. It is used in astrology (9 planets), numerology (9 numbers), Vastu and Feng Shui (grid of 9) and in traditional Islamic, Chinese and Hindu yantras. Power generation formula of Pyramid Yantra is shown in the illustration.

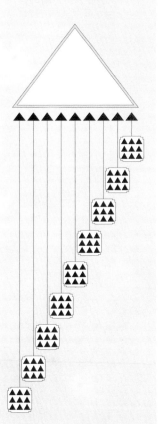

The bottom 81 PyraSpace adds power to the center 9 pyramids of PyraPlate. And this together with the top one is the addition of 91.

The Law of Central Axis

We know each bounded space is different in its identity. But each of these spaces are well connected by a divine axis or cord which is called the Central Axis. This central axis is like the thread of a necklace where each bead is a different identity in its own but when connected to each other through a thread, becomes a beautiful necklace. The center of each space is very important. Communication is done by this center of each space through the central axis. In this cosmos there is a maze of spaces but each is well connected with the others. Communication can be done from the higher to the lower level i.e. from brain to cell and from lower to higher i.e. from cell to brain. In the same way communication in the space occurs from any known microspace to the outside space and vice-versa.

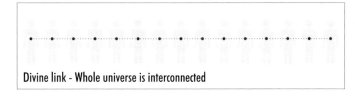

Divine link - Whole universe is interconnected

Pyramid yantra is a known multiple space instrument used for correction of disharmony. A space in this instrument is well connected through its center to the other spaces. The center of this yantra communicates with the center of the room in which it is placed. The center of the room communicates with the center of the house. And the center of the house communicates with the center of the man residing there. So central axis and center unit is very important in divine communication link. Any coding done at the central space of this yantra communicates to the centers of peripheral spaces in the cosmos as well as your own center. (One of the coding method is shown on pg 82 to 85).

PyraCenter (PC) - The Master Key

In simple words, the core or center of any particle, object, instrument, system, cell or living being is called "PyraCenter". It can also be known as the master control center of each and everything existing in the universe. PyraCenter and its interconnectivity with other centers is the base of PyraVastu practice. PyraCenter is a highly sensitive area for any interaction within and around.

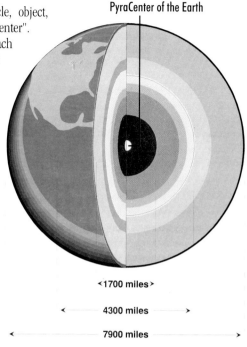

PyraCenter of the Earth

<1700 miles>

4300 miles

7900 miles

Let us see some examples for better understanding. Sun is the PyraCenter of our solar system, Nucleus is the PyraCenter of an atom, and DNA is the PyraCenter of a cell. Likewise if we study in a broader aspect, a Prime Minister or President is the PyraCenter of a country or a hard disc is the PyraCenter of our computer, etc. Here from all these one aspect gets clear that for any work to be done at lower or higher level, program is to be initiated at the PyraCenter. In PyraVastu the art of initiating a program at the PyraCenter is of prime importance. So we must learn this art of knowing and programming the PyraCenter.

Now we must again make this clear in our minds that PyraVastu is a completely new and revolutionary technique. Therefore, its theory and operating laws may also be quite different from the conventional techniques. The approach of PyraVastu is quite similar to that of Vastu and Feng Shui. Its methodology is different yet its effects are complementary to both these techniques, and vice versa.

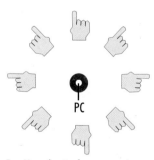

PyraVastu begins from center, it is inner pole technique.

End results of all these techniques may be the same but starting point of PyraVastu is completely opposite. As we have known earlier, Vastu and Feng Shui can be related to the Outer pole technique whereas, PyraVastu can be related to the Inner pole technique. So in PyraVastu unlike the other techniques, we begin from the PyraCenter, the subtle and invisible end.

Now let us understand PyraCenter in context of PyraVastu. In Vastu, Bhramasthala is the center space of any land on which building is to be constructed. Similarly in Feng Shui, a plot is divided into nine parts and the center is the area representing energy. But PyraVastu deals with it in as deeper aspect. Imagine a ninth part of the whole plot, which is quite a big area. Now divide that part further into 9 parts and consider the center of it. Go on dividing the center further into 9 parts. Ultimately you will reach a point where there is nothing or infinity. This is called the PyraCenter or 'PC' in PyraVastu. Another vital time center TC we have studied.

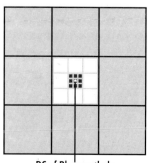

PC of Bhramasthala

Secret's of Jiten

The only way out is in!
Our ultimate center of bliss
and illumination is within.

Power of 7PC

Another important aspect of PyraVastu is its seven vital PCs. Vastu and Feng Shui emphasize on the floor and the central floor area. But PyraVastu deals with dynamics of the volumetric reality of an building. For considering any volume we have to see its boundaries. Say for a room, ceiling, floor and its four walls are its boundaries. In PyraVastu the volumetric center is very important. For its efficient and precise performance it has six satellites like centers in all six directions. These can be located at the centers of ceiling, floor and the four walls. All these six PCs collect the information from the surrounding and send it to the central PC. They also collect information from the central PC and pass it on to the surrounding.

Out of these six, three of them are Fa PCs and the rest three are Maa PCs. The PCs on Top, East and North are Fa PCs and those on the Bottom, West and South are Maa PCs. As we divide the six PCs into Fa and Maa, automatically the power axis for our working in PyraVastu is created. These six satellite Pcs and one central PC together form an important network in PyraVastu. PC and TC (Time Center are two master keys in PyraVastu.

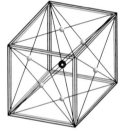

PC is volumetric center of the room or subtle space center in the air.

Seven power centers; four satellite on walls, fifth on top, sixth in bottom and the seventh the center in the space.

Center controls the whole volume by six sub-centers and three axis

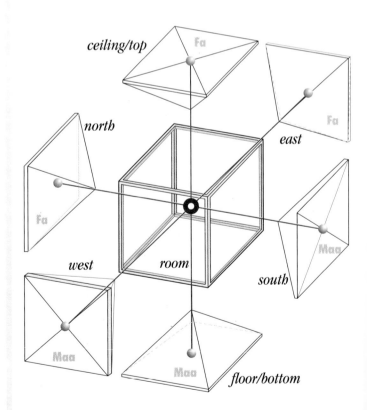

One center and effective pyramidal forces of other six

Scope of PyraVastu

As the application is more practical and very simple, the scope can be very huge. It gives miraculous results in many areas. Some are listed below.

Land

Today it is very difficult to get a perfect piece of land. This new PyraVastu gives us a powerful method for activation and simple method for correction. So now your plot for home, factory, shop or farm can be made in perfect harmony for optimum benefits.

Building

Buildings today have become more complex and irregular in shape according to the modern requirements and lack of space. Also it is just impossible to break or shift the walls physically. Now PyraVastu can shift rooms virtually or improve the shape energy!

Personal

Personal Vastu - a total new concept. For whom do we make all these Vastu corrections? For the Man who lives there. So why not make the Man, Vastu ok first. Only PyraVastu opens the new way to luck enhancement, protection for children, attract good fortune and many other methods for health, money and power.

Furniture

Many objects at home or office reflect their own specific properties on us. As we spend 80% of our life-time around these objects they must be in perfect harmony with us. It can be your office table or a bed or computer, Vastu correction is now possible with PyraVastu.

Vehicle

Vehicles and machines have become a part of your life in the new age of electronics and automation. So starting from your car to a machine at your home or factory; all these can be harmonized. PyraVastu works like magic in this active subject.

Wide Application

Vastu with pyramid yantra has a very wide application. This is due to the easy and practical solution it offers to every complex problem we face. You can explore the following with pyramid yantra.

Home & Protection. *Our first aim is to build a house, give shelter and protection to our family. Spiritual protection by PyraVastu for door and evil energy safeguard, page139.*

Kitchen & Health. *This is the heart of a house and it should be perfect according to vastu. If not, pay attention to method on page 141 for a happy and healthy family.*

Bedroom & Relationship. *We spend one-third life in our bedroom, so defects like evil mirror & attached w/c should be corrected. Also learn to energize the bed on page142.*

Office & Business. *Pyramids can be used for more success and business by applying simple PyraVastu remedies to your office or only your working table. More on page 156.*

Factory & Money. *Many difficulties like finance, labor and production can be solved by making your factory vastu okay. How to do that and make more profits on page 152.*

Shop & Sales. *PyraVastu for retail shops is a new way to increases you sales! Learn how to place pyramid yantra and make good sales on page no.156.*

Farm & Irrigation. *The main problem according to vastu is irregular shaped plot in case of farms. Now make your huge plot virtually Vastu ok by PyraVastu. Page 158.*

Personal Fortune. *New techniques to bring more luck and fortune by placing a pyramid yantra in your pocket! Explore more on page 162.*

Vehicle & Safety. *Drive safe with PyraVastu of your vehicle. Spiritually safe guard your self from accidents. And protect yourself from heavy machines in factories, page 161.*

...more. *Many applications for child-creativity, family-health and protection methods. Explore them and be a part of the PyraNet, like 25,00,000 others worldwide..*

Pyramid Yantra

By now you very well know that Pyramid Yantra is not a simple addition of pyramid and yantra. But it is a dynamic, precious, permutation combination instrument for special purpose or for solving a problem.

Prof. Dr. Jiten Bhatt has invented many such Pyramid Yantra for our day to day problems. Each instrument has a different formula, property and its operating laws. Here we will learn some of the basic Pyramid Yantra and simple technique.You are free to contact Dr. Jiten for advance tools and learning.

The figure on your right is of Pyramid Yantra - Multier 9x9. Other page: 143 Vastu Sleep, 151 Multier 9x9 -MAX, 157 PyraVastu Swastik, 164 Health 9x9 and many more.

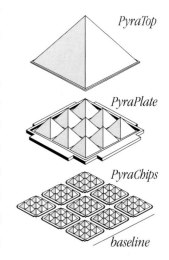

PyraTop

PyraPlate

PyraChips

baseline

Symbolic shapes used for Pyramid Yantra in following pages.

■	Multier pyramid (top view)	L	PyraAngle
⊠	Multier on ceiling (point down)	➡	PyraArrow
▲	Multier side view	⬢	Protect 9x9 - Outside
⚡	Energy 9x9 plate	⬢	Protect 9x9 - Inside
⊞	Bemor pyramid	卐	PyraVastu Swastik
◆	PyraStrip	◄■■■■■■►	Protect Band

Important Abbreviations used in following PyraVastu pages.

🔼 N	Magnetic axis	w/c	Toilet or bathroom
N W E S	North top in all plans	B	Basement
●	PC (PyraCenter)	G	Garage

Let's Start

Pyra Fire - Harmonize your space

Fire purification ceremonies are an integral part of many religions including Hinduism since time immemorial. For such fire harmonization 'Yagnas' were performed in special 'Kundas' (for details see pg. 59). Fire harmonization is a fundamental requirement for Pyravastu.

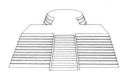

For Fire Harmonization -
◆ Take a square dish or a Pyrafire instrument. Square dish is to be taken because square is the base of everything and it produces stableness.

◆ Take 'Kapur' or Camphor. Place the camphor on your left hand and apply Fa Maa orientation to it (for details see pg.126)

Types of Fire instruments used for different purpose

◆ Another equivalent method is to use pure ghee with cotton wick and give FaMaa to the plate and ghee.

◆ Go to the center of any one room and light the camphor in the square dish or PyraFire instrument.

◆ Wait till the fire extinguishes.

◆ Perform this procedure in the center of every room and then in the center of the house.

◆ Avoid PyraFire in toilets and bathrooms.

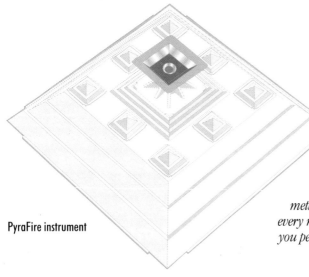

PyraFire instrument

This method of performing pyra Fire is very important as it helps in creating an awareness of harmony in each and every particle in the space where it is performed. This method can be done regularly - every year or every month or every week or even every day. If you perform Pyrafire religiously, major work in PyraVastu gets done.

PyraVastu for **Your Center (Brahmasthala)**

Brahmasthala is an important factor to be considered in PyraVastu, while constructing a house or any other building. The energy lines running through the center are also equally important. In ancient times people knew the importance of Brahmasthala and so, in temples and homes deities and holy tulsi plants etc. were located in the center. Every morning for charging the center, pooja of Tulsi was done. Activation is must. Also in PyraVastu, it is believed that if the Brahamasthala is 'hurt' by fixing of nails, pillars, pegs, heavy objects, etc. then the owner will be in trouble. So, Brahmasthala being one of the very important parts in a building, has to be safe-guarded and activated properly.

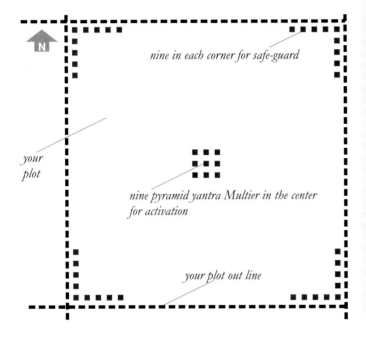

nine in each corner for safe-guard

your plot

nine pyramid yantra Multier in the center for activation

your plot out line

As soon a you purchase a land or a plot for your house it starts vibrating with you. Plot activation is must for fast growth and favorable effects from all directions. This figure shows the simple way to activate your plot.

You just have to place 9 Multier pyramids in the center and/or 9 in each corner.

The power of 9 Multier is ideal for a plot of 2000 sq.ft.

If the plot is bigger, then do the following; add 9 Multier for each 1000 sq.ft.

So if your plot is of 10000 sq.ft you have to place 81 in the center.

Plot Activation by 9 Pyramid Yantra

Install a set of 9 Pyramid Yantra Multier in the center of the plot. Dig a square pit minimum 1 feet deep and about 4 x4 feet.. Keep a distance of 6 inch between each Multier pyramid and they should be parallel to each other as shown in the Figure.

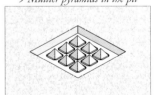
9 Multier pyramids in the pit

Safe-Guard your plot boundary, virtually!

Now you can protect your plot boundary without building a wall around it. This method is known as virtual plot safe-guard. Just place 9 Multier pyramids in each corner as shown in the figure above. You have to dig a pit of 'L' shape about one and half feet deep to place the pyramids into it. This is for square or rectangular plots.

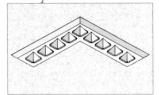
corner protection with 9 Multier

How to find Gravitational center

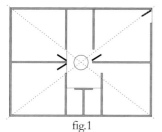

fig.1

To find a gravitational center or Brahmasthala for a square or a rectangular plot of a house is very simple. Draw two straight lines from the corners as shown in figure 1. Where they intersect is the center of the plot.

But if the plot or the plan is of irregular shape like in fig.2, paste it on a cardboard and cut the boundaries. Now make three points at different places like A, B and C. Make a small hole at all the three points. Now pass a thread from point A and hang it in the air as shown in fig.3. Draw a vertical line downwards from the thread starting from point A. Repeat the same with all three points one by one. The interaction of all three lines is your gravitational center.

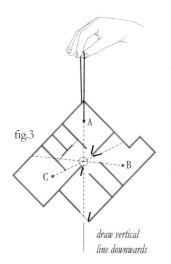

fig.3

draw vertical
line downwards

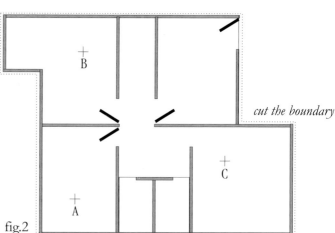

cut the boundary

fig.2

Correcting an irregular shaped plot

An irregular shape plot and land are not good according to PyraVastu. They slow-down progress and invite financial loss.

So it is more important to make an irregular plot to a square or a rectangular shape plot, physically or virtually by Pyramid yantra. Make a virtual rectangle by installing 9 Multier in each corner and activating the center by 9 or more in multiples of 9, i.e. 27, 81, 243, 405 and so on for bigger plots.

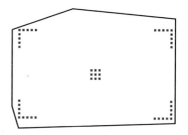

PyraVastu for **No-Center plot**

As seen above that the gravitational center is important. In some plots or buildings the center (Brahmasthala) is not located in the shape but it is outside. In such cases first divide the plot in to 2 or more parts by creating symbolic wall by placing pyramid yantra in line. Then treat each part as a single plot and charge it by 9 Pyramid Yantra Multier in the center.

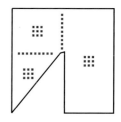

Center activation for Flats

What if you have a flat on the 5th floor and have no personal land? There is a solution for it too. You have to activate the center. Find the center, and fix 9 Multier pyramid on the ceiling. (see fixing method page 169-170.). If your flat or property is under construction you can just place 1 PyraChip under each tile of your whole house and forget the small defects of Vastu!.

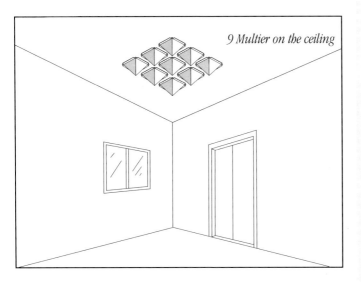

9 Multier on the ceiling

Adding power to Plinth for progress

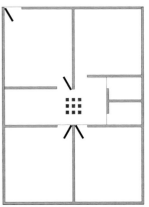

Power to center of each Tile

One of the most powerful yet easy methods is to activate the center of each tile. So place one PyraChip under each tile of your house before fixing it. And make each sq.ft a yantra.

New Wall center method

This is a new advanced concept of charging the 'Volume Center'. You can activate the center by placing Pyramid yantra on the center of any wall or ceiling. In short all 3 axis.

At the plinth level of any house or factory it is very essential to add more power if one needs fast progress. Secondly, in many cases the plinth is irregular in shape. So place 9 Multier in the center and also in the corners if irregular, or cut. If cut, it has to be virtually added and if extended it has to be cut-off by 9 Multier pyramids. All Multier pyramids are to be placed under the ground at about 1 feet and the distance between each should be more than 4 inches and less than 10 inches.

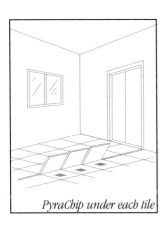

PyraChip under each tile

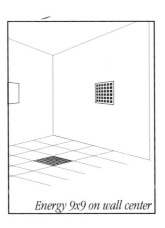

Energy 9x9 on wall center

What will you do when....
Wall, Staircase or a Toilet is in the center ?

According to a survey the following 4 are the most common Vastu defects found in more than 60% of small homes. But now you can easily rectify them with this new Cut-N-Throw method. First find the center and if there is a wall, stair, toilet or a pillar there, then use the following methods and clear the center.

Wall in the center?

This a common case where there is a wall of a room or a heavy object in the center. This has to be shifted. If it's an object you can move it physically but a wall has to be shifted virtually. Place 3 Multier on the wall (see fig.1.). Or you can fix Energy plate in the center and 4 PyraAngle at the corners, as shown in fig.2.

Heavy Pillar in the center?

A pillar in the center is not at all good according to PyraVastu. There are two solutions for this problem. The first is you place 8 Multier surrounding the pillar, in the ground or on the ceiling. But the better alternative is to virtually divide the house into two parts by using PyraStrip on the ceiling. And then activating both the centers separately.

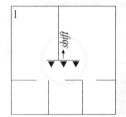

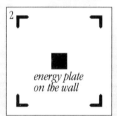

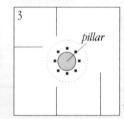

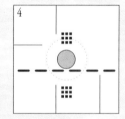

Staircase in the center?

Place eight pyramid Multier around the staircase if it is round as in fig.5. This will choke the effect of the stair on the center. These Multier are either to be installed under the flooring or on the top ceiling.
Secondly, if it is not practical to install pyramid under the floor you can cut virtually by fixing PyraStrips on the ceiling. (More detailed staircase correction on page no.146.)

W/C or Toilet in the center?

This is a very major defect and if possible the toilet should be removed from the center physically.
But in case it is very difficult to remove, it can be treated by placing 3 pyramids on the outer wall of the toilet, pointing the other side you want to shift virtually. As in fig.7 all pyramids are pointed towards north so the w/c will be shifted to south. (Or virtual cutting by PyraStrip fig 8.)

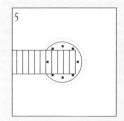

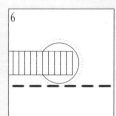

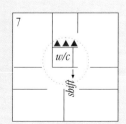

PyraVastu for **Your Main Door & Compound Gate**

Main door or the main compound gate plays a major role in PyraVastu. The perfect location on each side, as given below, should be followed for fruitful results. But if your door or main gate is in the wrong position as in fig. it can be corrected, activated or virtually shifted to appropriate positions by placing Pyramid Yantra.

north

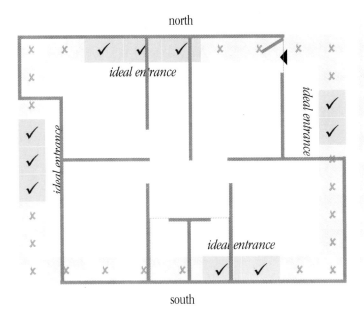

south

◀ This plan has a wrong entrance according to the law of Vastu.

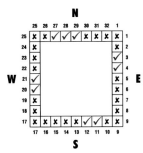

Correct position of door or main gate shown with right ✓ on each side. More details on page 106.

Door activation for good fortune

Activation of main door is a must. In olden days it used to be charged by auspicious symbols of 'Shubh-Labh', horse-shoe or by drawing a rangoli in the entrance.

But in the jet age we have no time and secondly we need faster and more scientific solutions to our problems.

You can activate your door by fixing 3 Pyramid yantra as shown, one on the top and 2 on sides. This is the most ideal position but if you do not have space on the top or on one side you can even fix it on the ceiling or on the side walls.

For more accurate results Bemor 9x9 is recommended. It can be programmed for the wish or personal purpose also. (Bemor has in-built 8-energy lotus plate.).

One other method is to fix one Protect yantra on the top and 2 Bemor by the side for protection from evil energy. (more details on page 194.).

Main door activation by three Bemor 9x9

Bemor 9x9

Main compound gate activation

The main entrance - the compound gate is also important. It should be in the correct direction. If not according to vastu it has to be activated by a set of 9 Multier pyramids. A set of 9 has to be installed near each pillar of the gate. So you need 18 of them. Note: these pyramids should be at a distance of minimum one ft from the gate pillar and inside the compound.
A set of 2 also works as a gate-guard and protects from evil energy.

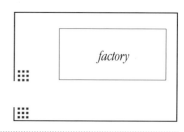

factory

Fortune lines for gate

This is another method by which you can increase your luck and fortune. It can be used to vastu okay the gates also. You have to dig a pit, 1 ft deep and 6x1 ft in length and breadth. Now place 9 Multier pyramids in a line one after the other as shown. This fortune lines are to be made near both pillars of gate. Both above shown method of 9 sets of pyramids and this fortune line can be used together also.

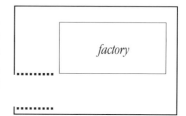

factory

Protection from evil energies

This is another method for the main house door. It is better to protect the door against the evil energies. Earlier it was done with a horse shoe or some yantra. Now it's time for a more scientific approach. Research shows that a Feng Shui mirror with pyramids can protect this very well. So place a Protect 9x9 (pyra Ba Gua see page 194) on top of the door as shown with 2 Bemor pyramids and protect your family.

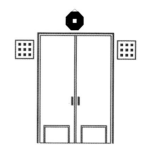

Virtual door closing method

Note: this is an advanced method, to be used by PyraVastu experts. It sometimes happens that a door is in the wrong direction and it is also not possible to close it physically. In this case this virtual door closing method is used. You have to fix 9 Protect Door Band on all three borders of the door and give FaMaa* to close the door. But once you close the door it must open in the right direction.

Door protection

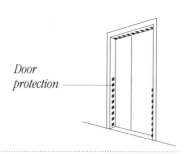

Opening new door!

After closing a door it is very important to open a new virtual door where you think is the perfect position according to PyraVastu. You have to make a virtual door by pyramids on a wall, fix an Energy plate in the center and 3 Bemor pyramids as shown and give FaMaa* to open a new door and bring good, harmonious energy in from that side. You do not have to draw the door on the wall but just imagine it in your mind.

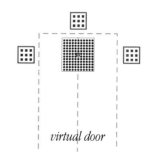

virtual door

* see more on 126 page.

PyraVastu for **Your Kitchen**

Kitchen plays an vital part in family health so it should be in the 'agni' corner of your house or restaurant. 'Agni' corner means the southeast direction.

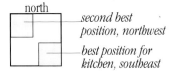
second best position, northwest
best position for kitchen, southeast

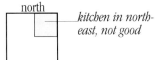
kitchen in northeast, not good

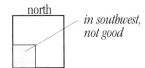
in southwest, not good

W/c in front of kitchen gate

If your kitchen door and w/c are facing each other it brings negative energy into the kitchen and reflects badly on your health. To block this negative flow you have to make a virtual partition by fixing Pyramid Yantra on the ceiling, facing down, between the two doors. You can use PyraStrip for this partition.

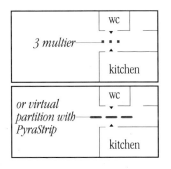

Cooking while faced in south

We become what we eat. So our food processing is a very important part. The person cooking should be in peace and perfect harmony. Always ensure that the person cooking should never face south.And if it is you have to fix a Multier pyramid on the south wall or Energy 9x9 plate.

Kitchen activation for family health

After the center of the whole house the center of each room is important, especially the kitchen. So by fixing 9 Multier pyramids on the ceiling or installing in the ground can give health to the whole family. This is must for restaurants and hotels for their all round progress.

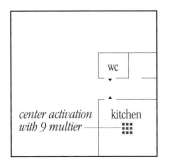

Fire-Water clash!

This is opposite element clash, it brings conflict in the family. Normally fire and water are on one platform or next to kitchen is washing area or a water tank. You can separate it by Pyramid yantra.

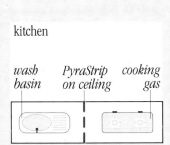
kitchen
wash basin / PyraStrip on ceiling / cooking gas

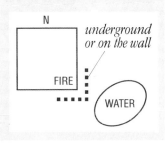
underground or on the wall

PyraVastu for **Your Bedroom**

*Bedroom is the place where you live one-third of your life. So it should be in the proper place
i.e. south-west, if not you must virtually shift it. Bedroom should be also well ventilated and with less
irregular shapes, walls and objects. There should be no clutter in the room.*

What if my bedroom is *not* in south-west?

Bedrooms and especially the master bedroom should be in south-west. But
if as in fig. it is in the north-east corner it has to be 'pushed' by fixing 3 plus
3 Multier on both west and south wall of the existing bedroom and the
place you want to shift.

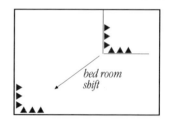

*bed room
shift*

Is a w/c attached with my bedroom advisable?

No, it should be separate. But if attached you have to virtually separate it
from the bedroom by fixing Protect Door-band on the wall of w/c. Never fix
or take pyramids inside a toilet or w/c.

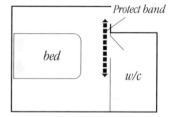

Protect band

bed

w/c

Can my dressing mirror create evil energy!

Yes, if left open. Specially all mirrors in your bedroom, if not treated, can
create health problems and body pain to persons sleeping in front of them.
First thing is place a curtain in front of the mirror or stick 9 Pyramid
Yantra to harmonize it.

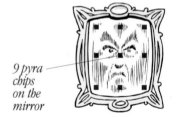

*9 pyra
chips
on the
mirror*

What happens if a door is facing my bed?

It is not advisable to place a bed in front of a door. The continuous flow of
energy from the door affects the health of the person facing it. One solution
is you close the doors while sleeping or protect your bed by 3 Protect
inside.

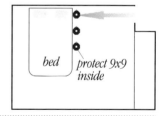

bed

*protect 9x9
inside*

A slant roof & beam on my bed generates stress?

The slope of the roof should be from north (low) to south (high) or from
east to west. If it is opposite or if too low in height it can make the person
more stressed. Fix a set of 3 pyramids on the wall where the roof is low or
under the bed.
If sleeping under a beam you have to fix 3+3 pyramids on the wall, just
below the beam to neutralize the effect.

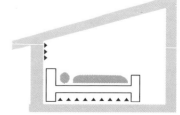

▲ Vastu Sleep

While you are at sleep your conscious mind is at rest. But let your sub- conscious mind help you to manifest peak performance...& new success in health, business and relationship.

◆

Core Theory: As we know the center is the most important in PyraVastu. So we must start with the most personal objects first. What could be more personal than a bed because we spend one-third of our life on it. So energize your bed first and make it a powerful yantra!

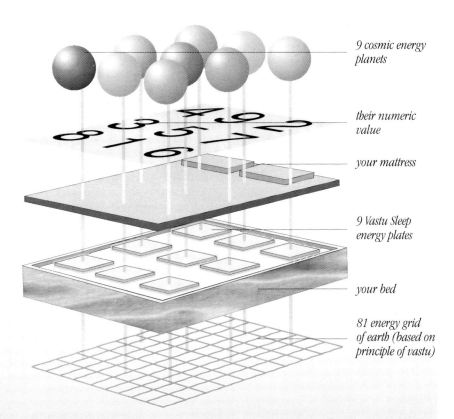

9 cosmic energy planets

their numeric value

your mattress

9 Vastu Sleep energy plates

your bed

81 energy grid of earth (based on principle of vastu)

This works on a 9 planets and the 81 Vastu grid principle. As we have studied, all the interaction is between the cosmic energy and the earth energy. The man is in the middle of this. So when you place 9 pyramids or 9 Vastu Sleep* plates under your mattress it starts working and the flow of energy starts passing through you.

Vastu Sleep* has a set of 9 plates with 81x9=729 pyramids on each plate. Also you can write a wish and place in the center plate's wish chamber.

Now you have to repeat your wish before you go to bed at night and let you sub- conscious mind work for you to get more health, wealth and power!

Vastu Sleep is a product of Personal Care with total of 6561 pyramid yantra for the whole bed.

Balcony and open terrace

The projection of your balcony or an open terrace should always fall in the north and east side, while the most ideal is north-east corner. If the balcony is in west or south side it has to be cut-off by fixing 2 PyraStrips on the inside wall of the projection. To fix Pyramid Yantra you can use a double sided adhesive tape or brass nails (iron nails are not advisable).

⋀
PyraVastu for your
Balcony, Basement, Garage & Toilet

After studying the main vastu correction of bedroom, kitchen and center one often ignores the importance of other rooms like basement, garage, etc. But you will be surprised to know that all these small rooms also affect you when not placed in a proper place according to vastu. Learn the proper positioning of each and then match them with your's. If wrong, correct them immediately.

Basements

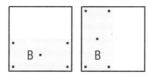

Basement in house, factory or shop should be located in north and east side and not in the south and west. So the ideal place is in the north-east corner of the building. But as shown in the example if the basement is in south or west directions, 'energy up-liftment' method is used. This is done by placing pyramids in the basement at the four corners and in the center.

Garage and servants room

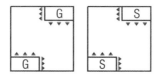

Servants room and garage should not be in north-east or south-west. But if it is already placed there and is impossible to change, you can cut the room by Pyramid Yantra. Just fix them on the outside walls as shown in the figure.

Toilet and w/c

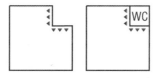

The ideal place for placing your bathroom or toilet is between center part of west or south. You should never face the sun when performing toiletry functions. WC should be never placed in the north-east side. And if it is already constructed in your house use the 'cut-off' method by fixing pyramids outside the toilet walls to remove the negativity.

Advance Learning

This page is for advance methods used by PyraVastu experts to shift rooms, cut-off basements, make a room virtually right angled and for many other solutions. If you do not understand, skip to the next page. Also some advanced instruments are shown in the side row which are intended to be used only under expert advice.

Advanced Tools for PyraVastu

PyraStrip, virtual partition and dividing tool. Must for cut-off method and closing door virtually.

Energize your personal space

You need to protect and energize your personal working space if you are not able to correct the Vastu of the surroundings.Fix 4 PyraAngle on the ceiling to protect your space and make it virtually okay.

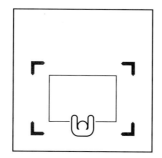

Basement cut-off

We have already seen a method of basement up-liftment. But now this is a new way to cut-off the underground room by PyraStrip. Fix 9 PyraStrips on all four walls, near the ceiling, and make a virtual partition slab.

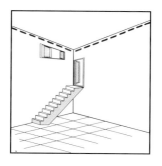

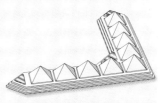

PyraAngle, virtual right angle creation. And arrow for virtual shifting.

90 degree for success

If all four walls of the room are of perfect right angles to each other, the room is 100% perfect according to Vastu. But if not, do not worry, now you can make your rooms 90 degree okay by fixing 4 PyraAngle on the ceiling near the corner. Note: Pyramids must face downwards.

4 PyraAngle on the ceiling

PYRON, a pyra-energy-on, 2in1tool for different purposes. Many types of Pyron are created for health, money, harmony, etc. (more on pg.201.)

Staircase Tips

It must be in clock-wise direction.

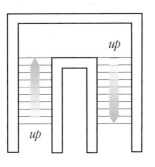

The first rule is all the staircase should go up in a clockwise direction. If it is a round staircase it is simple but when it is straight you have to follow the 'right-hand' rule. So when you climb the turn to go up should be on right side. But if it is opposite it is a defect according to Vastu and needs to be rectified.

Correct the defect by fixing one PyraStrip on each stair. This will generate a positive energy for each stair.

East to west and north to south.

'Not-to-be missed' tip is to check your staircase direction. It should start from either east of north and go up in the west or south. This will bring the harmonized energy of east and north to the upper floor. But if it is the opposite you may end up in a serious trouble. The best is change the staircase side physically. But if not possible correct it by Pyramid Yantra. Fix 3 Staircase 9x9 on the first three steps as shown, and protect the whole stair.

Staircase 9x9

staircase should be in south or west

It should never be in north-east direction.

The load of the staircase should never be in the northeast side of your house, factory or and building. As northeast is a corner for activity and higher energy the load of the staircase can choke the good energy flow. To correct it spiritually you need to place 3 Multier on the side or install a set of 9 under the staircase if possible. This will energize the object. The ideal place is south or west part of your property.

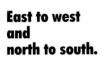

Risers in staircase must be in odd numbers.

Now stop reading and go near your stairs and count the number of risers! If it is odd in number i.e. 3,5,7,9,11 you are lucky. But if it comes to even numbers like 4,6,8 etc then you need to correct. Do not worry, it is simple to correct. Just cut one stair by fixing a PyraStrip on the side of either the first stair or the last. By this 'cut-off' method you will make the number odd. The whole staircase can be cut-off if in the wrong position.

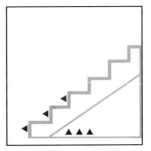

New Pynergy flow method

This is a new and more practical method of Vastu correction by the energy flow. Instead of finding small defects of Vastu and correcting them, just energize your house or workplace with proper Pynergy flow and feel the miraculous results!

Pynergy flow in a room

This a new method by which you can circulate the flow of energy from the main entrance to the whole room. Place a Pyramid yantra Energy 9x9 plate in front of the main door and a second at the same height from the ground as shown. This will bring the Pynergy to the end corner also.

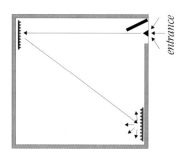

Energizing the whole house with Pynergy

As seen in the figure below, now you can even energize the whole house.

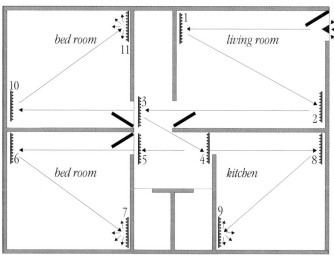

This is an ideal plan, in your house position may differ.
Do not take energy in toilets.

Start from the main entrance, place a Pyramid Energy 9x9 plate in front of the door (above 6 feet from the floor is ideal) Now bring the energy to the center by placing plates 2 & 3. Similarly you can even take the Pynergy to all rooms as shown by placing plates, 4 to 11.

Similarly you can energize your office, factory, shop or it can be used for hospital and huge complexes also.

If the area of the room/hall is bigger than 500 sq.ft you need more than 3 in each room.(i.e. in multiples of 3,6,9 and so on.)

Individual room energizing

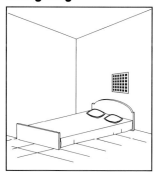

Pynergy flow method is very effective for energizing all hotel rooms, hospital rooms or each cabin of big offices.
Also for huge complexes and office receptions. This is good for shops (more on pg.156).

PyraVastu for **Irregular shaped plots**

Plot is the first thing which starts vibrating with you so it is more important to understand it thoroughly. Here are some examples where plots and building are of more irregular shape.

square   round   rectangular   triangle

PyraVastu for **Irregular corner plot**

To remove the defect of irregular shape 'strong center method' is used.
Method 1. Multiply horizontally, instead of 9 pyramids increase to 27 or 81.OR **Method 2.** If the space is less multiply vertically. Place the first layer, cover it with mud in such a way that only the tips of all 9 Multier pyramids are visible. Now place the second layer of 9 on it and so on.

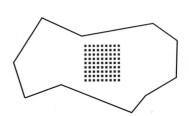

PyraVastu for **Diagonal plots**

Plots located diagonally to the magnetic axis need a 'virtual rotation'. Install an arrow of 9 Pyramid Yantra in the direction you need to rotate. For better result make 4 arrows in same direction and also activate the center. The fig. shows clockwise rotation,but you can even rotate it anti-clockwise by reversing the direction. Virtual rotation is also possible with existing building on it.

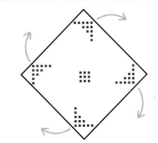

PyraVastu for **90 degree correction**

According to Vastu a 90 degrees angle of each plot corner is a must, but if it is more or less as shown, it is not good. To correct this make a energy angle of 90 degrees with Pyramid Yantra and install in the ground. You can take 9 or 27 Multier pyramids depending on the size and defect. This 'virtual right angle ' is applicable to rooms and objects with sharp corners.

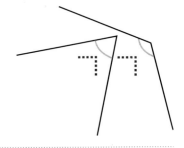

PyraVastu for **Extended plots**

A plot with extended south-west is not good. It brings ill health, mental unhappiness, accidental injury and reduces prosperity. To overcome this, make a boundary of Pyramid Yantra Multier inside the ground so that the plot becomes equal. Maximum distance between each pyramid should be 3 ft. and to boost more power it could be minimized to 1 ft.

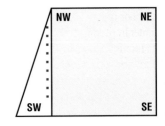

PyraVastu for **Squeezed plots**

If your plot is between two big plots its a squeezed plot and is not good, for it brings poverty. Such plots need to be released of energy to reduce the choke. Two boundaries on both sides of the adjoining big plots are to be energized. In such cases the boundary should be strong with more number of Multier pyramids in multiples of 9.

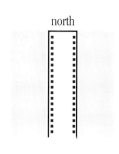

PyraVastu for **Slope correction**

Slope is an important aspect of the plot. To get natural beneficial energy south and west should be high. If it is opposite, as shown in fig. correction is a must. Install 9 Multier Pyramid Yantra in 'L' shape in low side to protect and 9 in square in high side to harmonize.

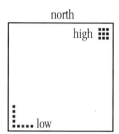

PyraVastu for **Corner cuts**

Corner cut plots and rooms are not good according to vastu. Specially the north-east corner should never be cut. But if you are not able to change them just do the correction by PyraVastu. If it is a plot make a boundary with pyramids at the corner. In rooms, fix them on the corner walls.

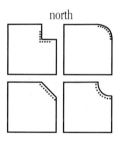

PyraVastu for **South-west reduction**

Install Pyramid Yantra inside the plot to make the shape equal. Because a plot with reduction at south-west leads to mental restlessness, financial loss, ill health and loss of position or reputation. The boundary should be in multiples of 9 (i.e. 9,18,27...).

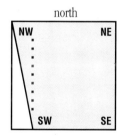

PyraVastu for **Irregular shape building**

In many buildings Vastu defects of shapes, cut corners, extension and many other irregularities are found. To correct them, a geometrically perfect shape like square or a rectangular is to be made by installing Pyramid Yantra in your ground.

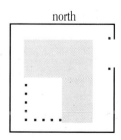

How to add more power!

You can increase the power depending on the intensity or the strength of correction you need. The following are a few methods for adding more pyramid yantra if the plot is too big or to get more benefits.

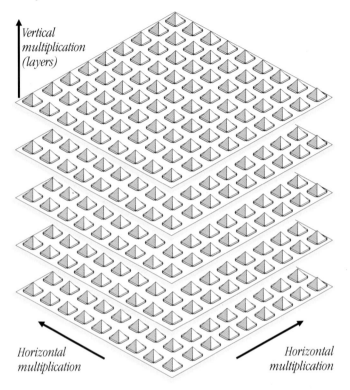

Vertical multiplication (layers)

Horizontal multiplication

Horizontal multiplication

Add layers for more benefit

This is for center activation of a very big plot or if the defect is more. You have to place 81 Multier pyramids in one layer and place such layer one under the other. You can extend upto 9 such layers. The figure shows 5 layers each of 81, so total 405 Multiers. The pit has to be 9 feet deep and 6 inch of gap between each layer.

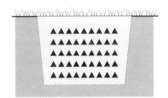

Eight directional benefit yantra

Other method is to install 9 Multier pyramids in all eight directions and one set in the center. This set of 81 is called Vastu kit. (Vastu kit is a product & TM of Personal Care Systems, Baroda).

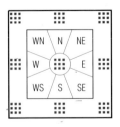

Double up your protection power

You can double your protection by installing 2 parallel lines of Multier pyramids. One inside and other outside your plot or both inside your plot. You can even increase 'L' lines to 3 on each side.

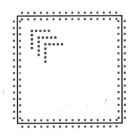

More fortune lines for progress

Instead of single fortune line you can add one or two more for fast progress. But all depends upon the size of the plot and intensity of your problem.

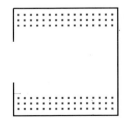

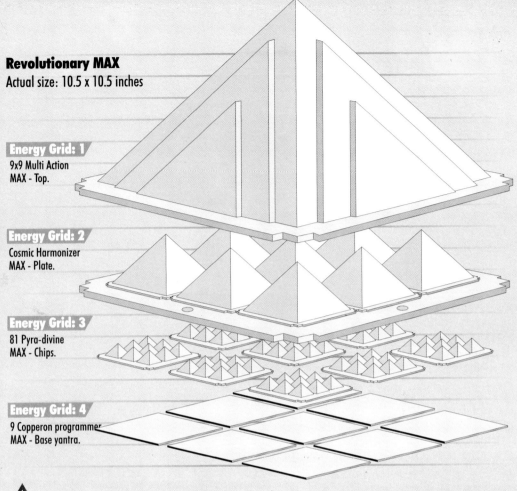

Revolutionary MAX
Actual size: 10.5 x 10.5 inches

Energy Grid: 1
9x9 Multi Action
MAX - Top.

Energy Grid: 2
Cosmic Harmonizer
MAX - Plate.

Energy Grid: 3
81 Pyra-divine
MAX - Chips.

Energy Grid: 4
9 Copperon programmer
MAX - Base yantra.

Result Maximization method

This totally new Multier Max is precisely developed to maximize your PyraVastu results. Powerful action is due to the synchronization of dynamic advanced techniques and finer harmonic setting of each layer, Multier Max creates a unique potential for PyraVastu correction. Better results in PyraVastu obtained by it are not only due to its accurate dimensions but also due to the superfine tuning between each vibratory frequency of all its components.

This has become possible only because of intense research by an experienced Bio scientist, PyraVastu inventor and world-renowned master, Prof. Dr. Jiten Bhatt. He always thinks that instrument must be simple, practical and result oriented. He takes utmost care in developing Pyramid Yantra so that we can save time, effort and money spent to get desired results.

Installing Max saves five times the space usually required by multier original. For placing 81 units of multier original, you require 9'x9' which comes to 81 sq feet area. But with the new Multier Max for the same results you only require nine Multier Max which makes 4'x4' i.e. 16 sq feet. One another advantage of this Multier Max is that, unlike the six-inch space to be left between the two original multiers, only three-inch space is to left between the two Multier Max. Just one Multier Max is to be used in place of nine original multiers yet the results obtained would be far much better than the previous one. This tool is exceedingly effective for huge projects like farms, factories, society, hospitals and big complexes.

16 Tactics for your Factory

This is a complete start-up plan for your factory but on a spiritual level. These 16 valuable tactics can change your business destiny and this step-by-step learning can create wonders. The following are the stages a new person may face when starting a factory, but if you are already a factory owner you need to skip a few of the early stages.

tactic
tactic
tactic
tactic
tactic

To get the right project

This the first step to start a factory or a business - putting the project on paper. This file is the most important asset for you and at this stage when you have no plot or building. Start activating your project file to get a winning start.

Action

Place a PyraChip on each project file you need to submit. You can either stick it on the top, as shown or inside. This will boost your dream project to reality.

Getting finance & bank loans

Finance is the biggest problem. To get finance at a proper rate and time is also important. You can lubricate the flow of finance by spiritual powers!

Action

Fix or place a Pyramid Yantra on the top-left corner of your bag or working table.(See also 156.)

Speedy start with plot activation

Plot for the factory is the starting point. Activate it and get a quick start!

Action

You have to find the center of the plot. Place 9 Multier if the plot is small and 81 if the plot is big. If the plot is too big or of an irregular shape you may need more pyramids in multiples of 81. Plot activation can be applicable even if your factory is already built. You just have to find the center of the plot or the building. And charge it with Multier pyramids.

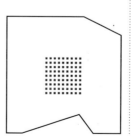

Protect plot from environmental competition

What is environmental competition? This is the stress developed on a spiritual level, because as you buy a plot or a building it starts interacting with you, the factories around and other environmental forces.

Action

A virtual protecting wall is must. Install Multier inside the boundary as shown. One feet inside the ground and at a 3 ft. distance between each other.

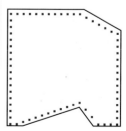

Check levels for fast progress

It is found in some industrial plots that some parts are lower or higher than the normal level. It is not advisable and can be a vastu obstacle, which can delay your progress. So make a perfect level if possible physically, but if not, use following.

Action

Charge the center of the low part only by installing 9 Multier pyramids and a 'L' shaped 9 Multier as shown. This method can be used both for lower and higher levels.

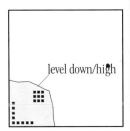

level down/high

Money matters & plot extension

Your plot should never be extended or reduced from south-west. This brings mental restlessness, accidental injury, financial problems and loss of position or reputation.

Action

Install 9 pyramids in a line 3 feet from each other and 1 ft. inside the ground. It should be in a straight line and if the plot is big in size you can place them in multiples of 9 i.e. 18, 27, 36 and so on.

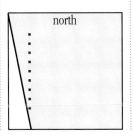

north

Your building activation

As you start constructing your building you need to activate your plinth, the center and all other Vastu defects if you have already built your building.

Action

Building activation is as simple as of the plot. You have to find a gravitational center of your building and charge with minimum 9 Multier pyramids. You can even correct other Vastu defects if they exist.

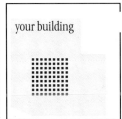

your building

Powerful - entrance

Entrance is the most important element in Vastu and Feng Shui. As all energy flows in from the entrance, you must pay proper attention on it and place it in a perfect direction if you are constructing a building. But what if you have already built a building with a wrong entrance gate?

Action

The main compound gate can be charged by placing two sets of 9 Multier pyramids near the pillar of the gate. To charge the door fix 3 Bemor pyramids on the top of the door. But if the door or the gate is big you need more than 18 pyramids. (More entrance understanding on page 139.)

entrance

Machine - Labour harmony

The most common problem in a factory is the machine and labour. You can harmonize them as follows.

Action

To get optimum result from a machine you must install pyramids under it before installation or on the main controls after installing.
For the safety of the person and to make them work in harmony, place a personal PyraCard in the pocket of each worker!

Protection from adjoining factories

You have to protect your factory from the adjoining factories. One is to do this physically by a wall and other is virtually by a PyraWall.

Action

Install a border in your plot to the side adjoining the factory or a place with more disturbance. This will block and protect your plot from negative energy.

Electricity never in northeast

Take care that all electric transformers and junctions are not placed in the north east corner of your plot. But if these are already placed, try the following.

Action

Block the energy with 8 Multier around the transformer or by a line under the ground. If the capacity of the transformer is big, use more pyramids. (See page 150.)

Charge your manager`s cabin

You can bring more harmonized energy in the managers' cabin so that they can take right decisions.

Action

All energy comes from the entrance. You have to flow the energy to the cabins you want by Pynergy method.
(see page. 147.)

PyraCard in the pocket

your factory

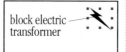
block electric transformer

virtual protection

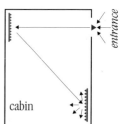
entrance
cabin

Production and products

Production and products are the heart of each and every factory. It is most important to get a perfect and saleable production. You can energize them with pyramids too!

Action

Install pyramids on your production track or the place where the production is made. Command accordingly.

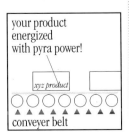

your product
energized
with pyra power!

xyz product

conveyer belt

Sell off your ready stock

After all this you must sell the goods at a good price. As per vastu your ready stock should be in the north-west part of your factory. So, if you are planning a factory take care that your store for ready stock comes in the north-west or go virtual!

Action

If your stock is in the wrong part shift it by placing Multier pyramids either on the walls or inside the ground.

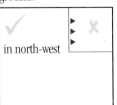

in north-west

Harmony with partners

If you have partnership in your company, you must see that all partners act in a perfect harmony with each other.

Action

Use a PyraChip in the pocket or the bag and charge it for the purpose of perfect harmony. You can also use a harmony yantra technique shown on page 212. Or to be more specific use a Harmony 9x9 with a photo of both persons in it.

Harmony 9x9
for perfect harmony

Restart your sick unit

PyraVastu offers miraculous results in restarting a sick unit. Because it adds more power to the plot of the building itself.

Action

The one most powerful method is to energize the plot with the eight directional benefit pyramid yantra. you can also activate the building by center activation method by 9 or 81 Multier pyramids.

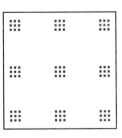

PyraVastu for **Retail Shop & Office**

The first important factor for a retail shop or office is its entrance and the second is the main cash box and then the shop. So these things should be perfect. But if not, make it ok by Pynergy.

Bring Good Luck from door

Fix 2 Bemor pyramids and a Protect 9x9 on the main door or shutter of your shop for good luck and protection.

Lion and Cow shape benefit

Lion shape plot is broader from front and narrower at back. The Cow shape plot is vice-versa. Lion shape is good for shops & Cow shape for home. So, make them accordingly.

make your shop Lion shape

Energy support behind you

For maximum support first sit in such a position that a wall is at the back of your chair and to add power fix one or three Swastik Gold plates at the back.

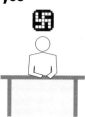

Pynergy in Cash-box

For maximum cash flow, place a Multier pyramid in your cash-box itself and let the Pynergy work for you!

Increase your money flow!

Your desk should be of a perfect rectangular shape without any cut or sharp corners. If it is so you need to place a Pyramid Yantra on the far left corner of your table, from whereever you are sitting. This is the corner of money and will increase your money flow. But if that corner is cut on your desk or is loaded with papers and files, it will bring financial losses. So first of all clear the corner and charge it with Pyramid.

As shown in the figure the 4 number is for finance. Other numbers are also related to a specific purposes. Similarly you can place a pyramid and charge your personal desk.

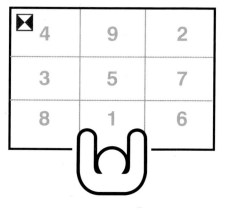

4	9	2
3	5	7
8	1	6

1-Career, 2-Relationship, 3-Wisdom, 4-Wealth, 5-Health, 6-Helpful people, 7-New projects, 8-Knowledge, 9-Fame. (More details on page 188.)

PyraVastu **Swastika**

This is an extraordinary combination concept of PyraVastu. Swastika is an auspicious symbol beneficial for home, office, ashrams, spiritual centers and work places. The effects of Swastika are well known, in addition to regular uses, the new PyraVastu Swastik has many more applications.

The power of Cross

A Swastika is based on two energy lines: one vertical and another horizontal making a cross, which is an universal symbol in many religions, in one or the other form. When we extend the energy of the cross in clockwise direction we get a Fa Swastika, which has small projecting lines in the clockwise direction. Likewise, if we extend the energy in anti clockwise direction we get a Maa Swastika, which has small projections in the anti clockwise direction.

The Fa Swastika is symbolic of the Sun and the Maa Swastika is symbolic of the Moon. One represents the starting point whereas the other represents the end point. Both are very powerful and potent in their respective areas of application. In this book we would limit ourselves to the Fa Swastika only, as for understanding Maa Swastika we need to have an advanced training.

A Swastika when formulated divides the space into four sectors. Each of the sectors has one PyraCenter (PC) and the center of the cross being the central PC. So each Swastika has five PCs. A very important aspect of this new Pyra Swastik is its ability to be programmed according to your requirements. This aspect makes it more personalized than any other swastika we use.

Clockwise and Anti-clockwise force

Benefits of Swastika are;
- Brings all-round prosperity and wellness.
- Creates purifying, divine and positive energy at the entrance, rooms, wall or objects.
- Unfolds worldly pleasures as well as spiritual upliftment.

You can program it for a variety of personal purposes like health, protection, relationship, success, career, business, education, fortune, peace and many others. It can be fixed on wall, ceiling or floor and can also be placed under the ground below our flooring. This is a very powerful positive energy tool used in Vastu correction.

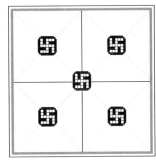

Five ideal positions on wall for Swastika in PyraVastu.

PyraVastu for
Farm and Irrigation

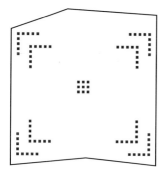

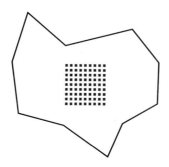

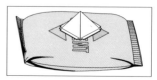
water flow

Protection is important

The first requirement for a farmer is to grow a good crop and to protect the farm. Protection becomes difficult because of the huge size of the farm. Now you can protect your farm with installing pyramids at the boundary of your farm at equal distance and in multiples of 9. For proper growth, charge the center.

Irregular shape is the main problem

The major Vastu defect seen in farms is that the shape is very irregular. This is one of the spiritual reasons for less progress and growth.
Install 81 or more pyramids in the center or divide the plot into proper parts. Note: In farms pyramids are to be installed about 3 feet deep.

Charging Water & Seeds

The best and most practical use of Pyramid yantra is to charge water, seeds and fertilizer for the crops. Just pass the water pipe upon 9 pyramids or make a special canal for the same. Seeds and fertilizer can be stored in a room powered with pyramid yantra or can be placed under Multier for 24 hours.

Activate your prime plants

Make your prime plants or crops a 'yantra'. Activate them by installing 8 Multier pyramids around them as shown and see the results. You can even protect the prime crop area by a line of pyramids around them.

More power farm

To make your farm a very powerful yantra, you can place more layers of pyramids as shown in the figure. But this is used for very big sized farms or farms with very irregular shaped boundary. 3 to 9 layers of 81 Multier each, which can provide a total power of 729 pyramids!

Advance Pynergy experiments

This is an advanced experiment, still in the research stage. Install pyramids inside the plants itself. You can install 9 PyraChips in the stem of a tree by cutting the bark. Then close it and let the Pynergy stay inside for ever!

around trees

around prime crops

your farm

5 layers of 81 each

inside trees

PyraVastu for **Societies & Townships**

New holistic solutions are offered to make a society or a big township Vastu okay, without changing the real plan. Try out these practical solutions to your complex problems.

Power entrance

Charge the entrance and the main road by a line of pyramids. This will let you start the project faster.

Holistic activation

Activate the whole area of 8 or 10 buildings at a time with pyramids in the center and at the boundary.

PyraVastu society

Add a selling feature to your project, that it is PyraVastu 'ok'. Because of very large sized plots in societies it is difficult to build each and every house correct according to the laws of Vastu. So make your society or township virtually okay by installing 81 or more Multier pyramid layers in the center and at the main entrance.(see page 150.)

Duplex trouble

In mirror-duplex houses if one is okay according to Vastu then the other is 100% wrong. This duplex trouble can be corrected by PyraVastu.

Shops facing south

In some townships there are all shops facing south. These have to be protected by Protect 9x9 or a common virtual wall in the front.

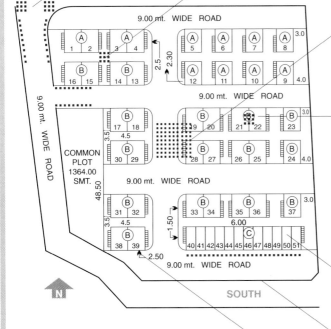

FAST TRACK

Forget all above mentioned techniques, just add power to each tile. This is most ideal for apartments and huge complexes.

Each door activation

Place 3 Bemor pyramids on each door to bring good luck and protection. Add a selling point of PyraVastu.

Outer boundary protection

This is the first and most easy step to start and complete the project. Install Multier inside the boundary.

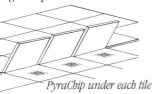
PyraChip under each tile

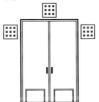

society plot

Protection Method 1: **For Main door**

Main door protection and activation is a must. A minimum of 2 Bemor pyramids and Protect outside in the center has to be fixed. And one Protect inside the house above the door. This will harmonize the flow of energy in the house or your office and bring good luck.

The same protection method can be used for shops and factories.

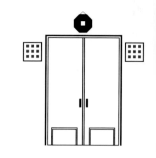

Protection Method 2: **For Object in the entrance**

There should be nothing in front of the main entrance or main gate. It could be an electric or telephone pole or a tree or some pillar or rock which blocks the gate of your shop or house. This is very bad. A stream of filthy water in front of your factory is a clear loss of wealth. To protect this an 'energy wall' is a must inside your gate. (see fig.)

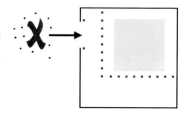

Protection Method 3: **For Roads**

The plot should not be at Y or T junctions i.e. it should not face a road or be on the junction of two roads. In such plots, the bad energy of the road is to be protected by two walls of Pyramid Yantra, one inside the plot and the other outside.

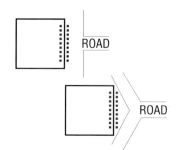

Protection Method 4: **From Religious places**

Do I need to protect my plot from religious places too? Yes, because harmony is a must. Too much positive energy is also not good. Install a border in your plot to the side adjoining or facing a temple or church. The border should be in your plot inside the ground.

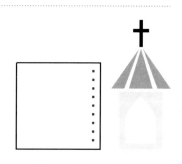

Protection Method 5: **For Object in the compound**

Many objects in our compound produce inharmonious energy if not in proper positions. As in fig.A a tree is in the north-east corner, it should be in south-west. Similarly in fig.B a water tank should not be in south-east. To correct this a 'trapping method' is used by placing Multier pyramids around the object underground.

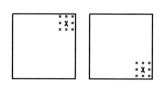

Protection Method 6: **From High-rise**

The plot should not be in neighbourhood of any high-rise buildings, hospitals, marriage halls, courts, burial or a cremation ground. In all such cases your plot needs protection as mentioned above. Number of pyramids depends on the plot length and intensity of disturbance. To boost more power, distance between each pyramid should be 1 ft.

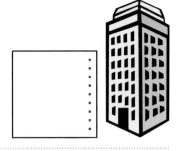

Protection Method 7: **For Corner clash**

If corners of two building or sharp edges of object face each other it is inharmonious for both individuals. Also it increases the stress and spoils the relationship. A 'L' shaped border of Multier pyramid is to be installed for protection.

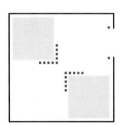

Protection Method 8: **For Locker and Safe case**

You can always place a Pyramid Yantra in your business bag or purse for super success, also in cash box and important drawers to improve the flow of money. It can also protect your locker at home and in the bank.

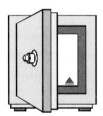

Protection Method 9: **For Vehicles**

Amazing, Vastu for vehicles!
It is very essential to make the vehicle in harmony with you by fixing Pyramid Yantra on your car and scooters for protection, safety and efficiency. You can also save petrol by fixing on engine, carburetors and petrol tank. This is also recommended for highway truck owners as an anti-accident device.

Also a new Pyramid Yantra is developed by Prof. Dr. Jiten Bhatt for car protection. It can be used for all four wheelers. It has to be fixed on the dash board of your car.

In case of two wheelers small size pyramid can be fixed on the handle or the front number plate.

Protect 9x9 Car

⋀ Enhance your Fortune

Life is a perfect synergy of effort and fortune. Both have an equal yet complementing ability to transcend us beyond the ordinary in this journey through life. If your efforts are supported by fortune , you live better and accomplish more. Life is about balance in both and bringing that awareness in our life . Understanding this interactive balance is the essence of life.

Creating fortune is not just redirecting our efforts but rearranging both our present effort and fortune to restore the natural flow of life which is brimming with prosperity.

Effort & Fortune are the two wheels in our journey of life.

Magic of nine!

4	9	2
Wealth Money Fortune	Fame Prosperity Illumination	Spouse Relations Partnership
3	5	7
Wisdom Family Health	Health Balance Stability	Creativity Children Projects
8	1	6
Knowledge Intuition Motivation	Career Success Business	Friends Travel New Beginnings

Universal Harmony

As per the ancient Egyptian scriptures there are three worlds. They are- Ta, Dwat and Nut. The soul travels from Ta (Earth) to Dwat (Man) and finally reaches Nut (Heaven) , the spiritual realm.

Today our whole attention is on improving effort but we are missing finer and more important part i.e. fortune. Firstly we should find the missing components from our luck. Secondly we should find some way to improve them. There are numerous complicated methods to do so. Here we will learn a simple formula to enhance our fortune.

In this new simple formula developed by Prof. Dr. Jiten Bhatt we find the missing components using our birth date. Once we know which number's vibratory force is missing, we improve it using our powerful FaMaa symbol. A special pyramid yantra developed for this purpose is called "Pyra card". For checking your fortune and the missing components see next page.

Heaven
Man
Earth

Man is an integral part of Heaven and Earth

⚠ Fortune PyraCard

Thousands of people have changed their luck with Fortune Card. Why not you? It is so easy, you just have to follow these steps-

Find your missing force of destiny

◆ Write your birth date on a piece of paper.
eg. 25 - 06 - 1983

◆ Take the first number (say date i.e. 25) and add both the digits to get a single digit.
eg. $25 = 2 + 5 = 7$

◆ Do the same for the second and third number (Month & Year) eg. $06 = 0 + 6 = 6$
$1983 = 1 + 9 + 8 + 3 = 21 = 2 + 1 = 3$

◆ Now add the single digits of your date, month and year. eg.
$7 + 6 + 3 = 16 = 1 + 6 = 7$

◆ Write all the numbers seen in your date and only single digit numbers obtained by addition. eg. Here the given date is 25 - 06 - 1983.
So one digit numbers in birth date are - 2,5,6,1,9,8,3
Numbers obtained by addition are - 7,6,3.
Number obtained by addition of date, month and year is 7.

◆ Now check the missing number from the mystic Pyramid Fortune-Numbers (fig 1) eg. Here 4 is missing.

◆ Make FaMaa yantra (fig.2) with faith & confidence on the square on your base of fortune card corresponding to the missing number. See fig 3.

◆ In your case if more than one number is missing make FaMaa yantra in all those missing squares

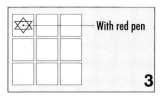

PyraNumbers for reference

1

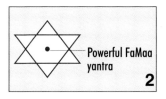

Powerful FaMaa yantra

2

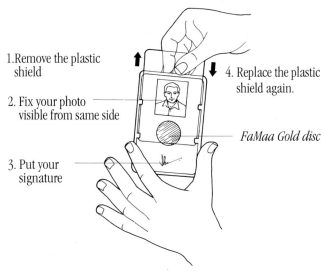

With red pen

3

What is PyraCard?

PyraCard is a revolutionary Pyramid Yantra conceptualized and originated by world renowned PyraVastu master Prof. Dr. Jiten Bhatt. It is based on oriental wisdom and modern research.

PyraCard empowers you to achieve both spiritual and materialistic wealth. It is enriched with a magical square, pyramid grid, 9 copper pyramids, beneficial cosmic colors, a gold disc and a FaMaa activator.

1. Remove the plastic shield

2. Fix your photo visible from same side

3. Put your signature

4. Replace the plastic shield again.

FaMaa Gold disc

PyraColors for Family Health

There are several ways of healing with colors, the usual ones being; Colored clothes, Colored silks, Solarised water, Food, Color Breathing, Color visualizing and colored lights. Here is an absolutely unique method - FaMaa color therapy. This new system of PyraColors are developed from integral effect of color, Pyramid Yantra, visualization and deep rhythmic breathing for health and wellness.

COLORS: The mere thought of them brings to our minds something more than what we just see; it is something we feel about each of them. Colors play an important role in our lives. Sunshine brings us joy and liveliness and every season has its own color.

Since time immemorial our ancestors have been worshipping the Sun from whose brilliance of pure light emerges all the different colors. We know that without light there is almost no existence of life and colors emerge from that very source of life. So, each color has its own individual impact on our mental, emotional or physical existence.

FaMaa Color therapy

red
blue / violet
yellow / orange
green

Colors have an innate ability to bring harmony and balance within our psyche and physique, when used accurately. Everything has a frequency of vibration with which it makes itself perceptible. Even our organs work in a certain vibration frequency, but in state of good health we usually never perceive them. In state of ill health or malfunctioning of any organ we start feeling the presence of that organ.

Colors have a very fine-tuning with the vibration frequency of our organs. They are absorbed through the subtle fields of energy around the human body known as "Aura". They are also absorbed through eyes and skin, as well as our seven energy centers known as "Chakras". Choosing a color that vibrates at a frequency needed to restore cells to balance is believed to initiate the process of healing. Colors revitalize and rebuild every organ of the body. They align mind, body and emotions and promote us towards spiritual development.

Let us see some common uses of these PyraColors-

1. RED: Use for- Anemia, Listlessness, Asthma, Paralysis, Blood dyscrasias, Physical debilitation, Bronchitis, Pneumonia, Constipation, Tuberculosis, increases circulation and stimulates nervous system. Do not use for- Emotional disturbances, Hypertension, Mental illness, Fever, Neuritis, Inflammation and any other cases where recession is required.

2. ORANGE: Use for- Asthma, Bronchitis, Respiratory diseases as a stimulant, Stimulates Thyroid, Depresses Parathyroid, Helps bone building, Cold, Mental exhaustion, Epilepsy, Prolapsed uterus, Gall stones. Do not use for-, Hyperthyroidism.

3. YELLOW: Use for- Arthritis, Rheumatism, Eczema, Flatulence, Indigestion, Diabetes, Physical exhaustion, Liver diseases, Depression, Paralysis, Paraplegia, Stimulates both motor and sensor nervous systems, Stimulates lymphatic system. Do not use for- Acute inflammation, Heart palpitation, Delirium, Neuralgia, Diarrhea, Over excitement, Fever.

4. GREEN: Use for- Laryngitis, Malaria, Acts as germicide or disinfectant in any infections, Back problems, Colic, Malignancy, Erysipelas, Neuralgia, Hay fever, Over stimulation, Heart problems, Syphilis, Hemorrhoids, Typhoid, Insomnia, Ulcers, Irritability, Venereal diseases, Helps create equilibrium. Do not use for- (Not known)

5. BLUE: Use for- Fever, Acts on skin as a stimulant in cases of burns, acne, ulcers, skin diseases, injury or abrasion, Diarrhea, Dysentery, Epilepsy, Inflammations, Goiter,

Headache, Hydrophobia, Hysteria, Insomnia, Menstrual difficulties, Acute rheumatism, Shock, Venereal diseases, Tonsillitis, Tooth infection, Whooping cough. Do not use- Cold, Gout, Hypotension, Muscle impairment, Paralysis, Chronic rheumatism, Bradycardia, any case where regression is not required.

6. VIOLET: Use for- Bladder problems, Bone growth and dysfunction, Cerebral meningitis, Concussion, Abdominal cramps, Mental illness, Nervous disorders, Neuralgias, Acute and chronic rheumatism, Scalp diseases, Sciatica, Skin diseases, Tumors, both benign and malignant. Do not use for- (Not known).

According to Prof. Dr. Bhatt, 3 Fa colors are Red, Orange and Yellow and Maa colors are Green, Blue and Violet. He has developed 6 Health Pyra color plates and a supporting plate with white color. This is Health 9x9 and it is used as a pair for health and healing.

Normally you use single white plate. But appropriate color plate at the required location and one white plate in the opposite side can give better results.

Health 9x9 for color healing,

	ACTION	INDICATIONS	ORGANS	QUALITIES
RED	Hot color, color with the greatest penetration, strongly stimulates the flow of blood.	Poor circulation, inflammation, chronic cough, asthma, anemia, eczema.	Heart, Lungs and Muscles	Love, anger, wrath, joy.
GREEN	Neutral color, treats chronic problems, sedative, soothing, relaxing.	Whooping cough, inflammation of the joints, tumors, ulcer, eye diseases, diabetes.	Lungs.	Contentment.
BLUE	Cold color, has a relaxing effect, valuable in treatment of all diseases involving heat.	Pain, congestion, hemorrhoids, warts, sleeplessness, frigidity, menopausal difficulties.	Pituitary gland, endocrine system, contraction of muscles and tissues.	Quietness, reserve.
ORANGE	Gives energy, makes joyful, color of the sun.	Pessimism, psychosis, depression, fear, arteriosclerosis, emaciation, tiredness.	Heart.	Joy, happiness.
YELLOW	Fortifies the endocrine system, makes chronic processes acute.	Diseases of digestive tract, strengthens the nervous system.	Liver, bladder, kidneys, stomach.	Intelligence, comprehension, cheerfulness.
VIOLET	Acts on consciousness, promotes awareness, prepares for meditation.	Lymphatic system disorders.	Spleen.	Meditation.

Frequently Asked Questions

Questions you have - answers you need. Following are the most frequently asked questions about PyraVastu and Pyramid Yantra. As usual, Prof. Dr. Jiten Bhatt has the most simple yet logical answers to them!

 How will I know if PyraVastu is working?

Things will start to change. They may happen on a subtle level. For example your happiness may increase or your attitude to life may alter. Things may also happen in a more tangible way, such as an unexpected phone call with a job offer, or an invitation to a party.

 Can PyraVastu help people who do not believe in it?

I have seen some immediate and powerful effects rewarding the work of self-confessed unbelievers. PyraVastu is not a form of magic. It works on the scientific principles of space and mind, and will have an effect whether or not people can feel it or know that it is being used. But if a positive mind and a strong faith is added it can give miraculous results.

 How long will it be before I begin to get results?

I have seen PyraVastu have immediate and dramatic effects, but it can also take time. Possibly the process is connected to our ability to adapt to change. PyraVastu can help you get the most from your life. But just as glowing good health needs careful attention to diet, exercise and lifestyle, PyraVastu will require a little time and care before you see dramatic results.

 What extra do I get from PyraVastu, compared to Vastu or Feng Shui?

The best part of PyraVastu is its most practical approach to match needs of the new-age man. Secondly there is no comparison with our traditional Vastu or Feng Shui as this is a new science and gives better solutions complementing both of them.

 Are there any equipment to measure the change made by pyramids?

Yes, it can definitely be measured. There are many types of tools and equipment with me such as Kirlian photography machine, Biosensor equipment and Bio-force meter. Also some simple instruments like dowsing pendulum & 'L' and 'Y' rods. But these need good experience and knowledge to handle.

Is this method used widely and proven to be effective?

I need not answer this question. Let the results speak. By today more than 2.5 million people are connected with this PyraNet and have discovered a new way to health, prosperity and power! Every day more and more people, Vastu experts and Feng Shui and Rciki masters are joining this movement. But do not go by my words, just try out a simple pyramid yantra experiment and expect a miracle.

" This revolutionary concept of Dr. Bhatt has changed my thinking out right and my fame and prosperity has flourished beyond my imagination".
Dr. Harshit Kapadia
Feng Shui column writer in Mumbai Samachar

" Learning and exploring new ways with PyraNet is really a marvelous experience. After this I am blessed by all round success."
Mr. Atul Joshi
Engineer & PyraVastu expert
USA

" Being from a small village I had many doubts about this system. But today I can confidently say, PyraVastu works like miracle".

Dr. Jaykrushna Patel
Vastu expert and
Alternative therapist

" After I met Guruji Dr. Bhatt, I changed my business and started practicing PyraVastu. I enlighten my relatives to do the same."
Mr. Dilip Shah
Businessman from Ahmedabad,
India

If you have a real life miracle to share, let us know and Dr. Bhatt will print your experience in his new book.

What is PyraNet? And how can I be benefitted ?

PyraNet is a network of millions of Pyramid Yantra, developed by Prof. Dr. Jiten Bhatt and used by thousands of people world wide. So when you learn and use a Pyramid Yantra developed by Dr. Bhatt you become a part of this huge revolution. When each Pyramid Yantra communicates with the other and makes a huge energy network, results are automatic. Now as you are the part of this network and whenever you use or fix a Pyramid Yantra developed by Prof. Dr. Jiten Bhatt you start getting results due to the power of this huge positive network!

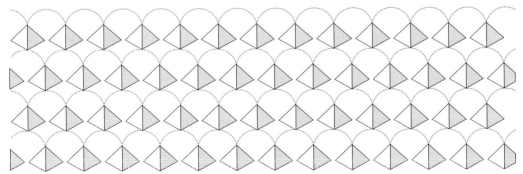

Positive energy PyraNetwork of millions of Pyramid Yantra

Is there any difference between 'Pyramid Yantra' and normal pyramids?

1+2 is equal to 3 and hydrogen combined with oxygen is equal to water. In the same manner this new method Pyramid Yantra is a powerful combination of pyramids and yantras. This power formula has no limitation like that of pyramid and yantra. So it can be placed in the pocket or on the wall or also on a vehicle. It can be made more personalized and can be placed underground for long duration without corrosion. Also Pyramid Yantra is a pure universal science for the common man and can be adapted by all religions or systems.

 # What is the ideal material in which Pyramid yantra is made?

As we are working on a more subtle level, the 'space'- akash-tatva is more important than the material used. Though the most ideal material in which a Pyramid yantra has to be made must be natural, as stone of the Great Pyramid, But we need 91 different chambers of Vastu and practically they cannot be created accurately in stone. So Neutron Polymer is used.
You also get the following benefits of the Neutron material:

Accurate dimensions
As it is die molded all the dimensions from inside out are the most accurate.

Neutral property
It is neutral in property so can be programmed as per your wish. The other metals are affiliated to some property. For example copper is affiliated to Mars, and gold to Sun so results may vary if used in PyraVastu.

Anti-Corrosion & Long lasting
When we place 9 pyramids under the ground it must stay there for life. In this case this Neutron plastic can stay without corrosion,completely intact in all 91 space chambers for long.

Air tight chambers
Each chamber inside a Multier 9x9 is air-tight and it is also a non-porous material.

These are a few of the many advantages of Neutron Polymer in which these Pyramid Yantra are made. But remember, material is less important, more important is the accurate space captured in each pyramid.

 # Yantras are made in metal, then why not Pyramid yantra?

Pyramid Yantra are not 'only' yantra but a powerful combination of both pyramid and yantra. They work on advance principles of space and information. Also when we study pyramids, not a single is made of metal. They are either of stone or some non-conducting material only. So whereas traditional yantras can be made in metal but not Pyramid Yantra.

Can I use a copper or gold Pyramid yantra?

Copper and gold have good properties. But when we make a Pyramid yantra completely from them all 91 space chambers are short circuited. To avoid the short-circuit problem, copper or gold has to be used partially or in appropriate place or proportion. The best examples are million of temples where only a small copper or gold yantra is fixed at the bottom and the tip of the temple. The whole temple is not made of copper. So if you need to use copper or gold in Pyramid yantra, use it in a small proportion at the base.

Short circuit in case of copper

In a copper pyramid all 91 space chambers are ⚡ short-circuited.

 ## As copper is a good conductor, can it not grasp more cosmic energy?

Firstly, one must understand that we are working on the ether level and we do not need the gross electricity conducting property. And also subtle level cosmic energies can penetrate through any conductor or non-conducting material. So the conducting property of copper does not play an important role in Pyramid Yantra.

All Pyramid yantra are in white color. Is there a specific reason?

As white is a universal receiver of all colors so all visible as well as invisible colors start interacting with it. So there is no need of a specific color. But if one needs a specific color property according to color therapy,one can use colored pyramids.

How to fix a Pyramid yantra for Vastu correction?

As you know Pyramid yantra has no limitations. It can be placed in your pocket or on your vehicle and machinery. So in Vastu corrections they can be used on the wall or even on the ceiling upside down. They can go underground or can be covered by false ceiling also.

 Fixing on wall

 Fixing on ceiling

 Underground

Give me more details about fixing Pyramid Yantra - Multier 9x9.

We will start with the more frequently used Pyramid Yantra - Multier 9x9. As shown in the figure Multier pyramid consists of three main parts 1.The bottom nine PyraChips with 81 pyramids, 2.PyraPlate with nine pyramids and 3.The top with one pyramid. Thus this pre-programmed Multier pyramid contains a total of 91 different pyramid space chambers.

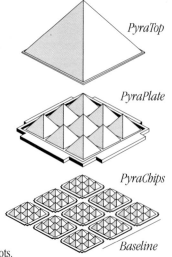

PyraTop

PyraPlate

Now before installing you need to stick all 9 PyraChips at the bottom of PyraPlate with an adhesive. Then press fix the PyraTop on the plates. This set is ready to install, give FaMaa (place this pyramid in left hand and place your right hand on the top and create pure love from your heart. Now from your mind add your intense wish into it). This Multier pyramid is personalized and is ready to work according to your wish.

PyraChips

Baseline

Installing pyramids under the ground

In most case underground installation are for center activation for protection of plots. So in such cases you need a minimum of 9 such Multier pyramids. FaMaa orientation as mentioned above is to be given to minimum of one center pyramid out of all nine. Installing is simple. Dig a pit more than 1 foot deep and of an approximate size so at least 6 inch space is kept between each Multier. Make sure that base line of all pyramids match the magnetic axis. Now close the pit.

Fixing on walls and ceiling

The same Multier can be fixed on a wall or ceiling with a double-side adhesive tape. This tape sticks on both sides, so first cut a small piece and stick on the back of the PyraPlate and then remove the release paper and stick on the wall. Take care that the base line of the pyramids should be parallel to the ground or ceiling. On ceiling all pyramids will face down, as now relative earth is the ceiling and sky is the space down. There are also many types of Pyramid yantra that can be fixed on the wall for different purposes.

What are the minimum and maximum number of Pyramids I can use?

I personally feel micro is more powerful than gross and mind is more powerful than matter. So you can even get fantastic results by a small PyraChip if you have programmed it adequately with pure love and intense will. But practically speaking numbers do matter. The minimum pyramids you need is a set of 9 Multier (Vastu 9x9) in the center of each building. And minimum of 3 where the defect is to be corrected. But if the defect is in bigger area or intensity, the numbers of Pyramid yantra may increase. The highest number of Multier pyramids used in a single project is 4500 sets, because of huge property and many obstacles.

Go step by step. First update yourself with basic knowledge of Vastu and PyraVastu. Start from your home and then help your friends and relatives. Find the defect, place appropriate Pyramid yantra and note the results. While finding defect and correcting them follow this proven thumb rule: start with the center, activate the center. Now protect the main door, check the kitchen, bedroom and placement of w/c in a house. Practice in this manner with the reference of this book and when you have successfully completed 25 cases write to Prof. Dr. Jiten Bhatt, for advance training.

" *After using Pyramid Yantra - Multier 9x9 in my Vastu practice, results are far better*".

Dr. D. Poornachandra Rao
Leading Vastu Shastri

EXPERT'S OPINION

Advanced training programs are conducted by Prof. Dr. Jiten Bhatt for you to become a PyraVastu Expert.

 What are the different types of Pyramid Yantra developed?

Many types are developed for specific use and purpose. Some of them are shown in this book. They include Vastu Sleep for bed, Wish 9x9 for wish fulfilment, Harmony 9x9 to improve your interpersonal relationship. Many other types are developed such as Protect 9x9 for inside and outside, Vastu 9x9 for center activation and PyraStrip and PyraAngle for virtual corrections. Many more are under development.

 How can I get my Pyramid yantra and from where?

Pyramid Yantra are available with all leading Vastu experts, Feng Shui and Reiki masters and all health promoters of new-age energy tools.
In case you need further information you can interact with
Personal Care Systems (Pyramid div.)
PO Box 808 GIDC,
Makarpura,
Baroda -390010,
Gujarat, India.
email : personalcare@mail.com

Later heaven Ba-Gua
BA means 8, GUA means Trigrams

This powerful mystical symbol of change and environmental interaction can transform our life towards a new horizon.

6

"Feng Shui is the Chinese wisdom to understand universal energy and its effects. Its use enriches us physically, mentally, emotionally and spiritually."

Prof. Dr. Jiten Bhatt

Feng
Shui

⟁ The Creation of Life

Before time began, there was just an inconceivably large egg out of which P'an Ku was created.

When he emerged from the shell, darkness poured out of the egg, but so did light. All that was clear and bright rose to the sky and all that was muddy and heavy fell to the earth. Since he was afraid that the brightness above would fall onto the darkness below, he held the two apart with both his arms for thousands of years. He did so until finally he collapsed with exhaustion.

He offered himself fully to the world. His last breath became wind and clouds, his voice became thunder, his left eye became sun and right became moon, his limbs and torso became plains and mountains, his blood formed rivers and lakes, his muscles formed soil and tendons formed paths and roads, his hair and beard formed stars, fine body hair and skin became grass, trees and flowers, his bones, teeth and marrow changed to rubies, jade and minerals. Thus, he gave birth to all life.

P'an Ku brought order to chaos and so gave birth to all life.

What is Feng Shui?

Five thousand years old Feng Shui (Geomancy) has played an important role in Chinese, Japanese cultures and their progress. Now Feng Shui is becoming more popular all over the world due to its effective results.

Feng Shui's simple translation is "Wind and Water".

We know our existence depends on two sources of energy. First is nourishing energy from Mother Earth in the form of food. Second is cosmic energy from air in the form of oxygen or vital force from space.

Life force of the earth is circulated by water. Similarly subtle, energy circulation in space is governed by wind. Wind brings healthy energy and takes away bad energy.

So Feng Shui (Wind and Water) is the essential element in nature and in our life. But the story does not end here.

Feng Shui has its roots in 'Tao', which means the way of nature. Years of observation by Tao masters about flow of energy and universal rhythm contributed to the coding of secret laws of nature and its relationship with our bio-force.

In short, the idea is to understand how energy moves in our surroundings and how to harness this energy for happy, healthy and prosperous life.

Thousands of people have gained extremely beneficial results just by a small change. You also can have it by simple re-arrangement of desk, furniture, change in color and shape or placement of symbolic objects.

The Fundamental Principle is that when you are willing to change the outside, inner change has already started occurring. Our inner momentum reshapes our destiny and values of life.

Wind

Water

Dynamic elements that control chi around us.

Many ways to learn

There are many thoughts, schools and ways of practicing Feng Shui.

The first is the 'FORM' school. It is based on the contours of the landscape and its waterways in relation to a site or building. In modern days of urban civilization it is not a practical approach.

The second is the "COMPASS' or 'LO P'AN' school. This method gives less importance to landscapes. It is more of a mathematical approach. It uses I Ching and its eight trigrams, Chinese horoscope and numerology. This method is good but can be successfully practiced by long experience only.

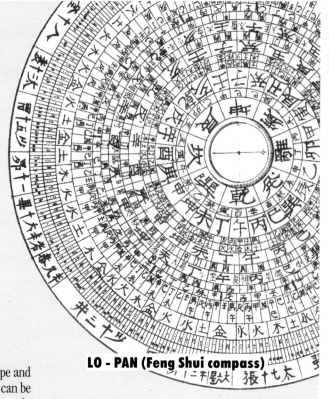

LO - PAN (Feng Shui compass)

The third is the 'INTUITIVE' school or the 'YIN-YANG' theory of feng shui. It deals more with the flow of energy in and around our houses. It also deals with how the residents of the house are tuned to that flow. This method can be easily implemented with a little experience.

There are many more like Water Dragon Feng Shui, Flying Star and Ba Gua school, etc. Remember no single method is complete yet, positive will and faith in one will definitely produce wonderful results.

Let's Start

Clear the clutter

No Feng Shui remedy or principles will help unless and until clutter is removed. Clutter is one of the commonest fault blocking healthy chi to act in our lives.

As a rule, healthy energy must flow without obstruction. Clutter is different than storage. Clutter is storage of useless objects. Check out if you have any clutter. Physical removal of clutter will produce positive flow of mental and emotional Chi and results in a healthy Chi that enriches life and brings happiness. Enjoy the clarity of life that comes with releasing the blocked energy.

Basic Feng Shui: Yin-Yang

The most powerful mystical system of change is through the creative interaction of yin and yang to unfold new horizons and transform our lives. Base of our existence are the two powerful forces: Father and Mother (FaMaa).

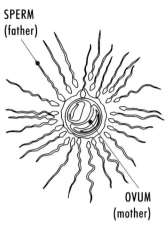

The basis of life is also Yin and Yang

To understand the mysteries of the universe and our existence, we have to deeply understand Taoism, the religion of China. They teach us "The Way"- inevitable, powerful and harmonious way of life and existence.

All matter has vibrations. The Hindus call it Prana, the Japanese call it Ki and the Chinese call it Chi.
The Universe is in a state of constant flow of this Chi around us. This flow is governed by descending yang chi from the Heavens and ascending yin chi from the earth.

When unseen chi is transformed into visible, it takes shapes and forms. This shape represents the property of energy for some purpose.

Here, in the fig. given below, circle represents Heaven chi, square sitting in the middle of Heaven represents Earth and central triangle represents the Man.

This is the Taoist symbolization of Heaven, Earth and Man.

In Taoist philosophy, everything is manifested by the combination of yin or yang. Even today, in the age of new millennium our most powerful tool - the computer also works on binary code (zero and one). All the information is the combination of zero and one.

Symbol of unity (yin and yang) according to Chinese philosophy.

Intuitive discovery by the Chinese, before 4000 years gave us the two basic codes and 64 hexagrams arising from them. These 64 hexagrams represent all possible stages of changes from birth to death. And just 40 years ago, science gave us the 64 codons of DNA, the genetic code for life. The basis of these hexagrams is yin and yang. Yin is symbolized by broken line and yang symbolized by continuous line. 64 permutations and combinations of these two is life.

In changing life, synergy of yin and yang and harmony between them is symbolized by the symbol of unity.

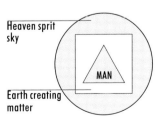

Symbolization of heaven-man-earth energy shape.

Without yin, yang cannot exist and without yang, yin cannot exist. They seem to be opposite but they are actually complementary to each other.

Yin within Yang
Yang within Yin
The cycle of life and death .

Binary code of life & Chi

YANG ▬▬▬▬
YIN ▬▬ ▬▬

Understanding this interactive balance of yin and yang is the heart of good Feng Shui. Practice of this good Feng Shui leads to personal happiness and success.

The basic principles of yin and yang can also be applied to the room. As yin is the female element of things, in Feng Shui, it refers to passive, serene parts of the room, part of room with no doors, windows or other openings. Yang being the vital male element of things, in Feng Shui it refers to vital area of action, part of the room with doors, windows or other openings. The aim of Feng Shui is to arrange the room in such a way as to create harmony in the room.

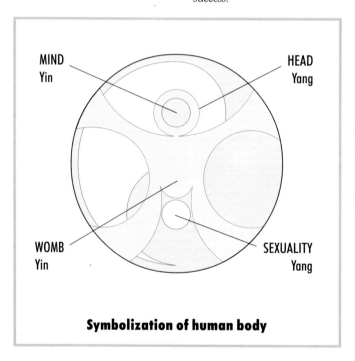

MIND
Yin

HEAD
Yang

WOMB
Yin

SEXUALITY
Yang

Symbolization of human body

Yin and yang are the basic energies of the universe. These energies are in constant swing according to months, years, seasonal changes, time, astrological conditions and internal flow of energies in our body.

Harmonious balance between the yin and yang

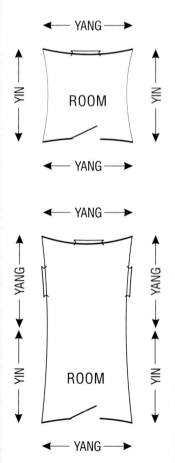

Let's learn more about basic Yin-Yang Feng Shui

We have already seen the constant swinging nature of yin and yang. Recalling that and considering your attributes from those given below you can judge your own personality and change your lifestyle accordingly.

Yin places: Forest, green land, shady trees, quiet mountainsides and serene sea sides.

Yang places: Cities, sunny places, flat landscapes, office buildings and uneven mountains used for climbing.

Yin outlook: The shady part of the house or building.

Yang outlook: The sunny part of the house or building.

Yin constitution: Tall, slim, generous features with thin frame.

Yang constitution: Stout, broad, sharp features with broad frame.

Yin mind: Imaginative, intuitive and creative.

Yang mind: Logical, ordered and quick- thinking.

Yin emotion: Kindness, sensitiveness, insecurity and depression.

Yang emotion: Ambitious, confidence, irritability and courageous.

Yin colours: Green, blue and pastel shades.

Yang colours: Red, yellow, orange and bright shades.

Yin shape and forms: Round, long, narrow and delicate.

Yang shape and forms: Square, angular, compact and sturdy.

Yin materials: Natural fabrics and wooden objects.

Yang materials: Synthetic fabrics and glass, metal and polished stone objects.

In China every mode of life is somehow linked to Yin and Yang . Even the numerology and numbers are yin or yang. Yin numbers are odd and yang are even. Zero represents nothingness i.e perfection and harmony. A favorable number of house, vehicle, phone etc. should be consisting equally of both yin and yang numbers.

Yin-Yang In practical use

Let's see how to apply the yin-yang theory in practise for everyday use.

• According to Feng Shui, in the center of the house maximum yin-yang energy is present and so when this part is used for applying yin-yang theory, it gives the best results. First of all remove all clutter from the center and other places in the house. Now perform pyramidal fire in the center of the house once a week at sunrise and at sunset.

• There are some places and corners of the house, inside and outside home that always remain shaded or dark, this can lower the flow of 'Chi'. So, place a small bulb in that place and keep it switched on all the time. In some other cases where there is much light at a place, put dark glass panes or films to lessen too much of 'Chi'.

• If you find some corner or room of your house or work place to be passive i.e. very less or no activity is done there, place wind chime or any other constantly moving object to balance its energy.

• If some rooms in your house are far too ventilated then lessen the ventilation. If some room is very less ventilated increase the ventilation to balance the energy in the room.

Like some of the applications of yin yang principle given here, you also can try applying others from the chart given on page 181.

Too Much YIN ?

Houses and buildings near graveyards, hospitals, prisons, slaughter houses, churches and police stations have too much yin as they are associated with yin energies of death. It is better not to live in such places but if you really cannot shift to other place, try out these simple remedies -

◆ Orient your main door so that it faces away from the yin structure or building.

◆ Do not have windows that open towards these structures.

◆ Paint your main door in bright red to signify strong yang energy.

◆ Make sure that the porch light is always on.

◆ Bring in sunlight which is yang. Cut down shady trees if necessary.

◆ Grow flowers in your garden.

◆ Put garden lights all around the house.

◆ Paint your fence or compound wall in bright color.

◆ Red roof also provides yang element.

◆ Introduce yang objects such as pebbles, stones etc. into the garden.

◆ Hang harmonious pictures which create balanced yang energy.

◆ Do not allow rooms to remain dark, cold and damp for longer periods.

◆ Placing red lanterns in hall or a crystal chandelier just inside main door promotes the flow of auspicious yang energy.

How to create YANG energy ?

Try doing these remedies -

◆ Repaint walls in bright colors.

◆ Bring in light. White walls are very yang.

◆ Change draping curtains with those with nets to allow light in the room.

◆ Use bright colors for furniture and bed sheets.

◆ Keep windows open.

◆ If trees are blocking, cut them back.

◆ Install plenty of lights and keep one on continuously.

◆ Keep radio, television or stereo on. Sound, bring in yang energy.

◆ Have vases of freshly cut flowers, dry or withered ones lower the Chi.

Too much YANG ?

Buildings that are constantly exposed to bright light or heat near electric transformer, high tension wires or near temple and places that are too windy are exposed to too much yang energy. It is good to avoid such places but if not, you can use these measures -

◆ Paint your door in any shade of blue.

◆ Select cool, yin colors for interior decoration.

◆ Avoid too much noise in house.

◆ Avoid too much light and never have a red light turned on.

◆ Introduce water features as a small fountain.

◆ Paintings of lakes and rivers.

◆ Maintain a good manicured lawn in your garden.

◆ Paint gates, fence or compound wall in black.

Sacred Om bell for harmonizing yin-yang energy.

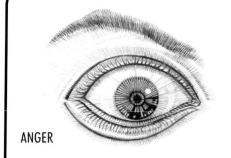

ANGER

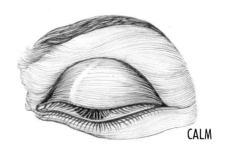

CALM

(FA) **YANG**	(MAA) **YIN**
HEAVEN	EARTH
SUN	MOON
MOUNTAIN	VALLEY
SUMMER	WINTER
DAY	NIGHT
BRIGHT DAY	CLOUDY DAY
SPIRIT	MATTER
MALE	FEMALE
FATHER	MOTHER
ABOVE	BELOW
OUTER	INNER
HOT	COLD
HARD	SOFT
DRY	WET
LIGHT	DARK
LIVELY	DULL
MOVEMENT	STILLNESS
NOISY	SILENT
FUNCTIONAL	NON FUNCTIONAL
POSITIVE	NEGATIVE
ELECTRIC	MAGNETIC
SHARPNESS	ROUNDNESS
CROWDED	LONELY
ACTIVE	PASSIVE
FLOURISHING	DECAYING

Five animal mystery

According to Feng Shui, houses are guarded by five animal spirits (Black tortoise, Green dragon, Red phoenix, White tiger and snake). All these have their own significance and importance. There are two methods - Yin method for graveyards or outside and Yang methods for living places. Here, we will talk about yang method.

Animal Attributes

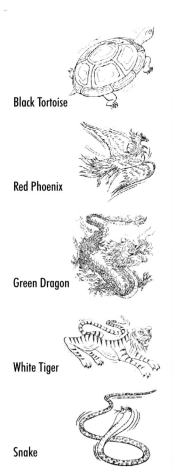

Black Tortoise

Red Phoenix

Green Dragon

White Tiger

Snake

1. Black tortoise - It rules the water. This side should be highest of all. It represents long life, endurance, security, patience and support.

2. Red phoenix - It rules the fire. This should be the lowest side of all. It represents beauty, inspiration, virtue, duty, capacity for vision and opportunity.

3. Green dragon - It rules the wood. It should be high next to the Black tortoise. It represents luck, good nature, benevolence, abundance, prosperity, strength and wisdom.

4. White tiger - It rules the metal. It should be high next to Green dragon. It represents male and yang energy in pure form, physical strength, essential for survival, protection from attack and defence.

5. Snake - It rules the earth, center and is the pivot around which all four seasons rotate. It should be neither high nor low. It is coiled in the center and protected by the four outer creatures. It represents receiving information and commands all the four forces.

Application

Start from your working desk. According to the five animal principle - The back of your seat is Black tortoise which means it should be highest because you need firm support from back. The front of the desk should be clear so that you get positive inspirations and opportunities come flying to you like the Red Phoenix. On your

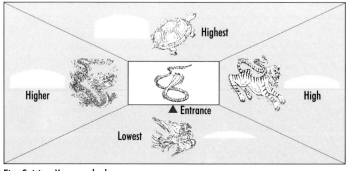

Five Spirits - Yang method

left is the White tiger which should have high cupboards but not higher than those on your right for bringing you protection and defence from evil. On your right is Green dragon which should have cupboards not higher than those on your back to bring you good luck. Similarly you can apply the same principle for your room, your house, your working place and all other places you can think of.

Five element Feng Shui

Second fundamental rule.

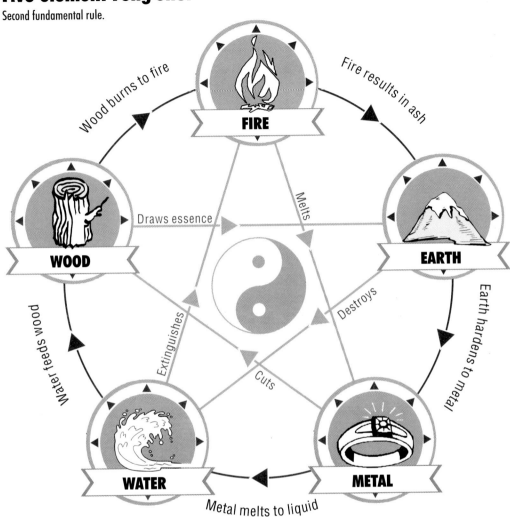

Secret of five forces

Thousands of years ago Fu Hsi and his followers declared that matter and energy were interchangeable.

Today, we understand it by Einstein's law of $e=mc^2$. The Universe comprises matter, energy and chi.

This is presented as the five basic forces or elements of all living things.

These basic elements are FIRE - EARTH - METAL - WATER - WOOD.

These five potent forces continuously interact with each other. This interaction works in two cycles, one of creation and other of destruction.

Constructive and destructive cycles

The five elements change in natural progression from one to another. This is the constructive cycle. In constructive cycle - fire results in ash or earth, earth hardens to metal, metal melts and creates water, water feeds wood and wood helps fire to burn. Here each element helps or enhances the progress of the other. This cycle creates harmony between elements.

But when these five elements change such that they check the progress, intensity and influence of each other, it is the destructive cycle. In destructive cycle - wood draws its essence from earth, earth destroys water, water extinguishes fire, fire melts metal and metal cuts wood. This creates disharmony between elements.

Use the Knowledge

Now that we have seen the five elements and their cycles, let us see how we can apply them to our house.

Divide the house into 9 equal parts. Each part has been attributed an element. Placement of objects in house should be in such a way that they correspond to the respective element.

WOOD	FIRE	EARTH
WOOD	EARTH	METAL
EARTH	WATER	METAL

If objects are placed such that they complement each other as in the constructive cycle, they enhance the property of each other e.g. If water objects like an aquarium or picture of water etc. are place in wood section of house then it enhances the property of wood. In case destructive cycle elements come together, they cut down the progress of each other e.g. If metal objects are placed in the wood section like wind chimes of metal furniture, it cuts wood. Hence there will be disharmony thus creating disturbances and troubles.

For example. If water element objects like aquarium, artificial waterfall etc. are placed in fire section of house it will create trouble. Similarly, disturbances can be created by wrong placement of wood in earth section, earth in water section, fire in metal section, etc.

You can make changes in your house or room to avoid disharmony or create harmony by placing right objects in right section.

Check Yours!

Check your element type from the method given below. First of all start with your house and working place (also see and relate with Ba Gua chart page 189). Check also of those around you - your wife, your children, your boss, your subordinate, your relatives and your friends. Do they form a creative cycle or a destructive cycle with you? By this you would come to know who helps in your progress. Understand your cycle and deal with people around you accordingly to improve your personal Feng Shui.

Firstly, find out your own element by the year you are born. Just see the last number of the year you are born in. From the chart below find your respective element and consider its attributes in the next chart.

FIND YOUR ELEMENT:

Last number in your birth year.	Yin/Yang	Corresponding Element
0	Yang	Metal
1	Yin	Metal
2	Yang	Water
3	Yin	Water
4	Yang	Wood
5	Yin	Wood
6	Yang	Fire
7	Yin	Fire
8	Yang	Earth
9	Yin	Earth

Attributes of each element

Relationship of shape with five elements

Use of five element shapes
(see page 24)

WATER: Intellectual, diplomatic, peaceful even in adversity, touched by art and beauty, nurturing, communicates well, intuitive, excellent negotiators, flexible and adaptable. Views things holistically, social and sympathetic. **Negative:** Fickle minded, over sensitive, intrusive, easily exhausted, fearful, nervous and stress-prone.

WOOD: Explorer, loves to be busy, hates to lose, versatile, energetic, outgoing personality, visualizing, artistic, enthusiastic, public spirited, nurturing, finish undertaken tasks. **Negative:** Impatient, angry and revengeful.

FIRE: Happy-go-lucky, passionate, committed, adventurer, loves change, active, stands for honour and fairness, leaders, inspire others to follow, dislike rules, innovative, hates boredom and humorous.
Negative: Impatient, exploits others and has little thought for their feelings, aggressive, destructive and violent.

How to use chart on next page.

This chart shows the properties of each element. Look into the chart to find out the physical attributes that each element possesses. Also you can use the chart vice-versa. Look for the attribute troubling you and find out which element is disturbed in you e.g.
- If you have knee trouble look into the chart, and find out which element has that attribute. Suppose it is the water element.
This means Water element is disturbed in you and hence treat it accordingly with help of that element and / or with aid of helping element according to constructive cycle.

EARTH: Diplomatic, loves people and to be of use, hates being ignored, resourceful, rhythmic and balanced, creative, wise, supportive, loyal, possesses inner strength, dependable. **Negative:** Nervous, anticipates non-existent problems, obsessional, prone to nit-picking.

METAL: Reliable, inspiring , careful, hates disorder and clutter, joyous, malleable, energetic, communicative, good organiser, independent, happy in their own company, intuitive and interesting people. **Negative:** Destructive, dangerous, sad, inflexible and serious.

Personal Five Element Feng Shui

	WATER	WOOD	FIRE	EARTH	METAL
Energy	Deep Sensitive Secretive	Energetic Impatient Competitive	Passionate Creative Self centered	Nurturing Balanced Diplomatic	Reliable Independent Reserved
Body organs	Kidney Urinary bladder	Liver Gall bladder	Heart Small intestine	Pancreas Stomach	Lungs Large intestine
Body parts	Low back Knees	Tendons Upper back	Eyes Hands	Muscles Synovial membrane	Skin Body hair
Body type	Big bones Wide hips	Short Energized	Slender Redness	Round Fleshy	Small bone Fair skinned
Facial traits	Ears, Chin Forehead	Eyebrow Browbones, Jaw	Eyes - tips, Corners & lines	Mouth, Cheeks Above lips	Nose, Cheek bone Moles
Emotion	Fear	Anger	Excitement	Worry	Grief
Physical emotion	Wisdom	Human kindness	Love	Instinct	Gratitude
Taste	Salty	Sour	Bitter	Sweet	Metallic
Colour	Black, Blue	Green	Red, Orange	Brown, Pink	White, Metallic
Needs	Water Time alone	Plants, Trees Focus	Color, Light, Heat Talking	Comfort Family	Order, Purity Boundaries
Values	Truth Spirituality	Work Intensity	Fun Variety	Helping Stability	Past / Future Aesthetic

The Lo Shu

The Lo Shu square is another important and most ancient symbol widely used in Feng Shui analysis. It is also called Magic Square as its nine chambered, 3 X 3 grid square features a unique arrangement of numbers from one to nine. It is unique because the sum of three numbers in any direction in the square, horizontally, diagonally or vertically, is 15. 15 is the number of days taken by the new moon to reach full moon.

The tortoise represents protection, longevity and wisdom.

The three-grid pattern corresponds to the eight sides of the Ba Gua symbol, and is associated with its eight trigrams. (This is discussed in detail later in the chapter). Lo Shu unlocks the time dimension for Feng Shui, and allows practitioners to decide precisely when is the best time to make changes to the site, home or interior decoration.

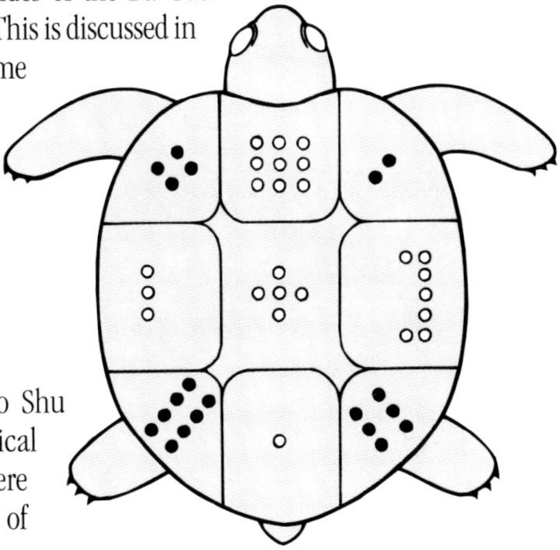

Lo Shu around the world

Chinese tradition says that the first image of Lo Shu square was seen by Sage Yu. He saw this mystical arrangement of numbers as white spots which were arranged in particular manner on the 9 grid shell of the tortoise emerging from river Lo in 2205 BC.

Lo Shu marking on tortoise

The ancient Indian system of astrology and yantra technique has created yantra squares. These planetary squares were used to generate signs that control the spirit of planets. The square of Saturn or 'Shani' has the exactly same arrangements of numbers as the Lo Shu square.

Shu is also the Egyptian god of atmosphere who along with Tefnut rules the wind and movement of clouds and moisture. This is very much of concern in Feng Shui.

Application

For practical use we would use the 9 chambered 3 X 3 grid square with numbers in each chamber instead of dots on the tortoise. In all further references of Lo Shu we will use the square as shown in the figure, alongside.

4	9	2
3	5	7
8	1	6

Lo Shu numbers

Understanding the Ba Gua method

In Feng-Shui, Ba Gua is a fundamental tool to determine the influence of directional energy. The Ba Gua represents the journey of life, the Tao, and we can use it to create comfortable living, working and leisure places.

Ba Gua is an eight sided diagram, with each side symbolizing an aspect of life such as family, children, health, friendship, love, travel, business and money.

To check Ba Gua, superimpose it over a land, building, room or desk. It highlights the missing and extending areas showing us which aspect of life is affected. When a corner or section is missing or extending, it indicates energy imbalance and corresponding aspects of life might also be disturbed.

We will see the effects of this missing and extending space later when we see the case studies.

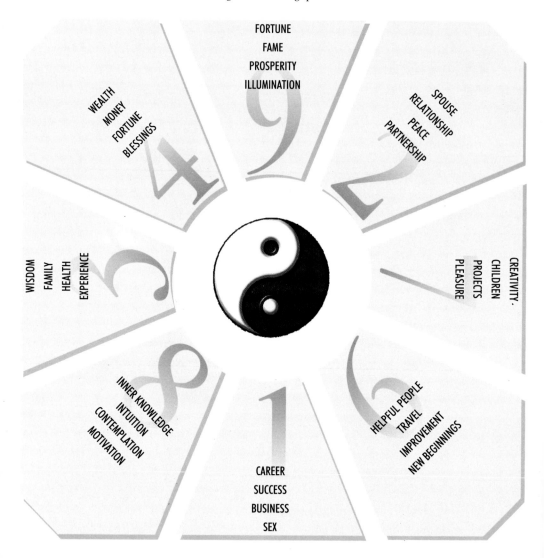

Practical application of Ba Gua

There are numerous methods of application of Ba Gua. However we adopt just one simple, easy to understand and the most practical method - The Front Door method. We will strictly and commitedly follow this method to achieve our aim of creating harmonious living according to PyraFengshui.

How to proceed?

Step 1 - Draw a basic ground plan of the plan you need to correct. Draw an outline of each floor with main rooms and doors into those rooms.

Step 2 - Draw Ba Gua along with numbers on a tracing paper as shown on opposite page.

Step 3 - Place the traced Ba Gua on the ground plan that you have. If you have more than one floor, you will need a plan for each floor.

Step 4 - Ba Gua should be placed such that 'number 1' side is parallel to the side of wall having the front door.

Step 5 - As referred earlier in this chapter there are some missing and extending sections in the plan of plot, house, room or desk. The missing areas are called negative spaces and extending areas are called positive spaces. (See the figure below).

Step 6 - You have to set your Ba Gua in such a way that the individual negative and positive spaces do not exceed 15%. Any space exceeding 15% has to be treated.

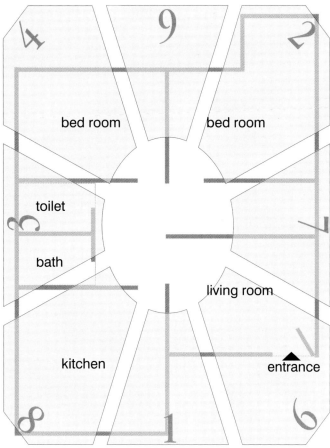

Your house plan overlapping with Ba Gua

Positive space does not usually pose much problem but negative space has to be compensated. Negative or missing space in 'number 5' or center is not to be interfered with. On the contrary it is desirable, The center has to be clear. Such internal courtyard is a general feature of a traditional Indian house and is also seen in some other cultures. Clear running water (not stagnant) in this area is good. Planting tulsi (basil) is also equally good, as seen in many Indian houses.

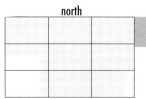

Gray part is house plan with nine grid. Empty space (white) is negative space and projected space (pink) is positive space.

What happens when you have negative and positive space in a building or a room.

	Result of negative space	Result of positive space
North	Difficulties in career - Creates weakness, depression and confusion.	Clarity of ambitions. Career blossoms. Beneficial especially to women. Excess positive space creates isolation and loneliness.
North-east	Feeling unstable - Creates forgetfulness. Not good for scholars.	Knowledge grows but there is increase in disagreements. Encourages greediness, boredom and insomnia.
East	Misunderstandings, ill health and loss of vitality.	Sense of maturity and success for occupants. Excess creates hyperactivity, over ambitiousness and carelessness.
South-east	Income is affected. Difficulties in business, confusion and accidents.	Prosperity and success. Excess creates oversensitiveness and tiredness .
South	Becomes self-conscious. Loses confidence, reputation and clarity.	Promotion and recognition. Excess creates conceit, notoriousness and emotional swings.
South-west	Feels unstable. Hard to find relationship. Difficulties for women.	Beneficial for women and romance. Excess creates slowness and over-dependence.
West	Difficulties for children. Loss of joy. Hard to save money. Emotional block.	Helps completion of projects, sociable and happy. Excess creates obsession for pleasure and tendency to greediness.
North-west	Not many helpful people. Lack of vitality. Difficulties for men. Children can be disobedient.	Concern for others grows. Financial soundness. Stimulates clear judgment. Excess positive space creates over controlling and self - righteousness.

Application of Ba Gua for your Compound, House and each Room

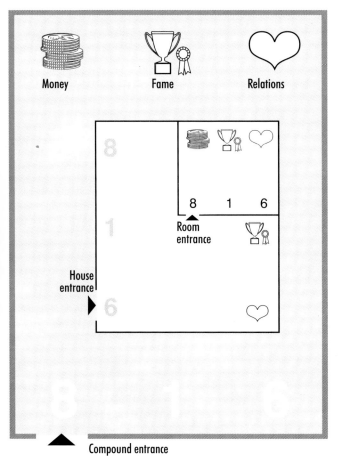

Compound entrance

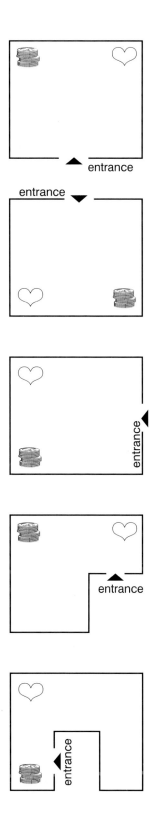

We have seen the front door method and its application on plan, on page no. 189. For simplification of the same method, take the following steps-

According to the method: Entering the plot, house or room, the front left corner represents the money area or space and the front right corner represents relationship area or space.

If you are dealing with correction of plot refer to the entrance of plot. If you are dealing with correction of house consider the entrance of house and not the entrance of the compound. Same applies when you are dealing with room correction. Consider the entrance of room and not that of the house.

A few examples are shown on your right on this page illustrating different entrances of the room.

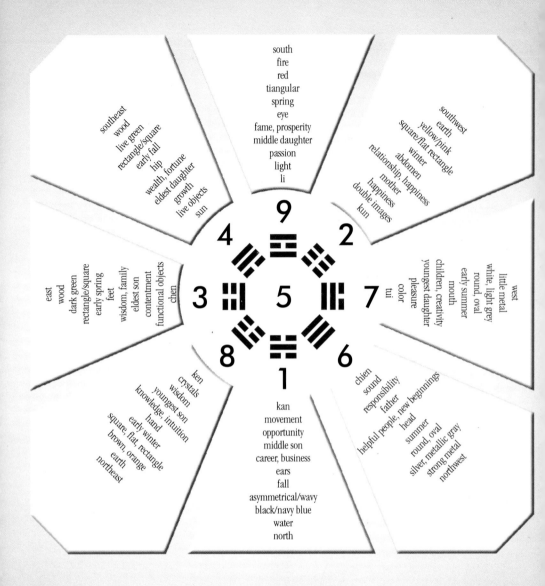

south
fire
red
tiangular
spring
eye
fame, prosperity
middle daughter
passion
light
li

southeast
wood
live green
rectangle/square
early fall
hip
wealth, fortune
eldest daughter
growth
live objects
sun

southwest
earth
yellow/pink
square/flat rectangle
winter
relationship, happiness
abdomen
mother
happiness
double images
kun

east
wood
dark green
rectangle/square
early spring
feet
wisdom, family
eldest son
contentment
functional objects
chen

west
little metal
white, light grey
round, oval
early summer
mouth
children, creativity
youngest daughter
pleasure
color
tui

ken
crystals
wisdom
youngest son
knowledge, intuition
hand
early winter
square, flat, rectangle
brown, orange
earth
northeast

kan
movement
opportunity
middle son
career, business
ears
fall
asymmetrical/wavy
black/navy blue
water
north

chien
sound
responsibility
father
helpful people, new beginnings
head
summer
round, oval
silver, metallic gray
strong metal
northwest

HOME BA GUA (DETAILED UNDERSTANDING)

This is an easy to use simple chart for your Feng Shui practice.

By using this Ba Gua chart you can understand the enrichments of each side of Ba Gua.
Compare your plan with this reference chart and you will come to know which enrichments you
are missing and what is to be done.
e.g. Segment 1- Trigram: ☵kan, Remedy: moment, Enrichment: opportunity,
Family relationship: middle son, Good for: career and business, Body part: ears, Season: fall,
Shape: asymmetrical/wavy, Color: black/navy blue, Element: water, Direction: north.

Understanding Trigrams

The universe is in a constant state of change through the creative interaction of yin and yang. This unceasing pattern, if changed, is reflected by the 8 trigrams and their 64 possible combinations known as hexagrams.

Each trigram is made up of three lines. The line can be broken or unbroken. Broken lines are yin and the unbroken lines are yang. These eight trigrams reflect the gradual movement from absolute yin to absolute yang and back to absolute yin in a never - ending cycle.

These trigrams represent the qualities of each side of Ba Gua

K'AN - represents career, business, success, and our journey through life. It is associated with winter, its element is water and direction is North. Its number is 1.

K'UN - represents union, relationships, domesticity and maternal instincts, good spouse, partnership, peace and happiness. It is associated with summer, its element is earth and direction is southwest. Its number is 2.

CHEN - represents health, vitality, elders, growth, ancestors, family, wisdom and experience.

It is associated with spring and new beginnings. Its element is wood and direction is East. Its number is 3.

SUN - represents wealth, blessings, growth, gentleness, assimilation and fortune. It is associated with wind and spring. Its element is wood and direction is southeast. Its number is 4.

CHIEN - represents leadership, achievement, helpful friends, mentors, teachers, travel, improvement and new beginnings. It is associated with autumn, its element is strong metal and direction is North-West. Its number is 6.

TUI - represents creativity, joy, children and projects. It is associated with autumn, its element is little metal and direction is West. Its number is 7.

KEN - represents knowledge, wisdom, intuition, contemplation and motivation. It is associated with winter, its element is earth and direction is North-East. Its number is 8.

LI - represents illumination of self, reputation visibility, fame, fortune and prosperity. It is associated with summer, its element is fire and direction is South. Its number is 9. Number 5 is in the center with symbol of unity. Female is represented by K'UN and Male by KEN.

▲ Protect 9x9 - Outside

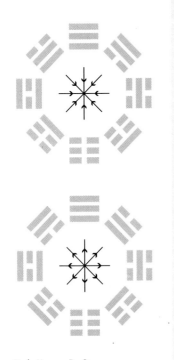

Early Heaven Ba Guas-
Two different opinions!

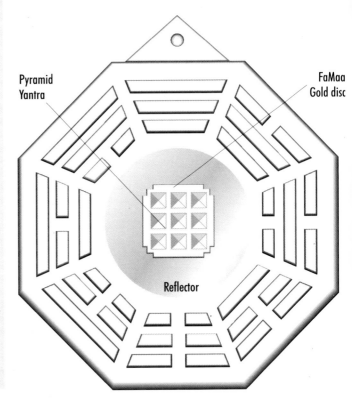

Pyramid
Yantra

FaMaa
Gold disc

Reflector

Prof. Dr. Jiten Bhatt's Pyramid Ba Gua

There are many schools of thoughts and numerous opinions regarding Ba Gua. Dr. Jiten Bhatt, after years of experience of using different Ba Gua, has designed this versatile pyramid Ba Gua. He created this special Ba Gua which has a pyramid yantra and a gold plate in the center. This special provision in center is made to pre-program your pyramid Ba Gua before applying to make it personalized and hence more effective.

It is an unique instrument made for the first time in world for bringing protection and good luck. It is must on every door. It helps to protect your house from Sha Chi- too many shining objects, sharp pointing corners or incomplete construction of next building, heavy transformer outside house or water on wrong side, etc. It not only protects but attracts helpful energies to bring you good luck. This Ba Gua has to be fixed only outside the house - one, three or more in number depending on the strength of the affecting Sha chi.

Protect main door.

Protection from road Sha Chi.

Object in the entrance.

⚠ Protect 9x9 - Inside

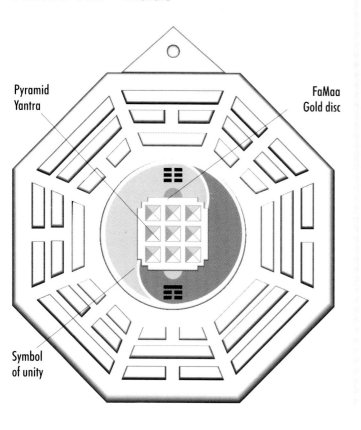

Pyramid Yantra

FaMaa Gold disc

Symbol of unity

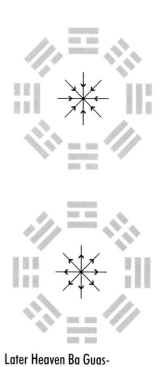

Later Heaven Ba Guas-
also has two different opinions!

Prof. Dr. Jiten Bhatt's Pyramid Ba Gua

Not only does Sha Chi affect from outside the house, inside our houses too we have many Sha Chi affecting us adversely. The previous Ba Gua cannot be used inside. Hence Dr. Jiten Bhatt has designed another pyramid Ba Gua for using inside the house. It guards us from any Sha Chi or killing energy shooting at us. These killing energies are usually caused by hostile objects or structures that represent poison arrows. These objects in our houses are the staircase, sharp corners of a room, beam overhead, pillar in the center, narrow passages, w/c attached to bedroom, etc. These strike Sha Chi.

This Pyramid Ba Gua is to be used only inside the house to protect us from Sha Chi in the house. It also can be programmed according to the need so as to attract positive energies to bring in good luck.

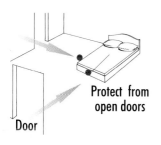

Protect from open doors

Door

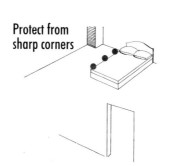

Protect from sharp corners

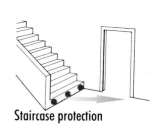

Staircase protection

Balancing Chi

For Chi to bring you health, good luck and prosperity it should be allowed to flow in its natural way. Chi can be obstructed, confused, accelerated or stagnant in your living or working place due to numerous reasons. You can correct this badly flowing Chi by providing suitable remedies and enhancements.

By using Ba Gua decide which section of your plot, house, room or desk requires to be corrected or enhanced. When you have decided on which section to work, then you need to decide exactly what type of remedy or enhancement is required there. Then apply it accordingly. You can either stimulate by using the remedy for that section or enhance the enrichment by using the remedy of its supporting element from the constructive cycle of elements (pg.183). Use remedies and enhancements with awareness in such a way that they create harmony, beauty, cleanliness and balance.

9 Simple Remedies

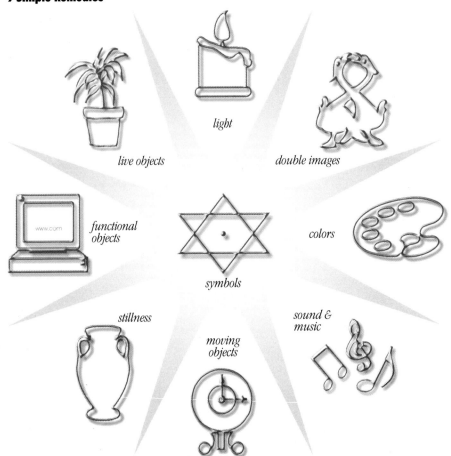

live objects

light

double images

functional objects

symbols

colors

stillness

moving objects

sound & music

Light

This remedy includes mirrors to deflect bad Chi, lights to brighten dull Chi, candles to warm up cold Chi. Do not keep lights in such a way that you can see bare bulbs. It is used as remedy for 'number 9' section of Ba Gua or to enhance fame and prosperity.

Double images

It includes using two similar flower vases, painting of two birds, objects with mirror symmetry, two teddy bears, etc. It is used as a remedy for 'number 2'' section of Ba Gua or as an enhancer of relationship and happiness.

Color

This remedy includes anything from color of walls to prints and paintings. Bright colors accelerate chi and pale colors slow down too much accelerated chi. Bright and lively colors are used for 'number 7' section of Ba Gua and enhance children's creativity.

Sound

This remedy includes wind chimes, bells, radio, harmonious music, ticking clock etc. If a clock is placed it should be seen that you always keep it at right time. It is used as a remedy for 'number 6' section of Ba Gua or as an enhancer for helpful people and making new beginnings.

Moving objects

It includes fluttering flags, flowing water, fountain and smoke from incense stick, clocks, mobiles, hammock etc. Mobiles, whether of natural fabric or not, should be light enough to be moved by breeze. Remedy for 'number 1' and enhances career and business.

Stillness

It includes still objects like statues, crystals, heavy vae, sculptures, etc. This would slow down Chi that is too fast. Hence, useful for places of study that need peace and relaxation. It is used as a remedy for 'number 8' section of Ba Gua or as an enhancer of knowledge and intuition.

Functional Objects

It includes tools and electric devices like television, electric toaster, computer phone, etc. Care should be taken not to overdo them as these are strong remedies. It is remedy for 'number 3' section of Ba Gua and enhancer for family and wisdom.

Live Objects

This remedy includes fishes, pets, plants, herbs, fruits, and vegetables. Dried flowers are considered dead and hence should not be used. Also plants and objects with life should not be left unattended or allowed to get dusty. Remedy for 'number 4' and enhances wealth and fortune.

Symbolic objects

Chi deals with the subconscious more than the physical and hence symbolic correction is more powerful. More on next page.

Chinese Secret Symbols

The Chinese strongly believe that patterns and symbols generate favourable future. They always use such symbols on wall hangings, ceilings, carpets, murals, pillow cases, flowers, tiles, table-cloth and furniture for happy life.

Beauty & Good Luck

Luck

Well Wishing

Wealth & Happiness

Prosperity

Symbol	Significance
Elephant	Wisdom
Vase	Peace
Phoenix & Dragon	Balance of Yin & Yang
Lotus	Endurance & Uprightness
Water Ripples	Wealth & Heavenly Blessing
Clouds	Heavenly Blessing & Wisdom
Gold Pieces	Wealth
Flowers	Wealth
Tortoise Shell	Longevity
Bats	Luck
Cranes	Fidelity, Honesty & Longevity
Deer	Wealth
Bird	Double Happiness
Fruit	Luck
Fish	Success

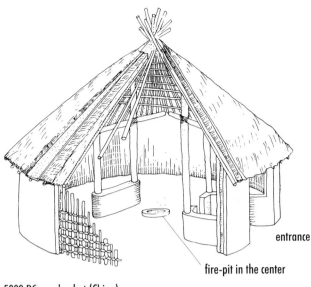

entrance

fire-pit in the center

5000 BC wooden hut (China)

Mystic Symbols

Symbols have the power to transcend us beyond our imagination by an making impression over our sub-conscious mind. Our ancestors who lived a primitive life never had to worry about houses and their construction. They believed in the merits of simple living. They lived a natural life and allowed their inner feeling to be expressed. Their huts were small but symbolic in shapes that resonated with universal energy. Later they started decorating their houses with beautiful symbolic designs and basic vibrant colors at the entrance to attract positive Chi. They were happy and satisfied. Tribals still follow them using their basic symbols.

Today with our complicated houses, we feel the need of techniques like Vastu and Feng Shui. Even after applying them we are still under stress and tension. These techniques no doubt bring about balance, harmony and awareness. But, they should be concerned with enhancing our choices, not condemning them as is usually seen. You know how you feel good over a certain table in the restaurant and not over the other. There is always a 'feel good' factor or instinct which moves us to a place of more comfort, more ease and a greater sense of personal power.

Symbols emerge from the core of our consciousness on which we agree from the base of our heart. Symbols can be anything, just two lines crossing each other. But when it makes a cross, faith and emotions of millions of people are related to it. Each individual is different by origin

Religious Cross

Symbolic design

Chinese Dragon

and thought, hence there are also different types of crosses and other symbols. One who believes in one kind of cross does not have the same faith in the other. The Chinese dragon produces wonderful results in China. This may be because the symbol of Dragon is in their culture, religion and everyday life. It resonates with them more deeply and spiritually. It may arouse emotion of fear in someone of non-Chinese origin and hence for him, it does not work. However auspicious the dragon may be for the Chinese, what may work for one may not work for another.

Faith and confidence in the symbol is very necessary. Select a simple symbol such that it touches your heart and with which your consciousness fully agrees. Your symbol should be individualized and personalized. You should not only know, but be aware of the meaning of the symbol you use. Until and unless it induces an inner vibration which positively and completely resonates with your consciousness, a symbol will not work.

But symbols can be anything, as our ancestors believed in it and so for them, the footmarks of their guru or saint were enough to be worshipped. As time passed, we found more detailed symbols like those on the feet of Lord Buddha, Lord Vishnu, etc. These are nothing but symbols with a message. Simplicity should be our answer to the problems we face every day. Working with symbols is not about re-arranging rooms and furniture. It is working with the sixth sense for the ultimate result. According to the Chinese tradition, there are 3 types of Lucks - Heaven Luck, Man Luck and Earth Luck.Symbols influence Man Luck and enhance Heaven Luck. Symbols influence our spirit. Hence believe in symbols that come to you naturally and effortlessly. They need not only be from your origin and religion. They can be something you adore very much. Something that has beauty, shape, rhythm and symmetry also becomes a symbol, only that your consciousness should agree to it. Symbols are a blend of inner perception and shapes, they are not magic wands. But they can bring inner harmony with more ease. By applying symbols, there is nothing to be lost and everything to be gained.

Another similar art of healing where symbols play a vital role is Reiki. It is easy to learn and apply by weekend courses. As we all are a part of universal life force it is our in-built ability to become a Reiki-channel. You just have to learn a few simple systematic steps and obtain finer attunement from your Reiki master or a PyraReiki master.

Lord Vishnu's feet

Lord Vishnu's feet
with auspicious symbols

New Feng Shui tool
Prof. Dr. Jiten Bhatt's - PYRON - with its mystical powers can enhance the essence of life including prosperity, marriage, health, career opportunities and luck. PYRON is the discovery of Dr. Bhatt's intense research on Pyramid, Vastu, Yantra and Feng Shui.

Double Energy - Multiple Results
This first time ever! The design of PYRON imparts double benefit as it has in-built Pyramid Yantra with 9 pyramid and 81 base pyramids. Also to add more power it is enriched with 9 pre-programmed copper discs at the bottom (pre-programmed for the purpose). Plus, at the top of your PYRON is a computer-uplifted specific 'silver code' to solve your every day problems.

Pre-programmed, Easy & Ready to Use
PYRON, due to its multiple benefits, gives you easy solutions to all Vastu, Feng Shui and Chi management methods. PYRON has a wide range of more than 36 yantras, each with a specific purpose and a programmed computer 'silver code' on top of it. Choose one or more according to your wish and purpose.

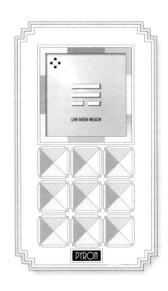

PYRON **NEW INVENTION!**

OM has 1001 meanings.

⋀ Power of OM

It is the fundamental nature of human beings to seek explanations for mysteries of life. To express these mysteries symbolic language is used, but still it is complex web and it is multiplicity can be understood only with full faith.

The symbols usually exist in nature and have a geometrical value, volume, sound, energy and its effect is much deeper. Symbols connect us with reality and the laws governing it in a direct way.

We very well know that one well illustrated figure is like thousand words. Same is with a powerful symbol; it offers hundred of meanings. It can transform us into a new dimension and each time gives a new message as per our mental, emotional and spiritual condition. Miracles can happen if we have whole hearted faith in them and they can be a bridge between the present and beyond. It is the witness of both.

A fire, for instance, symbolizes warmth, light, creative power, life force and masculine strength, initiation, activation, devotion, sacrifice, sacredness and many more meanings.

An interesting example is OM (pronounced as 'ohm'). This powerful sound or vibration is omni present and is the essence of Veda. OM is the mother of all sounds and represents strength, new vigour and energy. The best symbol of God, an ideal idol to worship in our inner temple. Seed of all mantra, the light of sun and moon and prime cause of entire cosmos. OM is life, prana and it is in all abilities of man and other creatures. So it is the supreme truth and present in the whole cycle of evolution.

In Hindu religion OM has 1001 meanings. The real secret meaning can be realized by right attuning of mind and emotions.

.......the man who understands a symbol not only 'opens himself ' to the objective world, but at the same time succeeds in emerging from his personal situation and reaching a comprehension of the universal ....Thanks to the symbol the individual experience is 'awoken' and transmuted in to a spiritual act.

- Mircea Eliade

Symbols for Prosperity, Success & Wisdom.

Occult Eight

In Hindu religion all auspicious works must begin with name of "Shree Ganesha". Lord Ganesha has infinite power which can be projected in all 1008 directions of working. Each directional purpose is symbolized by a different name of Lord Ganesha. When the special coded mantra with the statue of Lord Ganesha is kept in the house it becomes the symbolic solution of the problem. Some of the symbolized names are given below -

1) *'Santan Ganpateya Namaha'*
   For couples not having children.

2) *'Avighnay Namaha'*
   For removal of any obstacles in life.

3) *'Gyanrupay Namaha'*
   Helpful for children in studies.

4) *'Siddh Lakshmi Manoharpraya Namaha'*
   For increase in luck of financial matters.

5) *'Chintamani Charvanlalsaya Namaha'*
   For elimination of tensions.

6) *'Siddhivinakaya Namaha'*
   For success in every work.

7) *'Sumangalaya Namaha'*
   For increase of happiness and prosperity in home.

8) *'Mrutyunjaya Namaha'*
   For help in curing uncurable diseases.

ASHTA-VINAYAK
Symbols for Prosperity and Success

Ashta Mangal

Eight auspicious shapes.

Indian Symbols

In India many symbols are used in daily life, they are from simple to the most complex. Symbols in India are the outcome of mythology, religious beliefs, traditions, philosophy and emotions.

The most powerful symbols used are those of the five elements. This is shown by the five basic energies which are very important in 'tantra', 'healing' and 'spiritual' work. Also, other important symbols are those of the seven chakras of the 'yoga'. Nine planets and symbols of God and Goddess, with its functional abilities shown by different symbol.

Rangoli: must for every home

Rangoli- These are beautiful patterns made with colored powders on the threshold of the houses. It brings upliftment of spirit, wards off evil energies and gives protection.

One other very important symbol of India is the 'Rakhi'. It is tied on the right wrist of brother by the sister. This is a symbol of protection, unending love and affection. Besides these, there are other symbols used on specific occasions that have different meanings and some of them are shown here, alongside.

Note: More on Swastik and its practical use in Vastu on page 157.

Energetic Forms

Beautiful representation of these energy forms are visualized in the Islamic religion. There are simple 99 formulas, each with a wonderful influence on us. Combination of sound, form and meaning to generate definite perception within and around us. Below are a few of the 99 master keys.

ALLAH
He is Allah, there is no God but Him

AR-RAHĪM
The Merciful

AS-SALĀM
The Source of Peace

AL-MUHAYMIN
The Protector

AL-'AZIZ
The Mighty

AL-'AZIM
The Great One

AL-WADUD
The Loving

AL-WAHID
The Unique

AN-NUR
The Light

AL-HADI
The Guide

Prayer Beads

An Islamic rosary is made up of 99 beads. This is because they stand for 99 of the Divine names. The hundredth name of the essence, can only be found in Paradise.

The triangle is one of the most powerful symbols for energy, dynamism, action and positiveness. The fundamental principle of electricity is based on triangle (Star & Delta connection) and in spiritualism. The triangle represents the *shakti*.

Our hands are full of healing power. So let's make use of hand and triangle in our daily life. You can transform positiveness into your self or any thing in innumerable ways by this symbol.

1) You have a dislike or allergy to a kind of food.

2) You are uncomfortable with your job place, colleagues, boss or if you have misunderstanding with a friend or relative.

3) You have a subject that is less liked and difficult or if you have any other kind of mis-coordination, then try this!

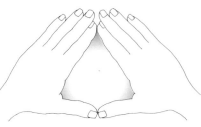

Your personal power-pyramid symbol

Keep your hands joined together with first fingers and thumbs touching each other as shown in the figure. This becomes your own 'personal' power symbol.

What you have to do is just to place the food, photograph of the person or subject book in front of you. Place your power symbol above it and look through it, think positively for 1 minute about the matter. You will attain fabulous results. If placing your object in front is not possible and if you are at a distance, make an affirmation about it on a piece of paper and follow the same procedure till you obtain required results.

Affectionate warm wishes.
This is your first book written with the aim of providing best health and prosperity. I have read all the pages, the scientific approach of Pyramid Yantra book is really praiseworthy.

Pandit Bhojraj Dwivedi
Author of more than 250 books on occult science.

EXPERT'S OPINION

7

"Pynergy flows in the core
channel of all things in existence.
The number of from applications
will crop up from thousands of
fertile minds. There are no
limitations to Pynergy".

Prof. Dr. Jiten Bhatt

What's
More...

FaMaa Health

The cat

A strange incident happened a few days ago. A cat used to come to our house every day and create nuisance. I was asked to chase it off one day. I went towards it assertively. But to my surprise instead of running away, it just closed its eyes and put her paws in front of them. To the cat I did not exist, but reality was that I as a threat was there all the time. So is the case with all of us too. When facing a health, wealth or happiness problem, we all become 'the cat'. Even when having minor health problems we instantly and instinctively pop unnecessary medicines or look out for easy outer solutions, unaware of the fact that they may actually do us more harm in the long run.

By indulging in unnecessary medication or other temporary pleasures we feed 'the cat' in us. We close our eyes to the storm of ill health or negativity right in front of our eyes, in spite of knowing that it is bound to reach us some day. We then complain of sudden disasters. Such disasters do not happen just like that. They are a result of feeding 'the cat' everyday. All our concentration today is on curing the sick, our minds have become sickness or gloom oriented. We initially don't pay attention towards ourselves and then expect miracles to happen!

Pancha Kosha - The five bodies of man

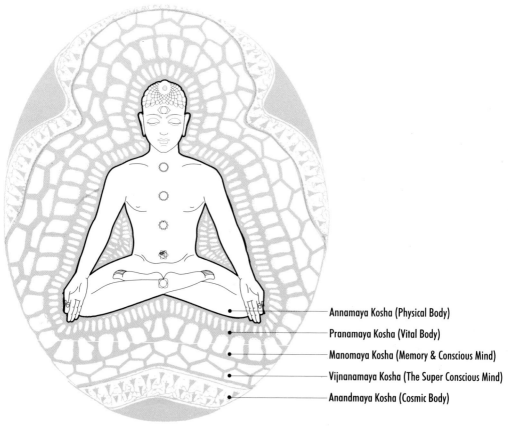

Annamaya Kosha (Physical Body)

Pranamaya Kosha (Vital Body)

Manomaya Kosha (Memory & Conscious Mind)

Vijnanamaya Kosha (The Super Conscious Mind)

Anandmaya Kosha (Cosmic Body)

We have to change our thought from being not sick to being well and healthy in the real sense. We were all born to be completely healthy and in harmony with the nature, experiencing joys every moment. Then why are we not happy? It is very simple, what you pay attention on, grows well. We pay attention to sickness, dissatisfaction, stresses, negative thoughts and overrated emotional crisis. In addition to that, we assault our bodies with chemical weapons in the name of medicines or momentary pleasures. Later on all these accumulate and present us with their precious gifts of depression, anxiety, diabetes, hypertension, cancer and many other such disorders.

Do we diagnose right?

Our diagnostic methods today are purely physical or physiological, making it a one sided approach. We all possess immense healing force within us to regain wellness. We just need to establish a simple formula to invoke that. There can be no better formula than creating balance in and around us.

Cosmic Egg - the seed of life and the serpent -a more esoteric symbol of -arousal of kundalini, principle of life cycle, fertility, attribute of wisdom, good and evil. Internal strength and power, temptation, medicine and healing, divine forces, and the earth energy.

The Indian wellness science, Yoga, says our bodies are a conglomerate of five bodies - Anandamaya Kosha (Cosmic body), Vijnanamaya Kosha (Super conscious body), Manomaya Kosha (Mental/ Conscious body), Pranamaya Kosha (Vital body), Annamaya Kosha (Physical body). These five interact within themselves and the cosmos beyond through the innumerable nadis. Thus they say we have five basic levels from where a problem can arise. This is the subtle division of the body. Diagnosis through these nadis can also give us vital information about the causes unknown to the science today.

"Power of Pyramid is unbelievable. It is a wonder instrument for upliftment of Body, Mind and Spirit".

Dr. Meher Master Moos
President, Zorastrian College
Prof. of Spectro Chrome-metry.

EXPERT'S OPINION

Secret's of Jiten

In this materialistic world we can't avoid science, maths, technology and economy, which are the base of our physical need. Health, music, mediation and prayers are our inner needs. For a happy and healthy life we need both.

Initiate a healing process

For healing we should balance all these five Koshas. These Koshas are very sensitive and can be disturbed by wrong thoughts, false emotions or improper living habits. For balancing these Koshas we have to provide it with the opposite. It does not mean physical or materialistic opposite, but in the sense of opposite that is complementary. A powerful positive thought or a potentized medicine or eating or exercising with total attention to the part, which requires it the most, is also a form of providing the opposite.

For implementing a powerful thought we require a re-enforcing instrument, which further amplifies its positivity. Pyramid yantra is one such forceful device. It helps enhancing the effect of thought throughout the channel of mind/heart-brain-spine-organ-cell. This positive thought is to be oriented by FaMa and Pyramid Yantra, which we have already seen in PyraVastu chapter. The Pyramid Yantra approach is holistic so it can be used solely or as a complementary enhancer to any other healing practice you follow.

Interpreting Vitality

Let us begin with a simple and practical method of diagnosis known as Applied Kinesiology. Here the person raises his/her right hand with palm

facing upwards. Ask someone to press your hand downwards by the palm. You have to offer resistance. Tell the other person to note the amount of resistance. Now put the food item or object, which has to be checked for suitability in the left hand and repeat the procedure. Compare both the resistances and then you would be able to know the suitability according to the increase or decrease of resistance. Positive suitability increases resistance whereas unsuitability decreases your resistance.

You can also check the vitality of your chakras using this method. Place the left hand on the chakra and ask someone to press down your right hand. Do the same for all the chakras and note at which chakra you offered less resistance. Now apply FaMaa to that chakra.

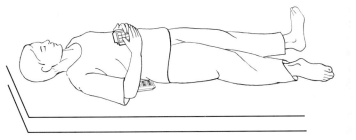

The Technique

◆ Sit calmly at a place or pause and relax before starting your meals or exercise.

◆ Give all your attention to the part or organ of your body that needs balance. It can be your ill organ or just a place where you tend to put on more fat. It can even be your medicine.

◆ Gently touch it with both your hands or and place a Pyramid Yantra there.

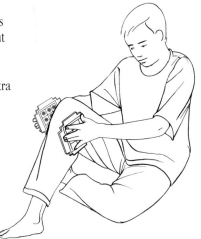

◆ Now give FaMaa orientation for a few minutes.

◆ You can transform positivity for wellness at the core of the system.

This method can help you enhance the condition of your mind, body, emotion and spirit. Make it a part of your daily routine and see the difference. Pyramid Yantra with FaMaa orientation immensely helps in creating a more lively, energetic, healthier, happier, harmonious and prosperous life.

"The best management evolves from a healthy body and a sound mind. One tool that I use for my fitness is Pyramid Yantra 9x9".

Dr. N.H. Atthreya
Top Management Consultant
Director, MMC School of Management

EXPERT'S OPINION

Harmony Yantra

In spite of all your materialistic achievements your wife or your children are not happy with you. May be in spite of all your efforts your husband does not seem to be happy. Situations and people may differ but the bottom line is that you may be missing happiness. Why do we face numerous such problems with others and ourselves?

Happiness is not a simple task. Conventional medicine would not be able to offer you anything here. This according to them is not an illness and hence no cure exists for it.

Lack of happiness is the result of disharmony. To gain happiness we must firstly establish harmony between two people or harmony within ourselves. Harmony 9X9 is one such uniquely designed device developed on the principles of Pyramid Yantra. It helps you initiate harmony between two persons or two organs requiring it.

Harmony - FaMaa chart

Fa	Maa
As per relations	
Father	Mother
Husband	Wife
Male	Female
Father	Son
Father	Daughter
Mother	Son
Mother	Daughter
Elder Brother	Younger Sister
Elder Sister	Younger Sister
Elder Sister	Younger Brother
Mother	Daughter- in- law
Mother	Son- in- law

Fa	Maa
As per age	
Elder Friend	Younger Friend
Elder Colleague	Younger Colleague

Fa	Maa
As per rank	
Boss	Employee
Manager	Supervisor
Supervisor	Worker
Senior Partner	Partner

Other uses

Harmony 9x9 can be placed under ground for harmony between two lands or building.

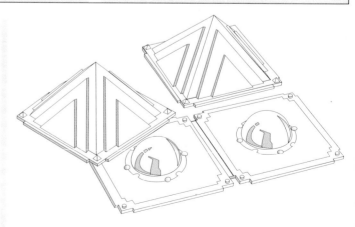

Pyra Reiki

The simple meaning of PyraReiki is PynergyReiki. We have already seen and understood the 'Pyra' part and the new Pynergy science. in the previous chapters. Now let us learn about Reiki and application of Pynergy to it.

Reiki (pronounced: ray-key) is a Japanese word meaning 'universal life energy'. Every living and non-living body radiates energy. This is the life force itself. But it has to be channelized properly for attainment of higher purpose of living. Dr. Mikao Usui is the originator of this concept of healing. Dr. Hayashi, his student, carried out Reiki and passed on this concept to a Japanese-American woman, Hawayo Takata, in the 1930s. In the 1970s she began teaching Reiki and she died in 1980. Now her grand-daughter, Phyllis Lei Furumoto carries out her work to spread Reiki. Today, more than 200,000 people have been initiated into it.

Reiki is simple to learn, effective a and popular form of natural healing. It uses cosmic force and symbols to channelize the life energy through the hands of the healer (we already know Fa - right hand and Maa - left hand) to the person being treated. Reiki helps in restoring depleted energy and relieving stress. It is also very useful in headaches, insomnia, digestive upsets, chronic aches and pains and in many other ailments.

Pynergy is not a religion but is a spiritual art. Similarly, Reiki is also not a religion but a spiritual energy therapy. Hence, Pynergy and Reiki go along very well. Both have many similarities as Reiki works on supreme awareness and emotional peace and Pynergy on FaMaa i.e. consciousness and bliss.

Learning Reiki has basically two parts - Reiki I and Reiki II (Reiki III and others are for teaching purposes). In Reiki I training, hand positions are taught and "attunement" or initiation is done. Reiki II involves further attuning and learning three symbols that have powerful healing effects. Once you have become Reiki II you can practice distance healing and help people anywhere.

PyraReiki is usually more beneficial to people after Reiki II. Now you can clearly understand, practice and appreciate the power of symbols. So with PyraReiki you can use the hundreds of practical techniques given in this know-how book.

PyraReiki results are fast, since with the use of scientific instruments you save a lot of your precious time. Secondly, you remain in constant touch with the person you are treating from distance. Thirdly, you become a part of the PyraNet (pg.167) and hence you have an easy access to the strong spiritual support created by millions of Pynergy users all around the globe.

Raku
The Lightening Bolt

Dai-Ko-Myo
Healing the Soul

Hon-Sha-Ze-Sho-Nen
Distance Healing

Sei-He-Ki
Emotional Healing

Cho-Ku-Rei
The Light Switch

Chart shows positions of
Health 9x9 used for Reiki
healing.

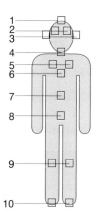

1. Head 2.Eyes 3.Ears 4.Throat
5.Lungs 6.Heart 7.Stomach
8.Lower Abdomen 9.Knees
10.Sole

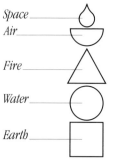

Space
Air
Fire
Water
Earth

Five basic Pyra Reiki symbols,
representing five shapes of stupa
and five elements.

Where and How to use PyraReiki:

PyraReiki and local healing

For local healing there are certain hand positions. There are numerous hand positions in Reiki, varying from 12 - 80. But here in PyraReiki we need just 10 basic hand positions (as shown in fig.)
Steps :

♦ Lie or sit comfortably in a calm and well-ventilated room.

♦ Start From the positions on head and proceed gradually to those on legs.

♦ Keep the Health 9 X 9 in position. Then keep your left hand on it, palm facing the Health 9 X 9 and then keep your right hand on it, similarly.

♦ Repeat the three symbols (Cho-Ku-Rei, Sei-He-Ki and Hon-Sha-Ze-Sho-Nen) one after the another.

♦ Apply PyraReiki to one position for 3 minutes. Usually there is no such time limit. Keep your hands in one position until your intuition directs you to the next point. But for practical purpose 3 minutes is the minimum required.

♦ For positions of legs you can sit and proceed. Keep your soles flat on Health 9 X 9 when doing that position.

Five Element PyraReiki

PyraReiki deals with the Five Element Tibeto - Buddhist theory. Any disturbance in any of the five elements in your body or surroundings can be easily brought into balance by PyraReiki. Here, Multier 9 X 9 is to be used along with the 5 symbols of Reiki corresponding to the respective parts of body. Keep Multier 9 X 9 on the part with disturbed element and apply PyraReiki similarly as for the local healing.

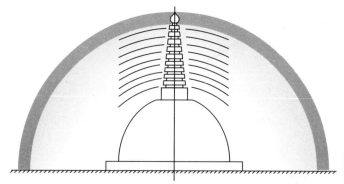

The Buddhist cosmology
showing the layers of invisible
domes enclosing the stupa

Chakra PyraReiki

Our eastern tradition has a subtle anatomy or an unbroken metaphysical understanding of the human as a whole interacting with our surrounding. The Chakras are important sensors of this subtle anatomy. They maintain relation of man with earth and heaven. We have 7 Chakras out of which 5 represent physical links, whereas the sixth and seventh represent the super physical links. For healing the chakras or meditating on them, use PyraReiki to influence them. Keep Health 9 X 9 on the area corresponding to the Chakra and give PyraReiki to it.

SEVEN MAJOR CHAKRAS & THEIR FUNCTIONS

Chakra	Gland	Organ	Function	Colour	Element
1. CROWN CHAKRA (SAHASTRAR)	Pineal	Upper Brain Right Eye	Spiritual Vision, Enlightenment	VIOLET	Ether
2. BROW CHAKRA (AJNA)	Pituitary	Hypothalamus Lower Brain Spine, Left Eyes Nose & Ears	Third Eye Intuition Clairvoyance Light, Telepathy	BLUE (Royal)	Ether
3. THROAT CHAKRA (VISUDHA)	Thyroid	Throat Upper Lungs Alimentary Canal Vocal Apparatus	Communication Self- expression Creative Energy Sound	SKY BLUE	Space
4. HEART CHAKRA (ANAHATA)	Thymus	Heart, Lungs Blood, Liver Vagus Nerve Arms	Consciousness Love Compassion Life Force	GREEN (Grass)	Air
5. SOLAR PLEXUS CHAKRA (MANIPURA)	Pancreas	Liver, Stomach Gall Bladder Large Intestine Spleen	Emotion Power Wisdom Action	YELLOW	Fire
6. SACRAL CHAKRA (SWADHISTAN)	Adrenal	Kidneys Bladder Legs	Anger / Action Sexuality Peace	ORANGE	Water
7. ROOT CHAKRA (MULADHAR)	Gondas	Sex Organs	Kundalini Security Physical Energy	RED	Earth

Color PyraReiki

For influencing the particular color of a Chakra you can also use Health 9 X 9 of that color (More on color healing pg. 164).

Wish Fulfillment with PyraReiki

In Reiki, we use a Reiki-box for this purpose. Now you can keep your wish in the wish machine specially prepared for this purpose (more on pg. 82) and apply the three symbols to it.

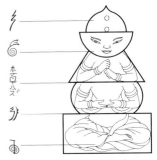

A Japanese drawing showing five parts of stupa, elements, chakras in the body and Pyra Reiki symbols

Symbolic Predication

Symbol	**What year were you born?**								
RAT	1996,	1984,	1972,	1960,	1948,	1936,	1924,	1912,	1900
OX	1997,	1985,	1973,	1961,	1949,	1937,	1925,	1913,	1901
TIGER	1998,	1986,	1974,	1962,	1950,	1938,	1926,	1914,	1902
RABBIT	1999,	1987,	1975,	1963,	1951,	1939,	1927,	1915,	1903
DRAGON	2000,	1988,	1976,	1964,	1952,	1940,	1928,	1916,	1904
SNAKE	2001,	1989,	1977,	1965,	1953,	1941,	1929,	1917,	1905
HORSE	2002,	1990,	1978,	1966,	1954,	1942,	1930,	1918,	1906
SHEEP	2003,	1991,	1979, ·	1967,	1955,	1943,	1931,	1919,	1907
MONKEY	2004,	1992,	1980,	1968,	1956,	1944,	1932,	1920,	1908
ROOSTER	2005,	1993,	1981,	1969,	1957,	1945,	1933,	1921,	1909
DOG	2006,	1994,	1982,	1970,	1958,	1946,	1934,	1922,	1910
PIG	2007,	1995,	1983,	1971,	1959,	1947,	1935,	1923,	1911

Say you are born in 1946, first find 1946 in the above chart. Find corresponding symbolic birth sign. Read the description of that birth sign on the next page. Year 1946 is the DOG, so read the properties of DOG, and find your characteristics.

RAT

Rats are well-mannered, charming, romantic, natural actors who can make others laugh or cry with equal ease and they also have a tendency to be nit-picking, manipulative, self tortured and self-pitying.

OX

Oxen are powerful, determined, weighty, charismatic, natural leaders, style-setter, brave, loyal, long-suffering, disciplinarians and bossy, stubborn, bad losers, stick-in-the-muds, jealous and rather oafish.

TIGER

Tigers are spontaneous, generous, sexy, brave, honourable, wise, noble, magnetic, profound, charismatic, hypersensitive, unyielding, rebellious, vain, live dangerously and to hell with the consequences.

RABBIT

Rabbits are refined, shrewd, scrupulous, calm, hospitable, clever, tactful, companionable - but they can also be moody, wimpish, hypersensitive, egocentric, jacks of all trades and somewhat withdrawn.

DRAGON

Dragons are vivacious, lucky, optimistic, intuitive, psychic, enthusiastic, generous - but sometimes demanding, disruptive, loud, egocentric, self torturing, over-impressionable and forcefully judgemental.

SNAKE

Snakes are elegant, intuitive, attractive, sympathetic, quiet, wise, serene and philosophical - but they also have the tendency to be self-critical, lazy, mean, possessive, underhand, disloyal and rather showy.

HORSE

Horses are charming, well-spoken, sensual, hard-working, tough, quick-thinking, companionable - and egocentric, insensitive, bullying, and weak.

SHEEP

Sheeps are home lovers, mild-mannered, artistic, delicate, peace loving, persevering, endearing - but also changeable, undisciplined, fussy, gloomy, unpunctual and are easily led.

MONKEY

Monkeys are witty, quick-thinking, incisive, clever, inventive, passionate, energetic, enthusiastic, vivacious, assertive, adaptable - and also deceitful, manipulative, two-faced, unfaithful and superficial.

ROOSTER

Roosters are full of vitality, frank, open, stylish, enthusiastic, adventurous, inventive, interesting, generous and confident - but they also have tendency to be braggarts, loud, caustic & changeable.

DOG

Dogs are brave, loyal, trustworthy, discreet, faithful, dutiful, generous-spirited, selfless, modest & conventional - but introspective, anxious, temperamental, self-righteous and extremely judgmental.

PIG

Pigs are truthful, loyal, sensitive, sympathetic, scrupulous, sensual, obliging, peace loving, refined and have sense of fair play - but sometimes naive, lazy, pushovers, gullible & insecure.

Now as we sail towards the end of our this journey of shapes and forms from simple to complex, known to unknown and visible to invisible, I hope you have picked up some pearls of personal enrichment that result in fortuitous opportunities coming your way. I wish these opportunites change your life, making you grow richer, healthier and happier.

Dr. Dhara Bhatt

⚠ About the Author

Dr. Dhara Bhatt is a homoeopath and a naturopath. She is also a natural clairvoyant and a divine healer. She started reading auras at the age of seven.

She has assisted Prof. Dr. Jiten Bhatt in his numerous workshops and programs all over India. She has herself conducted many workshops on aura reading, including the one at International Conference on Bio-energy. She has also visited the Pyramids of Egypt with Prof. Dr. Jiten Bhatt to experience and study personally the infinite powers of Pyramids.

Her diverse interests in learning have led her to study and practice PyraVastu, PyraReiki and Cosmic Meditation to learning languages like German and Russian. As an avid yet selective reader she has always loved books. she began to write herself to reach others. she offers her readers a simple, comprehensive and practical understanding of a concept.

**Dr. Dhara Bhatt recieves blessings from
Spiritual Guru H. H. the Dalai Lama**

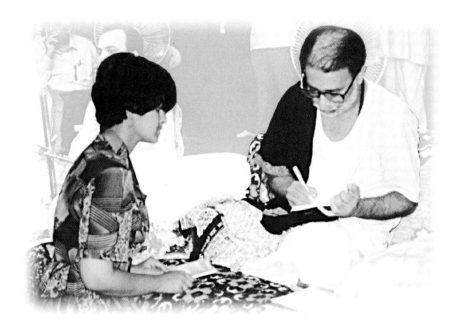

|| श्री ||

चि. धारा !

खूब जगो अने यशनि मने
खूब खीलो - आशीष !

बापु.

16-10-97

Dr. Dhara Bhatt being blessed by
Spiritual Guru Parampujya Shree Morari Bapu

Fact File

"I have obtained drastic enhancement in my life. My financial and property matters have improved. Also my son got a good job and my daughter is now happily married and settled in USA".

Dr. N. R. Vyas
Consultant - General Surgery.

"From my Dowsing experience I concluded that origin of problem is totally different from visible cause. Pyramid Yantra works effectively at root level".

Dr. Firoz Hakimji
Dowsing Expert & Spiritual Healer

"The dynamic methods of PyraVastu are a great boon to the field of Vastu".

Sushil Fatehpuria
Vastu Expert and Author of a book on Vastu.

"I used Dr. Jiten Bhatt's research oriented Pyramid Yantra for assured results in my practice".

Dr. Ravindra Kapadia
New Age therapy healer and Pranic healing master

"I tried Pyramid energy for my daughter during her pregnancy. She got wonderful result".

Dr. Chandrajit Mehta
Homoeopath

"Pyramid Yantra is an excellent tool for enhancing health and prosperity, when used with complete faith".

Swami Krishna Satyarthi
Spiritual and Meditation guru

"Pyramid Yantra brought a revolutionary change in my profession".

Dr. Harshad Kanakia
Cosmic energy and Color healing expert

"New systems of Pyramid Yantra is simple and easy to use, with marvelous results".

Dr. Sham Sunder
Scientific vastu Adviser

"Mystic powers of Pyramid Yantra is beyond imagination and gave me holistic upliftment".

Bhavesh Vadia
Truth Seeker

"Power of Pyramid Yantra has changed my life and business dramatically".

Bimal Bhatt
Successful Businessman

"PyraVastu has paved a new creative path for me. By practising it I have got amazing results in my own life. It has become a source of constant hope for me in bringing about change in lives of other people.

Hitesh Mehta
Energy Vastu consultant

"After studies I was very confused about future. Coming in contact with the Pynergy network has given me satisfactory financial and mental security. My life has completely changed since then".

Nirav Shukla
Budding businessman.

"Pyramid Yantra has helps remove all pain, misery and difficulties from our life. I have personally experienced its wonders".

Mahesh Desai
Businessman and Occult Science promoter.

"I am extremely happy after the installation of Pyramid Yantra in my home".

Sushmita Shastri
Housewife

"Reiki in combination with Pynergy gives excellent results".

Kalpana Diwan
Reiki Master

"Practising PyraVastu has given me numerous opportunities and professional tours abroad".

Mahavir Gandhi
PyraVastu practitioner

"PyraVastu has given me an invaluable chance to help others, making them happier".

Neeta Kothari
PyraVastu consultant

We need your advice!

Please spare a moment of your precious time to fill in the simple details below so that we can improve on our further publications. And also let us know your further interests and needs so we can divert them to appropriate agencies to serve you better!

Your first-hand feedback about this book on Pyramid Yantra.

Where would you rate the following on a scale of 5 where 1 is poor and 5 is excellent. Mark by a circle. ◯

New Knowledge input	1	2	3	4	5
Practical know-how	1	2	3	4	5
Personal satisfaction	1	2	3	4	5
User friendly reading	1	2	3	4	5
Design-Layout style	1	2	3	4	5

Personal suggestions:

Tools you need, information you require.

Please send me more information regarding the following. Please tick ✔

☐ More books and reading material on the same topic.

☐ Where & How to get products and tools shown in the book.

☐ Information on advance leaning through personal workshop and lectures.

☐ Where to find a PyraVastu expert.

☐ How can I become a PyraVastu expert.

☐ I am also interested in distance learning programs of PyraVastu.

Personal request:

Note:
The author is not responsible of providing the above requested information, but we on behalf of F.F.Publication will try our best and manage to provide you the information.

Be a part of the Pyra-Revolution!

Yes, I need to get connected into the Pyramid-Revolution, to spread the new concept of Pynergy to uplift the living of the society and the people around me.

What do I need to do?

You just have to list 3 friends of yours whom you think can benefit from this book.

We will send them complete information so that they can learn and explore the secret that you have already discovered.

Please write in clear handwriting the address of 3 friends, you think can explore this secret.

What are my benefits?

You will enjoy the following benefits;
- Will receive a personal certificate from the author.
- Latest information on new-age concepts of health and wellness.
- Advance notice of new books and products.
- Get special offer and preferred customer price on our products.

1

Name

Add

City

Pincode

2

Name

Add

City

Pincode

3

Name

Add

City

Pincode

your's

Name

Add

City

Pincode

Phone

Fax

Email

www

Please write below (in capitals) your name you want in your certificate.

Fill the information cut separate and send this page. Do not photo copy the page.

Send it to; F.F.Publications (info cell), 336/43 GIDC, Makarpura, Baroda 390010, India   www.pyramidyantra.com or www.jitenpyramid.com